D1256027

ON OUR MIND

ON OUR MIND

Salience, Context, and Figurative Language

RACHEL GIORA

OXFORD
UNIVERSITY PRESS

2003

OXFORD
UNIVERSITY PRESS

Oxford   New York
Auckland   Bangkok   Buenos Aires   Cape Town   Chennai
Dar es Salaam   Delhi   Hong Kong   Istanbul   Karachi   Kolkata
Kuala Lumpur   Madrid   Melbourne   Mexico City   Mumbai   Nairobi
São Paulo   Shanghai   Taipei   Tokyo   Toronto

Published by Oxford University Press, Inc.
198 Madison Avenue, New York, New York 10016

www.oup.com

Oxford is a registered trademark of Oxford University Press

Library of Congress Cataloging-in-Publication Data
Giora, Rachel, date
On our mind: salience, context, and figurative language / Rachel Giora.
    p. cm.
Includes bibliographical references and index.
ISBN 0-19-513616-0
1. Psycholinguistics.   2. Figures of speech.   3. Context (Linguistics)   I. Title.
BF455 .G525 2002
401'.9—dc21   2001006646

9 8 7 6 5 4 3 2 1

Printed in the United States of America
on acid-free paper

For my mother and father,
Esther and Arie Shapira

PREFACE

This book has been fun to write. It is not an individual enterprise. Some of my best friends have had a hand in shaping my ideas and nourishing the thoughts I tried to flesh out here. Whether they like it or not, I do hold them accountable. The list is long and unordered. I am especially indebted to Efrat Ben-Menachem, who first introduced me to the pleasures of researching. My dearest friends and colleagues—Mira Ariel, Asa Kasher, Tanya Reinhart, and Yeshayahu Shen—are particularly culpable. They are among the people who influenced me most, not the least by being such caustic critics, yet relentlessly helpful.

A great portion of this book was written while I was on my sabbatical in Santa Cruz, visiting with Ray Gibbs. Being in Santa Cruz was a marvelous experience. It allowed me, among other things, to share my thoughts with Ray, who is a most wonderful person and an admirable colleague and mentor. I cherish the countless hours we spent talking about our views and differences and about the topics that pervade the field. Ray Gibbs has been and still is a great source of inspiration, and his ideas certainly are reflected in my work. My Santa Cruzian experience also included my very dear friends Adam Ussishkin and Andrew Wedel, who always lent me their linguistic ear and never failed to be supportive and critical.

I have also benefited greatly from invaluable discussions with Ofer Fein—a colleague and co-author for several years—and from discussions and very valuable comments by Salvatore Attardo, Brian Bowdle, Hugh Bredin, Dan Chiappe, Herb Clark, Herb Colston, Seana Coulston, Carmen Curcó, Jack Du Bois, Steven Frisson, Dedre Gentner, Morton Gernsbacher, Paul Hopper, Dick Janney, Albert Katz, John Kennedy, Boaz Keysar, Teenie Matlock, Hoang Vu, Ellen Winner, Francisco Yus, Eran Zaidel, four anonymous reviews of this book, and numerous other people who I have read or talked to over the past few years. My discussions with several students—Ann Kronrod, Noa Shuval, and particularly Orna Peleg—have been inspiring and helpful in molding many of my views. I am no less indebted to Catharine Carlin, Robin H. Miura, and John Rauschenberg from Oxford University Press, and to copyeditor Cynthia Garver, for all their support and help. Particularly dear to me are the comments of an old friend and colleague, Jacob Mey, who read the final version with a hawkish but most benevolent eye.

My heartfelt thanks go also to my sister, Galia Shaham, and my sons, Ran, Etay, and Yoav Giora for their love and support.

The research reported here could not have been performed without support afforded by the Israel Science Foundation, the Lyon Foundation, and the Tel Aviv University Basic Research Fund.

It is a great relief, though, that the quest for truth must always fail so that any new theory is bound to be improved, reversed, or replaced by new thinking. The thoughts expressed here are also improvements on previous articulations of them in my earlier writings. The accomplishments of this book, therefore, are an invitation for a reform.

Asim Abu Shakra's art was selected for the book's jacket as a tribute to the Palestinian people and their struggle for a land of their own. The different ways the Palestinians and the Israelis perceive the cactus shed light on the themes reverberating in this book. For the Palestinians, the cactus is a salient symbol of their homeland. To the Israelies, its salient meaning is associated with their renewed identity as people native to Eretz Yisra'el (the land of Israel).

In the preface to Asim Abu Shakra's catalogue, Anton Shammas laments the tragedy of the Palestinian people by spelling out the appropriation of the indigenous symbol by the newcomers:

> And since the Palestinian cactus, if we don't let bygones be bygones, has long ceased to function as a thorny, succulent plant with thick, leave-shaped stems, as the dictionary would have it, and has become instead "a common nickname for those born in Eretz Yisra'el and raised in it [*tsabar*]", and nothing more—
>
> . . . .
>
> Someone had to transfer the cactus to the pot.
>
> Someone had to shake us and tell us that it's over and done with; that from this point on there is no return, neither to the map nor to the land—just being let on the windowsill. . . .
>
> It never occurred to anyone before:
> That here is the homeland for you, hanging on the wall.
> That only in this way it is possible to go on.
> That now it is possible to go on.
>
> —Anton Shammas, preface to *Asim Abu Shakra* (Catalogue, Tel Aviv Museum of Art, 1994, in Hebrew; my translation).

Credits

The poem appearing in chapter 2 is from Yona Wallach (1997), "Absalom" in *Wild Light*, p. 4; translated by Linda Zisquit; copyright 1997 by the Sheep Meadow Press; reproduced with permission.

The poem appearing in chapter 7 is by Efrat Mishori (1999), "The Wall of Motherhood" in S. Kaufman, G. Hasan-Rokem, & T. S. Hess (Eds.), *The Defiant Muse: Hebrew Feminist Poems from Antiquity to the Present*, p. 237; copyright by the translator, Rachel Tzvia Back, and the Feminist Press; reproduced with permission.

All citations from *Santa Barbara Corpus of Spoken American English* are copyright 2000 by John Du Bois; reproduced with permission.

Chapter 4, figures 4.1, 4.2, 4.3, 4.4, 4.5, 4.6, and 4.7 are from R. Giora & O. Fein (1999), "Irony: Context and salience," *Metaphor and Symbol*, *14*, 241–257; R. Giora, O. Fein, & T. Schwartz (1998), "Irony: Graded salience and indirect negation," *Metaphor and Symbol*, *13*, 83–101; reproduced with the permission of Lawrence Erlbaum Associates, Inc.

Chapter 5, figure 5.2 is from O. Peleg, R. Giora, & O. Fein (2001), "Salience and context effects: Two are better than one," *Metaphor and Symbol*, *16*, 173–192; reproduced with the permission of Lawrence Erlbaum Associates, Inc.

Chapter 5, figures 5.3 and 5.4 are from R. Giora & O. Fein (1999), "On understanding familiar and less-familiar figurative language," *Journal of Pragmatics*, *31*, 1601–1618; reproduced with the permission of Elsevier Science.

All citations from R. Giora (2002), "Masking one's themes: Irony and the politics of indirectness," in M. M. Louwerse & W. van Peer (Eds.), *Thematics in psychology and literary studies* are copyright 2002 by John Benjamins; reproduced with permission.

CONTENTS

ON OUR MIND

1

Prologue

We Didn't See; We Didn't Know

> There aren't six million Palestinians in the occupied territories, and the ideology of
> evil is different as well. Blunt and direct Nazi ideology is only found in the Mes-
> sianic centers of the settlers in the territories. The army and the government are just
> protecting the living space of the settlers. And the rest are just deeply disappointed
> with the Palestinians, who failed to grasp how profound our desire for peace is.
>
> But in Germany, too, most of the Germans were not Nazis. The majority just
> chose not to know.
>
> —Tanya Reinhart, *Yediot Aharonot* [an Israeli daily], 14 March 2001

For Israeli Jews, the coin *six million* is strongly associated with the six million
Jewish victims of the Holocaust. In spite of the negation marker (*There aren't six
million Palestinians*), the accessibility of the collocation *six million Jews* is not
diminished and allows for the analogy between the Palestinian and the Jewish
victims to be established rapidly, even before it is made explicit by the late context. This is just one example shedding light on how privileged meanings shape
the way we understand language. In this book, I explore the extent to which such
prominent meanings affect our linguistic and psycholinguistic behavior.

To give you an immediate grasp of the topics I address in this book, consider a few mundane anecdotes related to familiar routines and meanings foremost on our mind. For instance, although my telephone number is highly familiar to me, I find it difficult to recognize if someone segments it differently or
reads it to me from right to left. I might dial an unintended number—that which
I use frequently and which is consequently more accessible to me. Other exam-

3

ples may be even more embarrassing, such as when a person wishes to refer to her husband but uses her ex-husband's name instead.

Another commonplace experience I have with people's faces may also be suggestive. For example, in a movie theater I might bump into an old student of mine, who is not highly familiar to me: I might have seen her in the classroom, among 40 other students, once a week, a while ago. Though her face "rings a bell," I might not be able to identify her. Out of her "natural" environment (the campus? the classroom?), I have difficulties telling who she is. The memory of her face is not salient enough to me—not foremost on my mind—to allow a rapid recognition. In contrast, however, I should experience no such difficulties if, under the same circumstances, I came across a highly familiar face such as my son's or my best friend's. I would surely identify them instantly, without having to rely on contextual information for help. Their faces are so familiar—so salient—I can tell who they are regardless of appropriateness or naturalness of context.

The cartoon by Gary Larson (1984) shown in figure 1.1 may also be illustrative. It portrays the prototypical fear of monsters that almost every child has: a person is lying on the bed with some unfamiliar creatures underneath. However, while this might be our first preferred "reading" of the picture, this reading

THE FAR SIDE®   By GARY LARSON

"I've got it again, Larry ... an eerie feeling like there's something on top of the bed."

Figure 1.1 The monster under the bed. The Far Side® by Gary Larson © 1983 FarWorks, Inc. All Rights Reserved. Used with permission.

will have to be revisited when we see the caption: *I've got it again, Larry . . . an eerie feeling like there's something on top of the bed.* At this point, we have to discard our first adopted familiar (egocentric, human) perspective and take a less familiar, less frequent perspective—that of the monster who is under the bed. Having to reject a highly salient point of view in favor of an obscure one, which now seems just as "plausible," indeed allows for the funniness of the cartoon to get across.

The following poem, recently distributed on the Internet, explores the relations between such imbalanced perspectives. As the cartoon does, the poem ridicules our lack of flexibility in the face of variability and instability. It derides our automatic adoption of a "close to home" perspective, regardless of other likely possible alternatives:

(1)   *A Poem Written by an African Shakespeare*
      Dear white fella
      Couple things you should know
      When I born, I black
      When I grow up, I black
      When I go in sun, I black
      When I cold, I black
      When I scared, I black
      When I sick, I black
      And when I die, I still black.

      You white fella
      When you born, you pink
      When you grow up, you white
      When you go in sun, you red
      When you cold, you blue
      When you scared, you yellow
      When you sick, you green
      And when you die, you grey.

      And you have the cheek to call me colored?

Setting out from a salient, egocentric perspective results in reducing the multifacetedness and versatility of an outgroup member to a single feature ('black'). Even in the face of fluctuating circumstances, for the ('white') Self, the ('black') Other is always homogenous and invariable.[1]

Interestingly, this inflexibility of our salience-bound mind is also conveyed linguistically, through exposing the rigidity of word and concept meaning. Indeed, the first stanza challenges the conventional, most frequent, 'black' sense of *colored*. The second stanza amplifies the challenge by introducing the alternative, less salient (and also less euphemistic) senses of *colored* ('colorfulness', 'versatility'). Nevertheless, in spite of this massive attempt at revising the 'black' sense of *colored,* this sense is not shut out. When, at the end of the poem, we encounter *colored* ("And you have the cheek to call me colored?"—i.e., colorful), we do not activate 'colorful' exclusively. The salient 'black' sense is also invoked.

Language users are sensitive to degrees of salience. No wonder puns tend to spell out the less salient meaning of ambiguous words or expressions, trusting the lexical processor to activate the more salient meaning on its own accord and make the interplay between these meanings possible. Consider the advertisement *Don't leave without a good buy*, inscribed on an airport store, which calls for some interplay between the explicit, less salient meaning ('good bargain') of the homophone (a word having multiple meanings that share the same sound) and its more salient meaning ('good bye').

Or, consider how neologism in spelling by Maude Meehan (1991) (motivated by feminist awareness), inducing novel, nonsalient meanings (*men oh pause*, *men struate*), assumes that the salient meanings of these homophones ('menopause', 'menstruate') will pop up and highlight the differences between the various meanings:

(2)   *MEN OH PAUSE*
      and please take note
      I pen this semi-demi
      dithyramb
      in hope
      that I may set
      you men struate
      That sparse
      and very final show
      of red
      says only
      that a woman has bled
      not that she's dead
      or past delight
      in those
      hot-blooded lusty rites
      witch still transpire
      on any given night
      in grey and white
      haired womens beds

Some puns display the less salient meaning graphically, again, counting on the processor to avail the salient meaning spontaneously. For instance, the advertisement *GET A'HEAD* (fig. 1.2) portrays the less salient literal meaning of 'a head' graphically (and also via the misspelling), assuming that the salient meaning ('advance yourself') of *get ahead* will get across independently and automatically.

Jokes, as well as point stories—stories with a surprise ending—manipulate the very same tendency to opt for the more salient information first, although this time the process occurs in reverse order. Such discourses deliberately re-

Core Soft helps you
Get A'HEAD

Courses offered –

■ SAP R/3
■ Oracle
■ Oracle Financials
■ Oracle DBA
■ Unix
■ C, C⁺⁺
■ Visual Basic
■ Power Builder
■ HTML & Java
■ PeopleSoft

The **Final Word** in Technical Training...

Figure 1.2 Get ahead.

frain from spelling out the intended, less salient meaning, counting on its slower activation. No wonder we are caught off guard, so to speak, ignoring the less salient yet contextually appropriate meaning while accessing the salient meaning first, only to find out that this interpretation requires reinterpretation. For instance, when, in *And Now for Something Completely Different,* Monty Python (McNaughton, 1972) talked about "baby snatchers," they manipulated our tendency to activate the more salient interpretation first in order to catch us by surprise when eventually we find out that it was the babies who did the snatching (of adults).

Note that the practice of deliberately refraining from making the less salient meaning explicit (as in jokes) relies on the same assumption underlying discourses that make it manifest (as in advertisements). They all assume that, while less salient meanings are slow, salient meanings are accessed rapidly. Indeed, this sort of "reflex" is pervasive, irrespective of the fact that it may, at times, be "stupid" (Fodor, 1983), ignoring or resisting sensible behavior.

The following artifact conversation, taken from *The Opposite of Sex*—a movie by Don Roos (1998)—may exemplify our tendency to attend to what is salient to us first, even at the cost of erring. (On a somewhat similar view, see also Fodor, 1983: 70.) The conversation in (3) takes place between Lucia and Bill. Bill is Lucia's late brother's lover, and since Lucia is practically his housemate, Bill's familiarity with her lifestyle is detailed and extensive, inclusive of the fact that she does not date at all:

(3)   Lucia: I don't get sex.
       Bill: You should get out more.
       Lucia: No, I mean I don't understand sex. I don't get it, get it? Just it seems like a
       lot of trouble for not much.

Given Bill's background knowledge about Lucia, to interpret her as saying that she does not 'have'/'receive' sex may be somewhat less informative or relevant (Sperber & Wilson, 1986/1995) than the alternative 'understand' meaning of *get* that may make Bill's interpretation more "sensible." Bill, however, processes the meaning that is most accessible to him and fails to understand Lucia.

The superiority of salience over "sensibility" may be better illustrated by instances in which what we say falls short of what we mean. For example, in the following instances, the presence or absence of an explicit negation marker ('not') does not make a difference. In spite of the apparent inconsistency between (the negative) *couldn't care less* and (the positive) *could care less,* these frequently used collocations are interchangeable. Similarly, regardless of the (Hebrew) negation marker (*lo*), which appears in utterances such as *eix she-lo kor'im lo* ('whatever they do not call him') and *ma she-lo iye* ('whatever won't be') but not in their positive counterparts *eix shekor'im lo* ('whatever they call him') and *ma she-iye* ('whatever will be'), the meaning of the different members of each pair is identical.

Another instance of a linguistic behavior that "does not make sense" but which demonstrates that meaning salience reigns supreme, defying even "logic," is the evolution of the (Hebrew) masculine adjectives *koosi* and *kooson*. These were derived historically from the feminine *koosit* (meaning colloquially 'sexy'), originally a (chauvinist) "compliment" applicable to women only. Although the adjectives' root (*koos*) refers to a women's sex organ (originally an Arabic word), its masculine adjectives (*koosi, kooson*) are now used to refer to sexy men, in spite of the apparent incompatibility. Conventionality and frequency of use thus allow for the word's sense to be divorced from its originally "sensible" meaning and assume a life of its own.

The question, of course, is whether such prominent and independent meanings would be activated even in the presence of highly constraining contexts favoring an alternative meaning. A look at the context in (4), taken from "Miss Furr and Miss Skeene" by Gertrude Stein (1922/1975: 42), might give us an insight into the nature of the question. The context in (4) is heavily weighted in favor of the "happy" meaning of *gay*. However, it is dubious whether, under whatever circumstances, that meaning would be accessed exclusively. For instance, would a gay person, who is highly familiar with the homosexual sense of *gay*, activate only the contextually compatible "happy" sense of the word, while shutting out the contextually incompatible homosexual sense?

(4)   Helen Furr had quite a pleasant home. Mrs. Furr was quite a pleasant woman. Mr. Furr was quite a pleasant man. Helen Furr had quite a pleasant voice quite worth cultivating. She worked to cultivate her voice. She did not find it gay living in the same place where she had always been living. She went to a place where some were cultivating something, voices and other things needing cultivating. She met Georgine Skeene there who was cultivating her voice which some thought was quite a pleasant one. Helen Furr and Georgine Skeene lived together then. Georgine Skeene liked travelling. Helen Furr did not care about travelling, she

liked to stay in one place and be gay there. They were together then and travelled to another place and stayed there and were gay there.

They stayed there and were gay there, not very gay there, just gay there. They were both gay there, they were regularly working there both of them cultivating their voices there, they were both gay there. Georgine Skeene was gay there and she was regular, regular in being gay, regular in not being gay, regular in being a gay one who was not being gay longer than was needed to be one being quite a gay one. They were both gay then there and both working there then.

The goal of *On Our Mind*, then, is to explore the effect of accessible meanings on speech production and comprehension. It aims to shed light, primarily empirically, on how, in addition to contextual information, salient meanings and senses of words and fixed expressions shape our linguistic behavior.

1. Processing Models

Few major proposals attempting to account for how we process information have captured the attention of researchers for the last two decades or so. While they agree that context affects language comprehension and production, they disagree on the temporal stage at which this information comes into play.

1.1 The Interactionist View

For most contemporary theorists, context effects are primary (Bates, 1999; Bates & MacWhinney, 1989; MacWhinney, 1987). Accordingly, a highly constraining context, strongly biased in favor of a certain interpretation, interacts with lexical processes very early on and enables that interpretation to be tapped directly and, on most versions, exclusively. This constraint-based view, dubbed "the direct access" or "interactionist" model, thus, assumes a single mechanism that is sensitive to both linguistic and nonlinguistic information. Consequently, in a rich ecology, comprehension should proceed smoothly and seamlessly, selectively accessing the appropriate interpretation, without involving a contextually inappropriate stage initially (see also Wilson, 1998).

For instance, Vu, Kellas, and Paul (1998); Vu, Kellas, Metcalf, and Herman (2000); and Martin, Vu, Kellas, and Metcalf (1999) showed that when the sentence context (*The biologist wounded the bat*) was sufficiently constraining (compared to *He located the bat*) and weighted in favor of one meaning ('flying mammal') of an ambiguous word (*bat*), that meaning was activated exclusively, without activating the contextually inappropriate alternative meaning ('wooden racket'). This was true even when the appropriate meaning was the less frequent of the two.

Similarly, in a rich and supportive context, for a nonliteral utterance such as *We have come a long way* to be understood, the comprehender need not compute the contextually inappropriate literal meaning of the statement (which depicts individuals walking up a long path) before deriving its metaphoric meaning. Rather, the nonliteral meaning is accessed directly. Likewise, in an ironically biased context, *Thanks for your help* would be understood ironically directly, without having to analyze the sentence's literal interpretation first (Gibbs, 1986a,b, 1994, 2001, 2002; Sperber & Wilson, 1986/1995; but see Hamblin & Gibbs, 2001).

1.2 The Modular View

The direct access view argues against "the modular view" (Fodor, 1983), which assumes modular architecture of mind alongside nonmodular, central, cognitive mechanisms. According to the modular view, linguistic information (among other types of knowledge) is encapsulated and does not have access to other systems' information when processed initially. Rather, initial input analyses are stimulus driven: they are automatic, rapid, and, on some traditional interpretations, exhaustive: all the meanings of a word are accessed upon encounter. The assumption that retrieval of meanings may be speedy and impervious to contextual and world knowledge effects predicts that contextual fit is accidental: at times, the output of the linguistic module would cohere with contextual information; at times, however, it would not and would require further inferential processes. When the latter holds, comprehension would not be smooth, but would initially go astray, with a later stage of revision and adjustment to contextual information. Integration, then, should not be always seamless.[2]

1.3 The Graded Salience Hypothesis

A third option is proposed by "the graded salience hypothesis" (Giora, 1997b, 1999b; Giora & Fein, 1999a,c; Giora, Fein, & Schwartz, 1998; Giora, Peleg, & Fein, 2001; Peleg, Giora, & Fein, 2001, in press; see also chapter 2 in this volume). This hypothesis shares a number of assumptions with the modular view, presuming two distinct mechanisms: one bottom-up, sensitive only to domain-specific (linguistic) information, and another, top-down, sensitive to contextual (both linguistic and extralinguistic) knowledge. However, unlike the traditional modular assumption, the graded salience hypothesis assumes that the modular, lexical access mechanism is ordered: more salient meanings—coded meanings foremost on our mind due to conventionality, frequency, familiarity, or prototypicality—are accessed faster than and reach sufficient levels of activation before less salient ones. According to the graded salience hypothesis, then, coded meanings would be accessed upon encounter, regardless of contextual information or authorial intent. Coded meanings of low salience, however, may not reach sufficient levels of activation to be visible in a context biased toward the more salient meaning of the word (for a different view, see Hillert & Swinney, 2001).

Contextual information may also affect comprehension immediately. A highly predictive context may avail meanings on its own accord very early on.

Nevertheless, it would not penetrate lexical accessing. Although it has a predictive role that may speed up derivation of the appropriate meaning, it would not obstruct inappropriate, coded meanings upon encounter of the lexical stimulus. Indeed, contextual information may be strong and even faster than lexical processes, so much so that it may avail meanings even before the relevant stimulus is encountered, fostering an impression of direct access. This may be particularly true when the stimulus is placed at the end of a strong sentential context, after most information has been accumulated and integrated, allowing effective guessing and inferential processes. However, it does not interact with lexical processes but runs in parallel (Giora, Peleg, & Fein, 2001; Peleg et al., 2001, in press). As will be seen later, assuming a simultaneous operation of the encapsulated, linguistic mechanism and the integrative, central system mechanism allows the graded salience hypothesis to predict when contextual information may be faster than, coincidental with, or slower than linguistic processes. Unlike the modular view, then, the graded salience hypothesis does not always predict slower contextual effects that result in sequential processes. Neither does it assume that activation of a whole linguistic unit should be accomplished before contextual information comes into play. Rather, across the communication path, context and linguistic effects run in parallel, with contextual information availing meanings on its own accord, affecting only the end product of the linguistic process.

Indeed, it is quite often the case that only contextually appropriate meanings are made available for comprehension. However, the claim here is that their exclusive activation is not a consequence of some selective compliance with contextual information but, rather, a function of their salience. For example, although my Hebrew name (Raxel) literally means 'ewe', this meaning most probably escapes anyone who uses my name as a referring expression. This, of course, has nothing to do with context effects. Rather, since the literal meaning of *raxel* is no longer in use, it is not salient enough, and hence of low accessibility. Similarly, it is quite plausible that the appropriate, computer appliance meaning of *mouse* would be the first to occur to a computer freak encountering *mouse* when involved in a discourse about computers. Contrary to appearances, however, directly accessing the appropriate meaning of *mouse* is not a matter of compliance with context but a matter of the accessibility of that meaning or concept in the mind of that comprehender. A novice learning how to use a software, however, might activate (and benefit from) the literal meanings of *window, document, save,* and so on, since to her these senses are more accessible than the appropriate ones. Thus, findings showing that the intended meaning of conventional utterances (idioms and indirect requests) has been processed without any analysis of the sentence's literal interpretation (Gibbs, 1994: 89–90) need not attest to context effects and may very well be affected by meaning salience.

In the next chapters I explain the notion of salience (chapter 2) and look into how salient meanings affect ambiguity resolution (chapter 3), comprehension and production of irony (chapter 4), metaphor and idiom (chapter 5), and jokes (chapter 6). In chapter 7, I look into the role of salience in aesthetic novelty. Chapter 8 sheds a new light on contemporary research and attempts to reconcile the conflicting findings on literal and figurative language in terms of the graded salience hypothesis. Chapter 9 suggests possible extensions and implications of the various findings to theories of mind.

2

Salience and Context

Linguists, cognitive psychologists, and psycholinguists interested in the cognitive processes involved in language comprehension and production need mostly make do with observing the products of such processes—the linguistic entities speakers either emit or attempt to comprehend. But, at times, even these entities may be highly revealing about the nature of the unobservable processes. Consider, for instance, the text in (1). This is a very old riddle. However, even today, when I present it to my students in an introductory course on feminist criticism, it is still as effective as it used to be 15 years ago and is not resolved on the spot:

(1)   A young man and his father had a severe car accident. The father died, and the young man was rushed to the hospital. The surgeon at the emergency room refused to operate on him, saying: "I can't. He is my son." How is this possible?

What does that riddle tell us about the mind? What is (the mindset) ridiculed here? It is (among other things) our inability to instantly adjust to contextual information. Despite ample contextual evidence to the contrary (for instance, the riddle is presented in a course whose orientation is feminist; the immediate and explicit context eliminates the possibility that the surgeon is the young man's father, i.e., male[1]), it is the contextually inappropriate feature of *surgeon* ('male') that comes to mind first (and makes the riddle work). Redressing the "incongruity" or mismatch with context occurs somewhat later, when 'female'—the less frequent/stereotypical/salient feature of *surgeon*—is ac-

13

cessed (for empirical evidence, see Carreiras, Garnham, Oakhill, & Cain, 1996; Oakhill, Garnham, & Reynolds, 1999).

Consider yet another example. The other day, when I was shopping in the mall, I saw a shoe shop named *Body and Sole*. Despite ample contextual evidence supporting the shoe sense of *sole* (I was in a shopping mall, the window shop displayed shoes), I could not refrain from accessing 'soul'—the contextually inappropriate meaning of the homophon—alongside *sole*.

Or consider the following anecdote. Brigitte Nerlich, living in cold England, frequently whining about the cold weather, said to her husband one cold evening that she got cold feet. She knew while saying it that he would never in the world reply to her literal meaning and her literal intention to tell him that she had cold feet, but he would start a joke and comfort her and ask her what she was so worried about, which he naturally did (Nerlich & Clarke, 2001). Again, although the context was heavily biased in favor of the literal meaning of the idiom, it did not inhibit the idiomatic meaning.

This is one thing a product such as these anecdotes may tell us about the mind: the mind is rigid and, at times, error prone. Rather than accessing the compatible information exclusively, it opts for the most accessible information first. On most occasions, the accessible information is also correct—that is, contextually appropriate and compatible with the speaker's intention. On some occasions, however, it is not, and it will result in a search for a contextually compatible meaning.[2]

Has this folk theory about the mind (unveiled by jokes) gained any empirical support? Recently, Keysar (1994b, 1998, 2000); Keysar, Barr, Balin, and Paek (1998); and Keysar, Barr, Balin, and Brauner (2000) adduced evidence supporting the hypothesis that available information is accessed initially, regardless of contextual fit or speaker's intent. For instance, they showed that while searching for anaphor antecedent, the comprehender first accessed the candidate made available by the immediately preceding context, in spite of contextual information demonstrating that this referent could not be the one intended by the speaker. As illustration, consider the following example (taken from Keysar, Barr et al., 1998):

(2)   It is evening, and Boris's young daughter is playing in the other room. Boris, who lives in Chicago, is thinking of calling his lover in Europe. He decides not to call because she is probably asleep given the transatlantic time difference. At that moment his wife returns home and asks, "Is she asleep?"

Keysar, Barr et al. (1998) showed that retrieving the contextually appropriate referent of *she*—the one that could be intended by the speaker, the daughter—was slowed down when there was a more accessible, albeit contextually inappropriate candidate: the lover. The slower reaction suggests that the accessible, albeit contextually inappropriate referent was accessed and interfered with the retrieval of the contextually compatible referent. Such findings are consistent with the view that contextual information does not affect initial access: it does not preselect the contextually appropriate candidate (the daughter) while inhibiting the inappropriate one (the lover).

What is there about these meanings that makes them so privileged that even a highly biasing context is ineffective in blocking them? What makes them so salient, so foremost on our mind? The aim of this chapter is to point out some of the factors that make meanings unavoidable; more specifically, it aims to render precise the notion of salience so as to lay the foundation for the imminent discussions (in the following chapters) of the role of salience in language comprehension and production.

1. Salience

According to the graded salience hypothesis (Giora, 1997b, 1999b), for information to be *salient*—to be foremost on one's mind—it needs to undergo consolidation,[3] that is, to be stored or coded in the mental lexicon (for instance, the 'male' and 'female' features of *surgeon* in (1); the idiomatic meaning 'fear' of *cold feet*). Stored information is superior to unstored information such as novel information or information inferable from context: while salient information is highly accessible, nonsalient information requires strongly supportive contextual information to become as accessible as salient information. Information derived on the basis of given/stored knowledge (such as script-based or thematic-related knowledge), though predictable, is not salient and, at times, slower than when it is mentioned. For example, *The beer was warm* was read faster following *We got some beer out of the trunk* than following *We checked the picnic supplies* (Haviland & Clark, 1974; Gernsbacher, 1990; Sanford & Garrod, 1981). Similarly, meanings associated with a word that was mentioned in the text were shown to be primed instantly (about 300–350 milliseconds after onset of the prime). In contrast, inferences made on the basis of script or thematic information took longer to retrieve (about 500–750 milliseconds after onset of the prime; see Till, Mross, & Kintsch, 1988; Long, Oppy, & Seely, 1994). Specifically, immediately after reading *The townspeople were amazed to find that all the buildings had collapsed except the mint*, test words related to the contextually appropriate ('money') and contextually inappropriate ('candy') meanings of the target word (*mint*) were primed. However, a test word related to a thematic inference ('earthquake') took longer to retrieve (1000 milliseconds after onset of the prime).[4]

Salience is not an either-or notion, however. Rather, it admits degrees. The more frequent (Hogaboam & Perfetti, 1975; Liu, Bates, Powell, & Wulfeck, 1997; Neill, Hilliard, & Cooper, 1988), familiar (Blasko & Connine, 1993; Gentner & Wolff, 1997; Gernsbacher, 1984; Hintzman & Curran, 1994; Wiley & Rayner, 2000), conventional (Dascal, 1987, 1989; Gibbs, 1980, 1982, 1983; Ortony, Vondruska, Foss, & Jones, 1985: 587), or prototypical/stereotypical (Armstrong, Gleitman, & Gleitman, 1983; Rosch, 1973; Rosch & Mervis, 1975; Talmy, 2000: chap. 5) the information in the mind of the individual or in a certain linguistic community, the more salient it is in that mind or among the community members. Let us consider the relation of these factors to salience in more detail.

1.1 Frequency

Both (noun) meanings of *bank*—the 'financial institution' and the 'river-edge' meanings—are coded in the mental lexicon. However, for those of us who interact with commercial banks more often than with riverbanks, the institutional sense of *bank* is more frequently used and hence foremost on our minds—that is, salient. The more frequent the meaning, the quicker it is to retrieve (Galbraith & Taschman, 1969; Howes & Soloman, 1951; Just & Carpenter, 1980; Kawamoto, 1993; Rubenstein, Garfield, & Millikan, 1970; Seidenberg, Waters, Barnes, & Tanenhaus, 1984; Whaley, 1978; Zwitserlood, 1989).

The notion of frequency assumed here may be related to probability of occurrence recently investigated by scholars such as Burgess and Lund (1997); Carroll and Rooth (1998); Hindle and Rooth (1993); Jurafsky (1996); Landauer (1999); Landauer and Dumais (1997); Landauer, Foltz, & Laham (1998); and Lund, Burgess, and Atchley (1995). It may also be correlated with frequency of cooccurrence of meanings in the mental lexicon, which may but need not be correlated with frequency of occurrence at the referential or real world level. For example, the Palestinians' neologism, expressing their suspicion that "the Wye agreement" (occurred in Baltimore in October 1998) would turn into *a peace of paper*, hinges on the frequency of cooccurrence of *piece* and *paper* in the collocation *a piece of paper*. Although the discourse in which *a peace of paper* occurs abounds in repetitions of its components (*peace, paper*), the new coinage owes its meaningfulness to the frequency of cooccurrence of the linguistic components of *a piece of paper* that make up the lexicalized unit. This cooccurrence is frequent, regardless of the frequency of occurrence of concrete, real-life 'pieces' and 'paper', and it establishes the strength of association between the components of the collocation that accounts for its salience.[5]

1.2 Familiarity

The meanings of 'plant' and 'structure' of *tree* might both be coded in the mental lexicon. However, while both are familiar among linguists, the (syntactic) 'structure' meaning of *tree* may be entirely unfamiliar to lay persons (although they might have the notion of *family tree*). Similarly, since I am a female feminist linguist, I am more experientially familiar with the generic sense of the feminine gender (e.g., *her/she* in *The speaker must be relevant to **her** addressee. **She** should take his background knowledge into consideration*) than most of my students. Meanings may be frequent yet less experientially familiar to an individual, and vice versa (Gernsbacher, 1984). Or they can be familiar though less frequent (Wiley & Rayner, 2000). The more familiar the meaning, the quicker it is to retrieve (Blasko & Connine, 1993; Gernsbacher, 1984; Hintzman & Curran, 1994).

1.3 Conventionality

I need four fifteen-cent stamps is a more conventional way of requesting stamps at the post office than *I need the time* when asking someone to tell you the time; *A fine friend you are* is more conventionally sarcastic than *You are a fine/excellent friend* (Gibbs, 1982); *I'm afraid* is a more conventional way of hedging a piece of bad news than reporting on one's feelings ('I am frightened'; see Erman & Warren, 2001). Conventionality may be viewed as "a relation among a linguistic regularity, a situation of use, and a population that has implicitly agreed to conform to that regularity in that situation out of preference for general uniformity, rather than because there is some obvious and compelling reason to conform to that regularity instead of some other" (Nunberg, Sag, & Wasow, 1994: 492n). Whether conventionality is motivated or arbitrary makes no difference at this point (for a discussion of motivated and arbitrary conventions, see Gibbs, 1986a, 1994: 319–358; Lewis, 1969).[6] The more conventional the meaning, the quicker it is to retrieve.

1.4 Prototypicality/Stereotypicality

On encountering *bird,* comprehenders are more likely to access a prototypical (robin, sparrow) than a marginal (chicken, penguin) member of the category of birds, given similar frequency of occurrence and sometimes regardless of frequency of occurrence of real-life members (Rosch, 1973; Rosch & Mervis, 1975). Indeed, participants were faster to verify that a stereotypical member (e.g., secretary, nurse) is a *woman* than a marginal member of the category (boss, surgeon, comedian; see Armstrong et al., 1983). The more prototypical the meaning, the quicker it is to retrieve.

Are these factors (familiarity, frequency, conventionality, and prototypicality) correlated? Is any of these factors more weighted? Could these factors be subsumed under one category? Familiarity seems the more crucial factor (see Gernsbacher, 1984; Wiley & Rayner, 2000). Indeed, it is plausible to assume that a meaning that is either frequent, conventional, or prototypical/stereotypical is likely to be more familiar to an individual than is an alternative meaning low on these variables. Yet, this is not necessarily the case. For instance, a meaning may be frequent but experientially unfamiliar to an individual (see Gernsbacher, 1984). Similarly, a meaning may be infrequent (the 'structure' meaning of *tree*) but familiar to an individual (Wiley & Rayner, 2000). Such are meanings of "forbidden" words (four-letter words, taboo words related to, for example, sex), which must be foremost on our mind in spite of their infrequent use. Further, a certain word or utterance may be a conventional manner of speech under certain circumstances without being used frequently (for example, I may know the conventional way of asking someone to tell the time, although this may be a less frequent or familiar experience since I spend most of my time with intimates among whom politeness is rare; see Brown & Levinson, 1987). Similarly, two members (chickens; pigeons) of the same category ('birds') may be equally frequent or familiar (such as among farmers who grow both birds).

However one (pigeon) may be a more salient member in the category (of birds) on account of its prototypicality.

1.5 Gradability and Its Dynamics

Given that a salient sense of a word or an expression is the one directly computable from the mental lexicon irrespective of inferences drawn on the basis of contextual information, to what extent is salience a graded notion? It is graded in that it conceives of the lexicon as hierarchically structured. Although the various meanings of a word (*bank*) may be listed, one (the 'institutional' sense of *bank*) may be more salient, while the other (the 'riverside' sense of *bank*) may be less salient.

In addition, it is graded in that it assumes that the internal hierarchical structure of the lexicon is not fixed, but dynamic. For example, when the term *the West Bank* was first used by a metonymic extension to refer to the Palestinian territories occupied by Israel, it had a novel, nonsalient (though inferable) meaning. (The term probably started its career as 'the west bank of the Jordan River'). As of now, in a certain community of speakers, its salient meaning is its political sense (so much so that my spell-check won't accept the phrase in lowercase letters).

Or, take Swinney's (1979) notorious *bug* as another example (see also section 2.1). Possibly, it is undergoing a linguistic change—a reshuffling of salience—as might be deduced from the following title of an article in *Newsweek*: "Bugged by Y2K? Investors wonder what to do about their stocks, just in case the millennium bites" (August 1998: 48B). Comprehending *bugged* activates instantly both the 'concern' and the 'computer bug' meanings. As for the 'insect' meaning of *bug*, it seems quite plausible to assume that that meaning is now less salient, given that it catches us by surprise at the end of the sentence. Or take related examples. For people frequently interacting with computers, the salient meanings of *desktop, windows, folder, document, paste, inbox, mail, download*, and other such terms are metaphorical. Their literal meanings, once salient, have lost their priority. No wonder *mail* now denotes 'electronic' mail, while the 'post' system meaning is now a marked case, entitled *snail mail*.

1.6 Can a Constituent Longer Than a Word Be Salient?

Though salience relates primarily to lexical meanings, it is also concerned with the meaning of an utterance or message. Could phrases or sentences have salient/stored meanings over and above those of their individual words? Could meanings of whole phrases (*spill the beans; get cold feet*) be salient, too? Are they accessed alone? Are they accessed alongside the meanings of the individual words (or morphemes) that make them up? Would that meaning override the salient meaning of the individual words? According to the graded salience hypothesis, they would reach similar levels of activation if they are equally salient (see also Clark, 1979; McGlone, Glucksberg, & Cacciari, 1994). They would not, in case they are unbalanced in terms of salience, as is the idiomatic meaning of a familiar idiom relative to the literal interpretation of its individual words (Van de Voort & Vonk, 1995).

For illustration, consider the following example (originally in Hebrew, dated February 1998), in which both the intended, contextually compatible, literal meaning and the unintended, contextually incompatible, idiomatic meaning of the whole sentence were accessed:

Iddo and Omri (both aged 7 years, 8 months and both native speakers of Hebrew) are eating supper together. Iddo fetches himself a glass of juice out of the refrigerator.
(3)   Omri: I want to drink, too.
    Iddo's mother: Iddo, *totci lo et ha-mic* ('take the juice out [of the refrigerator] for him').
    Iddo (laughingly): ha... ha... ***le-hotci lo et ha-mic*** ('to take/squeeze the juice out of him'—a Hebrew idiom meaning 'drive one crazy'). (Mira Ariel, personal communication)

Iddo's laughter suggests that he has accessed the idiomatic meaning of the whole idiomatic phrase, as well as the compositional (literal) meaning. His amusement seems to disclose the computed discrepancy between the two (suggested, further, by the need he felt to repeat the idiom). Although the idiomatic meaning of the speaker's utterance was not the intended meaning, nor was it compatible with the context, it was not ignored; contextual information did not inhibit its activation.

This example suggests that a phrase or a sentence as a whole may have salient meaning(s) that will be activated automatically, irrespective of contextual information. Indeed, Giora and Fein (1999c) provide evidence consistent with the view that familiar idioms always avail their salient idiomatic meanings, even when contextually incompatible, as in contexts biasing their interpretation toward the literal meaning. Thus, subjects completed as many fragmented words related to the idiomatic meaning of familiar idioms (*on one leg,* meaning in Hebrew 'briefly') embedded in literally biasing contexts (*In the zoo, I saw a stork standing on one leg*) as they did words related to the literal (compositional) meaning. Further, they completed more fragmented words related to the idiomatic meaning of the idiom in the literally biasing context than they did words related to the literal meaning of the idiom in the idiomatically biased context. These findings suggest that the salient (idiomatic) meaning of the message was inescapable, despite the contextual bias towards the literal interpretation (see chapter 5 in this volume).

It is also possible, however, that highly salient idioms would activate their idiomatic meanings faster. Recall how Nerlich's complaint about her cold feet was entirely lost on her husband who took her only idiomatically. Empirical findings also suggest that salient meanings of fixed expressions may override those of their individual words. In Gibbs (1980), idiomatic meanings were activated rapidly: they were faster to process when the context was biased toward the idiomatic than toward the literal interpretation. Apparently the frequency of *kick the bucket* as a fixed, idiomatic unit exceeds that of its literal (compositional) interpretation, which relies on the frequency of the individual words, and thus makes the former more salient than the latter (see also Popiel & McRae, 1988; Van de Voort & Vonk, 1995). In the same vein, the degree of frozenness of idioms may index their salience—their storage as a lexicalized unit.[7] In light of these findings, it seems plausible to assume that some phrases may have salient (lexicalized) meanings processed first or in parallel with the meanings of their individual words (McGlone, Glucksberg, & Cacciari, 1994; Nunberg, Sag, & Wasow, 1994; for a review, see Gibbs, 1994 and Gibbs & Gonzales, 1985).

Evidence from other familiar, conventionalized phrases/sentences seems to be consistent with the assumption that meanings of phrases or sentences may be stored as discrete units. For instance, familiar metaphorical phrases/ sentences have been shown to be accessed initially both literally and meta- phorically (Williams, 1992)[8] and avail both meanings in metaphorically as well as in literally biasing contexts (Giora & Fein, 1999c). Similarly, familiar ironic utterances (*Tell me about it*) were shown to be accessed initially both lit- erally and ironically in the ironically as well as in the literally biasing contexts (Giora & Fein, 1999a), suggesting that their phrasal salient meanings were ac- tivated regardless of contextual information. In addition, familiar proverbs (*The grass is greener on the other side of the fence*) were shown to take equally long to read as their literal equivalents and to be processed literally and figura- tively, regardless of contextual bias (Turner & Katz, 1997; see also Katz & Fer- retti, 2000, 2001).

Would the compositional literal meaning of a sentence be salient? The compositional meaning of a sentence would not be salient, since it has not been lexicalized. However, to the extent that the intended, compositional meaning of a sentence relies on the salient meanings of its components, it would be easier to process than when it is not. Although the sum of the components' meanings is not listed in the mental lexicon as a discrete unit, when integrated into a sen- tence, this compositional meaning will be more accessible than is the composi- tional meaning of an equivalent sentence whose intended meaning hinges on the less salient meanings of its lexical entries. For instance, the meaning of the following *New York Times* headline (cited in Glucksberg, 2001: 16)—*Price Soars for Eggs, Setting off a Debate on a Clinic's Ethics*—is hard to get because its intended meaning relies on the less salient meanings of its components (the less salient 'human eggs' or 'ova' sense of *eggs*). Had *eggs* been replaced by 'human eggs', the difficulty of making up the compositional sense of the sen- tence would be reduced significantly.

Note, further, that the compositional meaning of a sentence (relying on the salient meanings of its component) is also more accessible than an inference or a conversational implicature drawn on its basis. Thus, the meaning of *What a lovely day for a picnic* in the context of a stormy day involves the implicature that the day is far from being lovely. This implicature is less accessible than the compositional meaning of the sentence, suggesting that the day is lovely (Giora, Fein, & Schwartz, 1998; Giora & Fein, 1999a). Recall, however, that some im- plicatures have become conventionalized, and are, therefore, salient (*kick the bucket; Tell me about it*).

On the basis of existing evidence, it is plausible to assume that some strings have stored meanings above and beyond the individual meanings of the words that make them up, but the measures prevalent in the literature have not been specialized to warrant a distinction between word and phrase/sentence level. For one, reading times of whole sentences might be particularly misleading in that they may mask differences in underlying cognitive process (Gibbs & Gerrig, 1989). Indeed, findings of equal reading times for metaphoric and literal target sentences which were taken to support an assumption of equivalent processes (Inhoff, Lima, & Carroll, 1984; Ortony, Schallert, Reynolds, & Antos, 1978) were shown to mask processing difficulty at the critical word level (Brisard, Frisson, & Sandra, 2001; Janus & Bever, 1985; chapter 8 in this volume). Similarly, attesting to the availability of a phrase or a sentence meaning by tapping word meaning (i.e., using words as probes) may not be sufficiently revealing about the meaning of the phrase or the sentence as a whole. As will be seen later, many of the probes used were related to a specific word in the sentence rather than to the meaning of the sentence as a whole (see Gibbs, 2002, for such a critique). In some cases this insensitivity is crucial. For example, if, when testing whether *kick the bucket* is interpreted either literally or idiomatically (or both), the probes used are 'die' (related to the idiomatic, message level sense) and 'jug' (literally associated with the word 'bucket'), then these probes measure different levels of meanings.

In sum, the graded salience hypothesis does not subscribe to any unified view of the mental lexicon as containing just one type of entry. It is consistent with the view that the lexicon accommodates specified, discrete entries for individual word meanings alongside underspecified meanings and senses. It is consistent with the view that word meanings may be distributed across layers of units representing semantic features in a network. It has no difficulty accepting that "each word is a constellation of semantic features so that subsets of these features participate in the meanings of other related words" (Vu, personal communication, 25 August 2000). Similarly, it has no difficulty accepting that the meanings of segments longer than a word (idioms, fixed expressions) are coded alongside the meanings of their components. It only postulates that coded meanings/senses are always activated upon encounter of the relevant stimulus, with less salient meanings not always reaching a threshold.

1.7   Measures of Salience

How can meaning salience be measured, then? What norming studies can be used to test the salience—that is, the accessibility—of meanings of words or collocations out of context? Measures of word frequency and probability are already available (Burgess & Lund, 1997; Carroll, Davis, & Richman, 1976; Carroll & Rooth, 1998; Hindle & Rooth, 1993; Jurafsky, 1996; Kucera & Francis, 1967; Landauer & Dumais, 1997; Lund, Burgess, & Atchley, 1995). Alternatively, frequency or familiarity ratings of both meanings of words and phrases can be collected from native speakers. This seems to be the most frequent measure used in the literature.

In our studies, we either measured response times to probes related and un-related to targets placed in neutral contexts (Peleg, Giora, & Fein, 2001, in press) or asked native speakers to act as lexicographers and write down the meanings of sentences and phrases (metaphors and ironies) that came to mind first and could illustrate the meanings of the stimuli in the lexicon (see Giora & Fein, 1999a). We also used completion of word fragments out of context to measure salience out of context (Giora & Fein, 1999c; chapters 4–5 in this volume). In word fragment completion tests, participants are asked to complete a fragmented word (b-tt-r) with the first word that comes to mind (*better, bitter, butter*). In addition, reaction times to probes related to the various meanings of the homonym[9] can also be collected out of context or in a neutral context. For instance, Williams (1992) measured response times to the various meanings ('strict', 'solid') of a polysemous word (*firm*) in the context of that word only. Giora, Peleg, and Fein (2001) measured response times to probes related to the various meanings of an ambiguous word in the context of a neutral sentence. Similar response times reflect similar salience. Different response times reflect salience imbalance.

2. Context Effects

Can a supportive context affect the accessibility of compatible meanings of a word or an expression? According to the graded salience hypothesis, top-down contextual processes can be predictive and affect the availability of meanings very early on. However, these guessing, inferential processes do not interact with lexical processes but run in parallel (Fodor, 1983; Giora, Peleg, & Fein, 2001; Peleg et al., 2001, in press).[10] Note, however, that some "contextual effects" are actually intralexical—that is, processes operating inside the input system (the mental lexicon) itself (Fodor, 1983: 81). For instance, a prior occurrence of a word semantically related to an immediately following word may affect ease of processing of that word (for a review, see Balota, 1994). Thus, in *I needed money, so I went to the bank*, the prior occurrence of the word *money* may speed up activation of the financial institution meaning of *bank*. In *Standing on the riverbank I saw some fish*, *river* may facilitate activation of the river-side meaning of *bank*. This kind of facilitation is usually referred to as *priming*. It is attributed to automatic spread of activation between related meanings in the lexicon.

The contextual effects assumed by the graded salience hypothesis occur when a strong and supportive context speeds up processes on the basis of previous knowledge and expectations regarding the progression of the text (Fodor, 1983: 75–78; Giora, Peleg, & Fein, 2001; Hernandez, Fennema-Notestine, Udell, & Bates, 2001; Peleg et al., 2001, in press; Rayner, Binder, & Duffy, 1999). For example, context facilitates word recognition: words may be recognized earlier in context than out of context (Grosjean, 1980; Marslen-Wilson & Tyler, 1980; Tulving & Gold, 1963; Tyler & Wessels, 1983, 1985). Context improves comprehenders' ability in a cloze procedure (where participants have to fill in missing words in a text; Schwanenflugel & Shoben, 1985). Cloze probability (the probability that the target is predictable in a context based on sentence completions) improved naming performance (Liu et al., 1997). Thus, in the absence of context, it might be difficult to discover what word *-epre-se-* corresponds to. But, having seen *After his wife died, John became very -epre-se-*, the task is much easier (Forster, 1989: 92), particularly when the target is placed in final position (Peleg et al., 2001, in press). Indeed, listeners were shown to derive an expectation about word meaning from the sentence context very early on. And when there was no incongruity involved, semantic integration began with only partial sensory information about the word identity (Van Petten, Coulson, Rubin, Plante, & Parks, 1999).

Importantly, the predictive contextual mechanism assumed by the graded salience hypothesis is such that allows for the anticipation of oncoming meanings and concepts rather than the specific words that have been selected to represent them (Peleg et al., 2001, in press). Thus in (4), contextual information affects the predictability of an oncoming effect on the basis of its strength of association with a given cause: reading time was longer for each oncoming string (*The next day his body was covered in bruises*) substantiating the effect as a function of relaxing the strength of association between that effect and the previous causal context (Keenan, 1978):

(4) a. Joey's big brother punched him again and again.
      The next day his body was covered in bruises.

     b. Racing down the hill Joey fell off his bike.
      The next day his body was covered in bruises.

     c. Joey's crazy mother became furiously angry with him.
      The next day his body was covered in bruises.

     d. Joey went to a neighbor's house to play.
      The next day his body was covered in bruises.

Other factors may influence context predictiveness. For instance, manifesting features that are salient in the target concept (for example, see the contexts in Martin, Vu, Kellas, & Metcalf, 1999, and Vu, Kellas, & Paul, 1998) or making explicit the meaning of the target word before that word is encountered (Rayner, Pacht, & Duffy, 1994) should contribute to the predictability of that meaning. Additionally, a given discourse segment may be predictive of the topic of the next discourse segment (Ariel, 1990; Giora, 1985a,b) as shown by Ortony et al. (1978) and Peleg et al. (2001, in press), though, again, not necessarily of the word selected to represent it.

Effects due to contextual expectations, background knowledge, or utilities are pre-lexical processes in the sense that they occur outside the input system (the lexicon). Although they show that "there exist *some* language-handling processes that have access to the hearer's expectations about what is likely to be said, they do *not* show that the input systems enjoy such access" (Fodor, 1983: 75).

Context may also have postlexical effects, influencing meaning selection and integration after the initial activation stage. Thus, context may suppress a contextually inappropriate meaning so that only the appropriate meaning would be retained for further processes (Fodor, 1983; Swinney, 1979), or it may maintain them both, depending on their function in constructing the intended meaning (Giora & Fein, 1999a,b,c; Williams, 1992; chapters 4–5 in this volume).

While context postlexical effects are widely acknowledged, exactly how contextual information constrains initial access of lexical information has been an important topic of research since the 1970s. (For an overview, see Gernsbacher, 1984; Gorfein, 1989; Katz, 1998; Simpson, 1984, 1994; Small, Cottrell, & Tanenhaus, 1988.) As will be shown later (chapter 3), much of the evidence adduced by psychological research of lexical processes is consistent with the graded salience hypothesis, which assumes that salient information should not be blocked even when contextually incompatible. While context may be predictive of certain meanings, it is deemed ineffective in obstructing initial access of salient information (Carpenter & Daneman, 1981; MacDonald, Pearlmutter, & Seidenberg, 1994; Rayner et al., 1994; Tabossi, 1988). Thus, while *river* in *riverbank* may prime the less salient 'riverside' meaning of *bank* (probably due to intralexical effects), it may not filter out the activation of its more salient, 'financial institution' meaning upon its encounter, in spite of contextual misfit (see chapter 3 in this volume). The main claim of the graded salience hypothesis, then, is that salient meanings are processed automatically (though not necessarily solely), irrespective of contextual information and strength of bias. Although context effects may be fast, they run in parallel and do not interact with lexical processes initially. This claim may be conceived of in terms of Stroop's study (1935), in which the instruction to readers to decide on the color of words (analogous to contextual information) did not inhibit access of the meaning of the words, which, when inconsistent with contextual information (color), induced interference (for converging evidence, see Binder & Rayner, 1998, 1999; Giora, Peleg, & Fein, 2001; Peleg et al., 2001, in press; Rayner et al., 1999; for a different view, see Martin et al., 1999; Vu, Kellas, Metcalf, & Herman, 2000; Vu et al., 1998).

Assuming distinct mechanisms that run in parallel allows the graded salience hypothesis to predict when contextual effects may be either faster, as speedy as, or slower than lexical processes (see also Giora, Peleg, & Fein, 2001; Peleg et al., 2001, in press). The next chapters will attempt to investigate these predictions by reference to comprehension and production of ambiguous, figurative, and literal language.

2.1 Measures of Context Effects

How can context effects be measured in relation to salience effects? Since a predictive context does not necessarily anticipate a certain word, but, rather, a certain meaning or concept, cloze probability tests (as used by Schwanenflugel, 1991; Vu et al., 1998) are not an adequate measure of concept predictiveness.

These tests focus on the predictability of a specific word from its previous context rather than on the predictability of a concept from that context. (They could be, however, if a range of words related to the concept were taken into consideration.) In contrast, reading times or response times are adequate. Consider, for instance, the following joke (taken from Coulson & Kutas, 1998):

(5)   By the time Mary had had her fourteenth child, she'd finally run out of names to call her
       (a) offspring [*Nonjoke ending*]
       (b) husband [*Joke ending*]

While *husband* and *offspring* had similar cloze probability (of 4% and 2%, respectively), *husband* took longer to read than *offspring*. Indeed, although the word *offspring* is quite infrequent and therefore unpredictable, the concept it represents in that context is not. In contrast, given the same specific context, the concept of 'husband' is unpredictable (requiring a "frame shift," to cite Coulson & Kutas). No wonder it took longer to read than *offspring*. Reading times, then, are better adept than are cloze probability tests at indexing concept availability and predictability.

Since salient meanings are assumed to be activated automatically, online measures, which reflect the moment by moment comprehension, must, in fact, be the best methods to test whether context may inhibit salient meanings. Among such methods are lexical decision tasks (such as when participants have to make a decision as to whether a probe is a word or a nonword) made upon encountering the key (ambiguous, figurative) word in the (context of the) target sentence. For example, upon hearing *bugs* in *The man was not surprised when he found several spiders, roaches, and other **bugs** in the corner of his room*, participants were presented with a visual letter string ('ant', 'spy'), displayed on a monitor screen. Having decided whether the letter string is a word or a nonword, participants pressed a "yes" or "no" key (Swinney, 1979). Naming is another task (see chapter 3 in this volume). Faster response times to related (versus unrelated) words presented instantly, regardless of context, reflect salience effects and lack of context effects at the initial access phase. In contrast, faster response to contextually compatible versus incompatible words reflects the superiority of contextual effects over salience.

Recording eye movements and fixations while participants are engaged in reading sentences naturally is considered a superior measure in that it taps very early processes. Moreover, unlike lexical decisions, it does not interrupt the natural reading course. An even more ecologically valid measure is recording eye movements with a head-mounted eye tracking system (i.e., a camera mounted on a lightweight helmet, which frees participants from the unnatural chin-fixated posture involved in traditional eye tracking methods; see Tanenhaus, Spivey-Knowlton, Eberhard, & Sedivy, 1995). Long eye fixations reflect processing difficulties, while short ones reflect ease of processing (for a review, see Rayner & Sereno, 1994; Rayner, Sereno, Morris, Schmauder, & Clifton, 1989; Sereno, 1995).

A similarly ecologically valid measure is moving windows (Just, Carpenter, & Wooley, 1982), which can unintrusively detect locus of online effects. In this self-paced, word-by-word reading task, each sentence initially appears to be constructed of dashes. When the participant presses the space bar, the sentence's first word appears in the dashes. With each subsequent press of the space bar, the next word appears and the preceding word reverts to dashes. Consequently, participants can see the length of the sentence and the relative lengths of the words, but they can only read one word at a time. The computer records the time between depressions of the space bar as the reading time for the word displayed during that interval. This procedure imitates the natural reading process and permits the computation of reading latency for each item in the target sentence and in the sentence that follows (attesting to "spill-over effects"—effects that occur a few words into the next sentence; Pexman, Ferretti, & Katz, 2000). Difficulties in processing may suggest, among other things, that a salient, though contextually incompatible meaning has been activated initially. It should be noted, however, that tracking eye movement or reading speed cannot disclose which meanings are involved. Nevertheless, even though none of these measures on its own provides conclusive evidence, altogether, they might adduce strong support.

3. When Do Salient Meanings Die Off?

The question as to how long comprehenders retain activated salient meanings may be particularly intriguing with regard to salient but contextually incompatible meanings. The assumption is that meanings are retained if they might be conducive to the interpretation process, but they are discarded (reduced below baseline rates) if they interfere with comprehension and fade if they have no role in comprehension (the retention hypothesis; Giora & Fein, 1999c and chapters 4–5 in this volume). Thus, the prediction as to when salient meanings are deactivated or die off need not distinguish contextually compatible from incompatible meanings. Rather, it should distinguish instrumental from noninstrumental meanings.

Findings in my lab (see chapter 4) show that salient, though contextually incompatible meanings that are instrumental in constructing the utterance interpretation may be retained longer than equivalent, contextually compatible meanings which are no longer instrumental. For example, the salient, literal meaning ('nice') of (unfamiliar) ironies (*What a lovely day for a picnic*) is retained longer in an irony-inducing context (a stormy day) than in a literally biasing context (a sunny day). While the literal meaning may be involved in constructing the ironic interpretation even 2000 milliseconds after offset of the target sentence, this is not the case with the literal interpretation of the same utterance. The literal meaning of an utterance embedded in a literally biasing context, it is hypothesized, is comprehended instantly. Having been accessed and integrated, the salient, contextually compatible meaning need not retain its initial activation levels and may begin to fade (see figure 4.6).

Salient meanings that disrupt comprehension tend to be suppressed (Gernsbacher, 1989, 1990; Gernsbacher & Faust, 1990, 1991). For instance, Williams (1992) showed that salient meanings ('strict') of polysemous words (*firm*) are activated initially but are deactivated in a context in which they are irrelevant ('firm bed'). However, meanings conducive to the utterance interpretation ('solid') are retained even when they are not intended (*firm teacher*).

It has been observed that some meanings are so salient, they resist suppression even when they are not instrumental to the comprehension process and might even divert attention. Such is the idiomatic meaning of idioms. Recall the anecdotal instances where *got cold feet* or *totci lo et ha-mic* were interpreted idiomatically in spite of contextual information to the contrary, affecting misunderstanding or laughter. Recall, further, how the contextually incompatible idiomatic meaning of an idiom intended literally was recycled for humorous purposes, possibly because it could neither be ignored nor suppressed (example 3 in this chapter). Similarly, idiomatically related test words were shown to be facilitated in a literally biasing context when measures were off-line (Giora & Fein, 1999c). In addition, in contrast to the suppression hypothesis (Gernsbacher, 1990), the ironic meaning of salient ironies was not suppressed in literally biasing contexts (Giora & Fein, 1999a; chapter 4 in this volume).[11]

4. What Salience Is Not

A number of central notions regarding meaning are prevalent in the literature, which should be distinguished from meaning salience. Researchers have discussed semantic meaning, enriched pragmatic meaning, literal meaning, salient features, linguistic meaning, explicature, implicature, grounded/embodied meaning, accessible entities, relevant meaning, and preferred interpretation. Is salience related to any of these notions?

4.1 Relevant Meaning

Is salient information identical to relevant information à la Sperber and Wilson (1986/1995)? According to Sperber and Wilson, information is relevant to the extent that it incurs contextual effects at a reasonably small cost. For instance, if I don't know what day today is and you tell me the day (upon my request), my set of contextual assumptions is increased. If you tell me that yesterday was Monday, I will be able to infer what today is and enlarge my set of assumptions, but I will have to invest more effort in the process. If I am not sure whether today is Tuesday and you confirm that it is, you have strengthened this assumption, so I feel more confident about it now. Or if, by mistake, I assume it is Monday and you correct me, your contribution is relevant to me, since it makes me replace a wrong assumption (that is, if I trust you) with a correct one, and so forth. All these are possible contextual effects. Some of these individual contextual effects are achieved at a small cost, which makes them more relevant than those that are more costly. Thus, the greater the number of contextual effects an utterance has in a given context, the more relevant it is in that context relative to a similarly effortful alternative that is poorer in contextual effects. Similarly, the less effortful the interpretation of an utterance in a given context, the more relevant it is in that context relative to a similarly productive alternative.

Given Sperber and Wilson's view that relevant information cost-effectively modifies comprehenders' cognitive environment, salient information need not be relevant. It may be, however, since it is accessed automatically, and on occasion it is also compatible with contextual information, seamlessly integrating with it while incurring contextual effects. On other occasions, however, it may not be since it is contextually incompatible and would not integrate with contextual information. Consider, for instance, the salient, literal meaning of (conventional and novel) metaphors and (conventional and novel) ironies which, though irrelevant—inducing no contextual effects—is nevertheless activated automatically and, on some views, retained for further processes (Giora, 1995, 1997b, 1998b, 1999b; Giora & Fein, 1999a,b,c; Giora et al., 1998). Such is also the central meaning ('solid') of polysemous words (*firm*). When embedded in a context biased toward their less central sense ('strict'), the central meaning ('solid') of polysemous words is activated and retained despite contextual incompatibility. When it is not related to the intended meanings, it is deactivated (Williams, 1992; see also chapter 3 in this volume). Salience, then, is indifferent to relevance.

At first blush, one component of relevance—the notion of accessibility—might seem akin to salience. According to relevance theory, accessible assumptions (assumptions made available by the immediate context) affect the relevance of incoming utterances by decreasing their processing load. Unlike the graded salience hypothesis, relevance theory focuses on accessible contexts. Although the graded salience hypothesis acknowledges the predictive and facilitative effects of contextual information, it is concerned primarily with the accessibility of meanings *out* of context—that is, with the effect of the comprehension process on highly salient/accessible context-free meanings. Thus, while relevance theory lays emphasis on the role contextual information plays in comprehension, the graded salience hypothesis underlines the role coded meanings play in the same process vis-à-vis contextual information.

4.2 Embodied Meaning

Is salient meaning an embodied meaning, a meaning shaped by our bodily experiences? Recent accounts of how we make sense of language point to the primary role grounded and embodied meanings play in language comprehension (Glenberg, 1997; Glenberg & Robertson, 2000; Harnad, 1990, 1993; Johnson, 1987; Lakoff, 1987; Lakoff & Johnson, 1980). Briefly, how we perceive and conceive of the environment is viewed as determined by the type of body we have, the structure of the environment, and our mind. According to Glenberg (1997), cognitive structures are embodied to facilitate action in and interaction with a three-dimensional environment: "Because language acts as a surrogate for more direct interaction, language comprehension must also result in embodied representations, which are in fact mental models". According to such action-based theory of memory, concepts become related not via associations but through separate patterns of actions that can be combined or "meshed," given the constraints of our bodies (Glenberg, 1997: 1; for similar proposals, see also Barsalou & Prinz, 1997; Prinz & Barsalou, 2002; Solomon & Barsalou, 1997; Wu, 1995; for a similar yet different notion of 'blending', see also Fauconnier & Turner, 1996, 1998).

Placing meaning within the constraints of our bodily experience with the world may give rise to the assumption (among others) that sense accessibility may be a matter of grounding (Glenberg & Robertson, 2000). But salience cannot be explained on grounding, nor is it overridden by it. As shown by previous research, similarly embodied linguistic expressions varying in salience induced different reading times. For instance, low-salience, novel uses of highly conventional expressions (*foot race* in (6b)) took longer to read than their salient, conventional uses (*foot race* in (6a)), despite their similar affordability (Gerrig, 1989):

(6)   a. *Conventional use*

The people of Marni, France, have an unusual celebration every year. Over four hundred years ago, Louis X visited their town. He started the tradition of having annual sports events. The town's teenagers race on foot all the way around the town. The older sportsmen race horses around the same course. The foot race is the more popular event.

b. *Innovative use*

Over four hundred years ago, Louis X visited the town of Marni, France. He started the tradition of racing snails in the town square. The town's people still gather every year for races of two lengths. By tradition, the short course is made just as long as King Louis's foot. The longer race is made the length of Louis's favorite horse. The foot race is the more popular event.

Similarly, in McGlone et al. (1994), familiar idioms such as *didn't spill the beans* were read faster than their less conventional variants such as *didn't spill a single bean*. In addition, familiar idioms (*spill the beans*) were read faster than their literal paraphrases (*told him all*) compared to their variants (*didn't spill a single bean*), which took equally long to read as their literal counterparts (*didn't say a single word*). Given that the meanings of these idioms and their variants converge in affordances but diverge in degree of salience, it is salience rather than grounding that can account for the difference in the reading times found here.

That salience is independent of grounding is even more evident considering that conventional language that lacks in affordedness is sometimes faster to read than less conventional language that does not. Consider, for that matter, some of the familiar idioms used by McGlone et al. (1994). These salient idioms do not involve more affordances than their literal paraphrases; in fact, they do not seem grounded at all, yet they were read more quickly than their (more grounded) paraphrases:

(7)   *Figurative expression*   *Literal paraphrase*
   - He had two left feet.   He was extremely clumsy.
   - It's raining cats and dogs out there!   It's raining hard out there!
   - He began sweating bullets.   He began feeling anxious.
   - You have to take his words with   You have to take his words
     a grain of salt.   with a whole lot of reservation.

Salient and grounded meanings, then, are independent notions.[12]

4.3 Semantic Meaning

The traditional view of pragmatics (Grice, 1975) assumes two levels of propositional meaning: the semantic level of "what is said" and the pragmatic level of "what is implicated by what is said." The semantic level of what is said pertains to the minimal meaning—the compositional meaning hinging on the meanings of the individual words that make up the proposition (plus disambiguation and reference determination) before drawing any inferences based on contextual assumptions. This meaning can be captured by truth conditions. Thus, "what is said" by *Jane has three children* is 'Jane has at least three children (and may have more)'. In contrast, the pragmatic meaning of what is implicated by what is said goes beyond what is said and incorporates extralinguistic information in conformity with the speaker's intention and a set of common norms (Grice, 1975). Accordingly, *Jane has three children* may convey the "generalized conversational implicature" that 'Jane has exactly three children'. It may also convey a "particularized conversational implicature" that 'Jane is married' when said to a person who inquires about her marital status. (For a review, see Ariel & Giora, 2000; Gibbs & Moise, 1997; Levinson, 1983, 1987a,b). Can salience be equated with the semantics of the sentence?

The Gricean view of speaker's meaning as divided between what is said and what is implicated has been criticized by proponents of relevance theory, notably Carston (1988, 1993), Récanati (1989, 1993, 1995), Sperber and Wilson (1986/1995), and Wilson and Sperber (1993). They argued that what is said is subject to the same inferential processes involved in determining conversational implicatures. They proposed that comprehenders must recruit pragmatic information to derive what is said. For instance, hearing *You are not going to die,* comprehenders do not take it to minimally mean 'You are immortal'. Rather, they interpret it as conveying the explicature—the meaning enriched by pragmatic inferencing—that 'You are not going to die now (from this wound)'. In a recent study, Gibbs and Moise (1997) lent empirical support to a revised view of the Gricean model. They showed that comprehenders opt for pragmatically enriched rather than semantically based meanings when asked to determine what is said.

To what extent do these findings have any bearing on the graded salience hypothesis? Recall that according to this hypothesis, the relevant distinction is between salient (coded or stored) information and nonsalient (unstored, inferred) information. Inferred (pragmatic) information that has become grammaticized may indeed be part of the lexical meanings of a word or a phrase and may be processed automatically upon encounter (Ariel, 1998, in press; Carston, 1988; Hopper & Traugott 1993; Traugott & König, 1991).[13] Noted examples are conventional figurative meanings of idioms such as *kick the bucket* which indeed were shown to be processed faster than their literal counterparts (Gibbs, 1980); ironic meanings of conventional ironies such as *very funny*, which were shown to be accessed initially, regardless of contextual information (Giora & Fein, 1999a); and conventional indirect requests, such as *can you pass the salt* (judged as almost literal, Gibbs, Buchalter, Moise, & Farrar, 1993), which were shown to be read faster than the same utterances used literally as questions (Gibbs, 1983; for a similar view, see Holtgraves, 1998).

Consider, further, other interesting examples in which the salient (intended) meaning is logically divorced from the less salient "said" or literal meaning, such as *fill in a much needed gap* where it is not the gap that is in need, but its filling, or *you are digging your own grave* where it is your deeds that will cause you harm but not the digging that will cause the death (see Fauconnier & Turner, 1998). Apparently it is "what is implicated" rather than "what is said" that made its way to the mental lexicon (see also section 4.7). Future research may tell which enriched pragmatic meanings have reached this entrenchment stage. Salient meanings, then, may be unrelated to semantic meaning.

4.4 Accessible Referential Meaning

Does meaning salience depend on referent accessibility? Accessibility theory (Ariel, 1988, 1990, 1991, 2000) accounts for the distribution of linguistic referring expressions (*she, the professor, Ann Smith, Smith*) in terms of the degree of accessibility of the concepts they are designed to retrieve. Speakers cue comprehenders as to which mental representations to retrieve, depending on their accessibility status. Thus, highly accessible entities (those most available to the comprehender by virtue of their recent mention in the immediate discourse) are marked by high accessibility markers (such as pronouns). Less accessible entities (such as those not mentioned in the immediately preceding context) are assigned relatively low accessibility markers (such as a name or a definite description). Pronouns thus signal that the representation in memory of the entity referred to is highly accessible, but definite descriptions mark a relatively low degree of accessibility.

Although salient information is accessible, it is not directly related to reference accessibility. It centers on sense accessibility rather than on the accessibility of the mental representation of a specific referent. For example, while the Clintons may both be similarly accessible entities, the sentence *Clinton attracted so much attention because she was Bill's wife* sounds "less natural" than *Hillary attracted so much attention because she was Clinton's wife*. Apparently, it is (still) more conventional to refer to men by last name and to women by first name than vice versa (Ariel, 1990; Coates, 1986, among others).

By the same token, referring to a baseball player by a definite description such as "the player" is more conventional than by a definite description such as "the glove." Though the entity referred to is the same and has the same accessibility status in both cases, accessing it following a less salient cue ('the glove') rather than a more salient clue ('the player') should take longer (as shown by Gibbs, 1990, whose example is cited here; see also chapter 8 in this volume):

(8)   Mr. Bloom was manager of a high school baseball team. He was concerned about the poor condition of the field. He also was worried about one athlete. His third baseman wasn't a very good fielder. This concerned the manager a good deal. The team needed all the help it could get. At one point, Mr. Bloom said to his assistant coach,
    "The glove at the third base has to be replaced." [*Less salient referring expression*]
    "The player at the third base has to be replaced." [*Salient referring expression*]

Reference accessibility and sense accessibility are distinct notions, then.

4.5 Feature Salience

The salience imbalance model proposed by Ortony and his colleagues (1985) to account for metaphors entertains a notion of salience similar to that discussed here, only, I suspect, somewhat more limited in scope. It centers on attribute rather than on meaning salience. Attribute salience pertains to "the prominence or importance of an attribute in a person's representation of an entity or category." Within the category of sleep-inducing drugs, for example, "the attribute *induces sleep* has high salience for all members" (p. 570). A salient attribute is thus one that can be readily brought to mind and is presumed to be more readily accessible than a less salient property (p. 587), occasionally due to conventionality. Although attribute salience may account for the representation of monosemous words, it is less adept at accounting for words with multiple meanings, including polysemous and ambiguous words.[14]

4.6 Literal Meaning

Is salient meaning literal? To be able to answer that, we have to look first into what scholars think literal meaning is. Admittedly, the bulk of research into figurative and literal language has focused on the figurative front, assuming, unwarrantedly, that literality is a unified, context-free notion. However, recent research into literality (Ariel, 1999a, 2002a,b; Gibbs et al., 1993), revealed that literality is not a well-defined, stable notion but is amenable to context effects. According to Gibbs et al. (1993), people's belief that literality is theory-neutral stems from conflating processes and products. The judgment that literality is a one-faceted notion rather than a continuum "is based on a *product* of linguistic interpretation and should not be taken as evidence regarding the psychological *processes* by which figurative language is comprehended" (Gibbs, 1993: 388).

Along similar lines, Ariel (2002a) proposes to replace the notion of literal meaning with a notion of contextual minimal meaning. She first suggests that the controversies over what constitutes literal meaning (Berg, 1993; Dascal, 1987, 1989; Gibbs, 1984; Giora, 1997b; Katz, 1977; Searle, 1978) stem from the different functions attributed to "literal meaning" by different theories. While psycholinguists are interested in the meaning that is accessed automatically (such as salient meanings) or derived by default processing mechanisms (Gibbs, 1984), linguists focus on the linguistic meaning (Ariel, 2002a; Sperber & Wilson, 1986/1995) that is grammatically specified and compositional but need not be truth-functional. Philosophers (Dascal, 1987, 1989; Searle, 1978), in contrast, seem to be interested in meaning product—that is, in what speakers are minimally committed to.

Minimal meanings may depend on context. For instance, Ball and Ariel (1978) found that *go for a walk or something* minimally meant different things in different contexts, such as a drive, a long drive, or going next door to see a movie (for similarly conflicting findings, see also Gibbs & Moise, 1997; Nicolle & Clark, 1999). Ariel thus argues against positing a rigid type of minimal meaning. Instead, she considers three kinds of basic-level meanings: one that is grammatically specified (in which the coded meaning is compositional and obligatory); another that is psycholinguistic (Giora's, 1997b, salient meaning); and an interactional, or a privileged, contextual meaning (see Ariel, 2002b).

Is salient meaning, then, a literally based minimal meaning? For illustration, consider the following example cited in Ariel (2002b), in which a judge ruled that a "burgundy" car satisfied an order of a "red" car, accepting the defendant's position that "the plaintiffs indicated 'red' without indicating a specific shade of red. . . . According to [the] Even-Shoshan dictionary definition, burgundy is dark red" (*Ma'ariv*, an Israeli daily, 15 July 1992). Ariel terms this interpretation of *red* a "wise-guy" interpretation. Indeed, 'burgundy' is a coded member in the 'red' category and constitutes part of the meaning of *red*. However, it is a marginal member. Though literally based, it is not a salient meaning.

Example (8) might give rise to the assumption that salient meanings are indeed literal meanings. However, salient (coded or stored) meanings, enjoying a privileged cognitive status, though they tend to, need not be literal at all. There is no reason why figuratively referring to a baseball player as 'the glove' would not become salient in the course of time, as have 'the leg' and 'the back' of a chair, or the 'running' of a vehicle or a nose. The intricate question of what is literal meaning (Ariel, 2002a,b; Gibbs, 1994; Gibbs et al., 1993) is irrelevant to the notion of salience. Though literal meanings tend to be highly salient, their literality is not a component of salience. The criterion or threshold a meaning has to reach to be considered salient is related only to its accessibility in memory due to such factors as frequency of use or experiential familiarity.

Since literality is distinguished from salience, it is necessary to be clear about what "literal meaning" alludes to within the framework of this book. "Literal meaning" refers to what is denoted by individual words, as well as to what is said by the compositional meaning of the sentence made up of these individual words intended nonfiguratively. When the compositional meaning of a sentence does not coincide with the linguistic/literal meaning of the sum of the words, "literal meaning" alludes to the explicature—that is, to the compositional meaning enriched by some pragmatic meanings.

Although the compositional meaning of an utterance intended literally is not coded in the mental lexicon, and is therefore not salient, it will, at times, be loosely treated as salient, in case the components that make it up are salient. Calling a literal interpretation salient is, then, only a shortcut. As mentioned earlier, the assumption is that an interpretation made up of the sum of its salient components is more accessible than an alternative interpretation that does not rely on the salient meanings of its components.

4.7 Generalized Conversational Implicature As a Species of Preferred Interpretation

"A generalized implicature is, in effect, a default inference, one that captures our intuitions about a preferred or normal interpretation" (Levinson, 2000: 11). Would such a preferred interpretation be salient? According to Levinson, generalized conversational implicatures are generated by heuristic devices (Levinson, 2000: 24). As such, they are not salient, since they are not coded or stored. They are, however, gradable with regard to accessibility (see also Levinson, 2000: 411 n.23): some are stronger or more easily generated than others. Indeed, some pragmatic meanings (inferences) have undergone consolidation (see also Horn & Bayer, 1984; Morgan, 1978; and section 4.3 in this chapter). Yet some might still be actually generated on the fly, in spite of their high frequency or preference. Thus, in the final analysis, only empirical measures would determine the degree of salience (or nonsalience) of generalized conversational implicatures (for such initiations, see Hamblin & Gibbs, 2001).

In sum, various factors, such as literality, metaphoricity, irregularity, and grounding, may account for the career of saliency: that is, for why some meanings would be used repeatedly to the extent that they become foremost on our mind. However, the graded salience hypothesis is indifferent to such motivating factors. It relates to the entrenchment status of stored meanings at a given time in a given community or, more precisely, in the mind of a specific individual, affected by exposure—that is, by such factors as familiarity, conventionality, and frequency of occurrence. It predicts that meanings an individual is highly familiar with will always be activated automatically in the mind of that individual, irrespective of contextual information.

5. Is the Lexicon a Dynamic or a Static Repository?

The graded salience hypothesis assumes that the mental lexicon is amenable to learning and change. Since learning "is an experience-dependent generation of enduring internal representations, and/or an experience-dependent lasting modification in such representations" (Dudai, 1989: 6),[15] the salience-ordered, hierarchical structure of the lexicon may be unstable and in a constant state of flux. It is hard, though, to predict the amount of experience and length of exposure necessary to consolidate a new meaning that would result in salience reshuffling. Some meanings are more resilient, others are more resistant to change (see chapter 1). Some experiences are highly effective: they don't require more than one exposure to make their way to memory. Others have less effect and require repetitive exposure to ensure imprinting. Research into meaning consolidation is limited. However, studies into the "career of metaphor" (Bowdle & Gentner, 2001; Gentner & Bowdle, 2001) show that, at times, even a limited amount of experience with a new stimulus may result in its consolidation, so much so that its original nonliteral simile formulation (X is like Y) gives way to a structure more typical of equivalent conventional utterances (X is a Y). In the research reported by Bowdle and Gentner, subjects were given three exposures to a given base term (*glacier*) used in novel similes (*Science is like a glacier*), which led to a small yet significant shift in preference toward the metaphor form (*Science is a glacier*). How salience shifts, then, is still a mystery. A recent study of the regularity in semantic change, however, provides invaluable evidence and insights into the mechanisms involved in the career of saliency (Traugott & Dasher, 2002).

6. Comprehension

How do meanings an individual is highly familiar with affect comprehension? To answer this question, let us consider a few examples. For instance, when Ray Gibbs and I read the following excerpt from a recorded conversation between a wife and a husband (Du Bois, 2000b, and see the appendix of chapter 5 in this volume for the full text; for details on transcription conventions used here and in the examples cited later, see Du Bois, Schuetze-Coburn, Cumming, & Paolino, 1993), we came up with two different interpretations for the conventional metaphor *grounded,* which has a number of conventional meanings:

(9)   PAMELA: I used to have this,
       .. sort of,
       .. % standard li=ne,
       that,
       ... % there were two things I got out of= .. my marriage.
       One was= a name that was easy to spell,
       and one was a %,
       .. (H) a child.
       (Hx) .. % ... that=,
       ... really got me **grounded**.

For Gibbs, who, as a psycholinguist, is currently preoccupied with embodied and grounded language, the meaning of *grounded* that came to mind was related to being established or based or of achieving a sense of stability. For me, a psycholinguist who is also experientially knowledgeable about motherhood, the more salient meaning of *grounded* was the one related to a punishment that limits one's freedom of movement (the most common punishment given to children on American TV series).

Or consider the following poem (originally in Hebrew) by the Israeli poet Yona Wallach (1997: 4, translated by Linda Zisquit), which depends on an allusion to a biblical character and story for its interpretation:

(10) *Absalom*
      One more time I must
      remember my son Absalom
      whose hair caught in my womb
      and it didn't come out for me
      to finish Absalom my son
      I construct the possibilities of my feeling
      pity floods me
      and the hunger that might be
      the wills of heredity
      and Absalom who wasn't allowed
      in another incarnation Absalom will be
      my lover and I'll sense traces of her
      when Absalom my lover
      is a bodily sensation or how my belly
      is empty of Absalom my son
      an arrangement of stars
      falling and a sword that strikes
      the magnet on her heart
      a precise feeling
      what will you fight
      and on what will the wind
      rest
      where will it carry you
      the wind my son.

For Hebrew readers of the poem, the choice of name for the aborted son—Absalom—is not accidental. Its salient meaning and referent—King David's beloved son—plays a significant role in the comprehension and interpretation of the poem. "My son Absalom," "Absalom my son" further echo David's lamenting the death of his most beloved son:

> The name alludes to the tragic fate of that son—his revolt against his father, his death while young, the terrible agony of the father, the topic of his eulogy, though he [the son] went out to fight against him [the father]. The analogy to the character of biblical Absalom does not hinge only on the choice of the son's name, but also on the morbid image of his death as a result of his hair getting entangled. . . .

The attitude of the poet to her son is ambivalent:

(10.1)   I construct the possibilities of my feeling
         pity floods me
         and the hunger that might be
         the wills of heredity
         and Absalom who wasn't allowed
         in another incarnation Absalom will be
         my lover and I'll sense traces of her

> The constructions of the possibilities of feelings, that is, the poetic creation, is the alternative to the birth of the son. The speaker does not deceive herself with regard to the happiness that the birth of this son may bring on her: Absalom is the handsomest, most beloved, most wonderful son, but he is also the most significant threat to the father's rule, or figuratively—to the creativity of the mother, and therefore, he is doomed to die before he is born. (Rattok, 1997: 19–20; my translation)

This specific interpretation of the poem relies on intertextuality—on the allusion to another, familiar text that allows for, or rather, compels this interpretation. Both Absalom's name and his tragic history are salient information (in the mind of many Hebrew readers). Their salience made them accessible, and the analogy-inviting context allowed for their integration into a coherent interpretation. Salience then is relative to an individual. What is foremost on one's mind need not necessarily be foremost on another's. Two individuals may be differently affected by the same text.

6.1   Initial Processes

Comprehension is viewed here as comprising two phases: initial activation and subsequent integration processes. Initial processes may be induced by both contextual information and meaning salience. For instance, when a prior context is highly predictive, it may avail the appropriate interpretation of a lexical stimulus very early on and, at times, even before that stimulus is encountered (as when we guess the end of a speaker's utterance). Regardless, however, upon encounter, the lexical stimulus still evokes its salient meaning, which might be either contextually compatible or incompatible (Giora, Peleg, & Fein, 2001; Peleg et al., 2001, in press). Such a parallel process, then, has two sources: contextual information and the mental lexicon. Parallel processing may also originate in the lexicon itself. When two or more meanings of a word or an expression are similarly salient, they are all accessed simultaneously. When they are not, however, access is ordered: more salient meanings reach threshold earlier.

6.2   Integration Processes: The Retention/Suppression Hypothesis

Some meanings, made available on account of their salience, may not be retained after their activation, since they cannot integrate with contextual information. In the following joke, *Two men walk into a bar and a third man ducks,* the salient meaning of *bar* ('pub'), activated automatically, needs to be abandoned and replaced by 'pole'—the less salient meaning of the word. If it is not, the text will make no sense (Gernsbacher & Robertson, 1995). Some meanings, however, will be retained despite their contextual misfit, either because they are instrumental in constructing the intended meaning, or because they are not intrusive, or because, being highly salient, they are difficult to suppress (see also Morris & Binder, 2002). For instance, the salient 'soul' meaning of *sole* invited by *Body and Sole* is retained for further processes, despite its contextual incompatibility. Its retention allows for 'sole' and 'soul' to be compared and implicates that the sole is to the body as the soul is (chapter 7 in this volume). The idiomatic interpretation of *cold feet* was difficult to suppress, however, when the idiom was intended literally and affected misunderstanding (see Nerlich & Clarke, 2001).

Thus, comprehension involves an initial phase in which contextually appropriate and salient meanings are activated—the latter automatically and independently of contextual information, the former as a result of a predictive context—and an immediate subsequent phase of integration in which the activated meanings are either retained for further processes or suppressed as contextually disruptive. This holds for any stage of the comprehension processes (see chapters 4–5 in this volume).

The extent to which salient meanings and contextual information affect language comprehension is the question that looms large in the various chapters of this book. In the next chapter, I will look into how salience affects ambiguity resolution vis-à-vis contextual information: that is, how we home in on the contextually appropriate meaning when we encounter words such as *bar* which have multiple meanings but only one that is contextually appropriate.

3

Lexical Access

> "There's a glory for you."
>
> "I don't know what you mean by 'glory,'" Alice said.
>
> Humpty Dumpty smiled contemptuously. "Of course you don't—
> till I tell you. I meant 'there's a nice knock-down argument for
> you.'"
>
> "But 'glory' doesn't mean 'a nice 'knock-down argument,'" Alice
> objected.
>
> "When *I* use the word," Humpty Dumpty said, in a rather scornful
> tone, "it means just what I choose it to mean—neither more nor
> less."
>
> —Lewis Carroll, *Through the Looking Glass*

Can we really constrain context to the extent that it would affect comprehension entirely so that only relevant meanings would be processed, neither more nor less? Can we really make context strong enough to allow for an efficient and frictionless processing, filtering out inappropriate meanings?

Quite a number of cognitive scientists and psycholinguists believe that the mind is flexible enough to accommodate contextual information to the extent that, when sufficiently constraining, it dominates comprehension entirely. This view, dubbed "the direct access model," assumes that human cognition is governed by a single, interactive architecture that benefits from both linguistic and extralinguistic information that activates compatible interpretations exclusively, so that comprehension proceeds seamlessly and effortlessly.

In contrast, the graded salience hypothesis (Giora, 1997b; chapter 2 in this volume) assumes that salient (conventional, frequent, familiar, prototypical) information should always be activated, regardless of any contextual information to the contrary. Although a predictive context may avail appropriate information speedily, it cannot obstruct access of salient information when inappropriate, since contextual and lexical processes do not interact initially but run in parallel. As illustration, consider the following conversation (cited in Ariel, in press), taking place between M and her husband W, who is interested in biology and genetics:

(1)   M: I wanted to talk with you about something, but I can't remember what.
       W: [*Notes sewing threads on the table*] It must have to do with thread (*Joking*).
       M: Yea, I wanted you to do Maya's jeans (*Joking*).
       W: You know, the first interpretation I got was *genes* with a *g*. (15 June 2001, reconstructed from memory)

Apparently the 'genes' sense of *jeans* that came first to W's mind was not induced by the highly constraining context (the sewing threads on the table which he noticed; the 'to do Maya's X' verbal context) but by a different mechanism that is sensitive to linguistic stimuli and responds automatically, regardless of context. In what follows, we will examine evidence adduced recently in an attempt to resolve this debate between lexical and context effects.

1. Lexical Access and Context Effects

Lexical access pertains to the rapid activation of word meanings operating when a linguistic stimulus is encountered in and out of context. A number of models have been proposed to account for how we process words with multiple meanings. According to the "exhaustive access model," all the word's meanings should be accessed at once, regardless of salience (frequency, familiarity) and higher level contextual information. According to the "ordered access view," access may be exhaustive but is sensitive to salience. The "interactionist, direct access model" favors a "selective access model," according to which processes vary when the word is in or out of context, suggesting that a strong context taps the appropriate meaning exclusively. The hybrid "reordered access model" assumes that both salience (frequency) and contextual information affect access of appropriate meanings.

The graded salience hypothesis is partly consistent with the exhaustive access model in that it maintains, among other things, that access of salient meanings should be invariant across contexts. The graded salience hypothesis is also partly consistent with the ordered access view, which maintains that access is exhaustive but sensitive to salience so that the more salient (frequent, "dominant") meaning is accessed faster than a less salient meaning. It also partly agrees with the hybrid reordered access model in that it allows contextual information to avail meanings but not to downplay the role of salient meanings (although it disagrees with the assumed interactive aspect of contextual effects). To disconfirm the graded salience hypothesis, it would be necessary to show that contextual information can exclusively activate less salient information, as maintained by the direct, selective access model.

1.1 Exhaustive Access: When All the Meanings of a Word Are Activated upon Its Encounter

The hypothesis that lexical access should be invariant across contexts has been proposed by proponents of the modular view (Fodor, 1983). According to the modular view, cognitive processes are either domain-specific or domain-general. Domain-specific processes are modular in the sense that, among other things, they are encapsulated—thus impenetrable to processes that occur outside the input system. Relevant to our discussion is the assumption that lower level processes such as lexical access should not be affected by top-down feedback from higher nonlexical level representations such as contextual or world knowledge. Lexical access is thus autonomous and, on some views, exhaustive: *all* the meanings of a word are activated at once upon its encounter, regardless of either contextual bias or salience. Contextual processes interact only with the output of the lexical processor. They influence integration of the output of the lexical processor into the text representation, selecting the contextually compatible meaning while discarding the contextually incompatible meanings (Cairns, 1984; Connine, Blasko, & Wang, 1994; Conrad, 1974; Gow & Gordon, 1995; Kintsch & Mross, 1985; Lucas, 1987; Onifer & Swinney, 1981; Picoult & Johnson, 1992; Prather & Swinney, 1988; Seidenberg, Tanenhaus, Leiman, & Bienkowski, 1982; Swinney, 1979; Tanenhaus, Carlson, & Seidenberg, 1985; Tanenhaus, Leiman, & Seidenberg, 1979; Till, Mross, & Kintsch, 1988; West & Stanovich, 1988 and references therein).

Studies testing this hypothesis used, among other tools, semantic priming effects. Priming effects are related to the facilitated processing found for a word and its associates following prior processing of that word. The repeated processing of that word or its high associates is shorter than that of an unrelated word (Meyer & Schvaneveldt, 1971). Indeed, in Swinney's (1979) study, words were shown to prime both contextually appropriate and contextually inappropriate test words. When, for instance, *bug* was heard in a context biasing it toward the 'insect' rather than toward the 'microphone' meaning (see example 2), both the (visual) compatible ('ant') and incompatible ('spy') test words were instantly facilitated. Both were shown to be activated initially (at zero interstimulus interval) in contexts biasing either meaning, irrespective also of salience (Onifer & Swinney, 1981). However, shortly afterward (three syllables later), only the contextually appropriate meaning was available, suggesting that contextual information affected only postlexical decisions, suppressing the contextually incompatible information while retaining the compatible meaning (see also Seidenberg et al., 1982).

(2)   Rumor had it that, for years, the government building had been plagued with problems. The man was not surprised when he found several spiders, cockroaches, and other *bugs* in the corner of his room.

It should be noted, however, that according to the modular view, context may prime a word meaning in case the prime involves associative primes. For example, *table*, occurring in prior context, may prime its close associate *chair* encountered later on. This priming is intralexical: it affects relation between words or meanings within the lexicon:

> A context that is associatively related and (temporally near) an ambiguous word could act on processing of that ambiguous word *within* the lexical module. This type of effect cannot be taken as evidence for interaction *between* modules. . . . To claim strong evidence against a lexical modularist position and in favor of some alternative type of interactive model, either a distant context (greater than 200 or so milliseconds) or a nonassociative context would have to be shown to restrict access. (Prather & Swinney, 1988: 296)

Indeed, when context exhibited lexical associates (*Although the farmer bought the straw*) and the test word was presented immediately, the contextually appropriate meaning was facilitated (Seidenberg et al., 1982; Tabossi, 1988). According to the modular view, then, context cannot restrict lexical access, although it can be predictive and may affect the degree of activation (for a similar view, see Oden & Spira, 1983).

Although it is intuitively implausible, most of the evidence adduced suggests that lexical access is independent of higher level processes. Neither sentence nor discourse context blocks the (initial) activation of meanings (Binder & Morris, 1995). The graded salience hypothesis is consistent with the autonomous, contextual impenetrability aspect of modularity, predicting that salient meanings should not be bypassed. However, the prediction of the graded salience hypothesis that more salient meanings would reach sufficient levels of activation before less salient ones cannot be accommodated by the strong (traditional) version of the exhaustive access hypothesis of the modular view (but see Forster & Bednall, 1976, and Swinney & Prather, 1989, about the possibility that the mental lexicon may be salience-based). Neither does it assume automatic suppression of incompatible meanings. Furthermore, it allows a strong context to precede lexical processes, without being interactive.

1.2 Selective Access: When Only the Contextually Appropriate Meaning Is Activated

The modular view (which does not allow information from different domains to initially interact) has been challenged by the view that strong context governs interpretation entirely. According to this view, contextual information—and even more so, heavily weighted contextual information—interacts with lexical processes very early on and activates contextually appropriate meanings exclusively. While preselecting the appropriate meaning for further processes, highly constraining contextual information blocks contextually inappropriate meanings (Glucksberg, Kreuz & Rho, 1986; Jones, 1991; Martin, Vu, Kellas, & Metcalf, 1999; Simpson, 1981; Simpson & Krueger, 1991; Tabossi, 1988; Tabossi

& Zardon, 1993; Vu, Kellas, & Paul, 1998; Vu, Kellas, Metcalf, & Herman, 2000). The graded salience hypothesis is inconsistent with such a selective, context-dependent model. Though it allows context to be predictive, it assumes that context is ineffective in blocking salient meanings.[1]

Indeed, some of the findings that seem to support selective access of contextually compatible information may have alternative accounts. Consider, first, the case in which context is assumed to inhibit activation of contextually incompatible, less salient meanings while preselecting the salient meaning (Tabossi, 1988). In this case, the salient meaning is also the intended one—the one compatible with contextual information. This coincidence of salience and contextual fit may be interpretable as supportive of a direct access process according to which contextual information activates the contextually appropriate meaning exclusively. However, it is not less plausible to assume that, as predicted by the graded salience hypothesis, the more salient information is accessed before the less salient meaning reaches a threshold. Since it is contextually compatible, integration processes are speedy. Here context comes into play *after* the more salient meaning has been accessed, and context integrates the appropriate meaning (see also Hogaboam & Perfetti, 1975). No interaction during access need be involved here.

Or take another example. In the study reported by Tabossi and Zardon (1993), idioms were initially processed literally. Activation of the idiomatic meaning did not occur until the idiomatic (key) word was processed. For instance, in *Finally Silvio had succeeded in setting his **mind** at rest*, facilitation of the idiomatic meaning occurred only after *mind* was encountered. This finding attests that the more frequent/salient (literal) meaning of *set* (available in more than the specific idiomatic context) was activated faster. It was not rejected because at that point it was contextually appropriate. Consequently, search for contextually appropriate meanings was not boosted, disallowing the less salient idiomatic meaning of *set* to reach sufficient levels of activation. This meaning, therefore, was not activated until *mind* was encountered. The constituent *setting one's mind* availed the idiomatic meaning, thereby facilitating the processing of *at rest*. Though these findings may contradict the exhaustive access version of the modular view, they are still consistent with its more moderate version (discussed later in this chapter), according to which lexical access is exhaustive but ordered by frequency. They are also consistent with the graded salience hypothesis, according to which salient meanings should be accessed automatically and revised in case of a misfit with the context.

In fact, most studies attesting to selective access found evidence in favor of contextual information that affects exclusive activation of salient meanings (Duffy, Morris, & Rayner, 1988; Glucksberg et al., 1986; Martin et al., 1999; Schvaneveldt, Meyer, & Becker, 1976; Simpson, 1981; Simpson & Kruger, 1991; Tabossi, 1988; Tabossi, Colombo, & Job, 1987; Vu et al., 1998, 2000). However, some of these findings may be explained by suppression (Gernsbacher, 1990). The mechanism of suppression is responsible for decreasing the activation of an inappropriate interpretation *after* that meaning has been activated (as predicted by the modular view). Suppression of the inappropriate meaning may occur via the enhancement of the selected appropriate meaning. Indeed, the suppression of the unselected meaning and the enhancement of the selected meaning can also explain Schvaneveldt et al.'s (1976) findings, which were taken to support selective activation of contextually appropriate meanings. Schvaneveldt et al. showed that recognition of the third word (*money*) in a string (*river–bank–money*) biasing the second ambiguous word (*bank*) in favor of one (riverside) meaning—the discordant condition—took no longer than its unrelated control word, when it instantiated the unselected meaning of the ambiguity ('financial institution'). In contrast, in the concordant condition, when the third word (*money*) instantiated the selected, enhanced meaning ('financial institution') of the ambiguous word in the string (*save–bank–money*), recognition was faster.

The selective access model may account for these findings. It can argue that *money* took long to process in the context of *river-bank*, since *bank* in this context could only mean 'river edge'. Hence, it could not prime *money*. However, in the context of *save-bank*, *bank* meant only 'financial institution' and therefore it could prime *money*, which, indeed, was processed faster. However, some crucial findings of Schvaneveldt et al. cannot be accounted for by a context-dependent view.

According to the selective access hypothesis, there should be no difference in reaction times between the recognition of a third word (*money*) related to the unselected ('financial institution') meaning of a homonym (*bank*) (in *river–bank–money*)—the discordant condition—and the recognition of the same third word (*money*) in a similarly unrelated context (*river–date–money*). According to the selective access hypothesis, *bank* in the context of *river* should have been interpreted *only* in terms of 'river-edge', with no recourse to the unrelated/unselected 'institutional' meaning of *bank*. As a result, the different contexts of *money*—*river-bank* and *river-date*—should have elicited the same reactions time to the 'unrelated' target *money*. This was not the case, however: the context of *river-bank* elicited *longer* reaction times, suggesting that the occurrence of *bank* in the context of *river* also activated the unrelated, salient ('institutional') meaning of *bank*, which, in turn, had to be suppressed.

As shown by Gernsbacher (1990), suppression comes with a cost. At times, it makes the suppressed meaning even more difficult to instantly retrieve than an unrelated meaning. For example, Gernsbacher and Robertson (1999) found that participants were considerably slower and considerably less accurate at verifying that the sentence *She blew the match* made sense after they read a sentence such as *She won the match* than after they read a neutral control sentence such as *She saw the match* or a meaningless control sentence such as *She prosecuted the match*. They interpreted this finding as attesting that the unselected meaning of *match* ('fire') in the 'contest' context (*She won the match*) was suppressed once the 'contest' meaning of *match* was selected: hence the difficulty of retrieving the 'fire' meaning of *match*, which should have been no more effortful than retrieving the 'contest' meaning of *match* had there been no suppression. The suppression hypothesis (see also Simpson, 1984), then, can better account for the various findings in Schvaneveldt et al. (1976), as well as for their replication in , for example, Hagoort (1989).

The different reaction times in the concordant and discordant conditions were also replicated by Balota and Duchek (1991) for healthy elderly individuals. However, in their study, individuals with senile dementia of the Alzheimer type produced a different pattern of response. They did not take longer to respond in the discordant than in the unrelated condition. In fact, they responded considerably faster to the third word (*money*) in the discordant (*river–bank–money*) condition than in the unrelated (*river–date–money*) condition. Balota and Duchek interpreted their results as attesting that these individuals exhibited context-insensitive activation of multiple meanings (as predicted by the modular view), inconsistently with the selective access model. However, these findings are better explained by a suppression deficit. Rather than assuming that healthy individuals do not activate multiple meanings in contexts biased toward one meaning of the ambiguous word (for a similar view regarding healthy elderly, see Stern, Prather, Swinney, & Zurif, 1991), it seems more plausible to assume that individuals with senile dementia of the Alzheimer type are (similar to) less skilled comprehenders. In Gernsbacher's studies, less skilled comprehenders did not show any deficit in activating multiple meanings of ambiguous words, but they were deficient in suppressing both contextually appropriate and inappropriate meanings (Gernsbacher, 1990, 1993; Gernsbacher & Robertson, 1995, 1999; but see Long, Seely, & Oppy, 1999).

In Simpson and Krueger's (1991) study, participants self-paced their reading aloud of context sentences that included an ambiguous word at the end. As the last word was read, the experimenter pressed a key that blanked the screen and presented the target either immediately, 300, or 700 milliseconds later. Simpson and Krueger used a naming task, which is assumed to be more rapid than lexical decision. Replicating findings by Simpson (1981), they showed that when the context (*This is not a very good spring*) was not biased toward either meaning ('coil'; 'summer'), the ambiguous word elicited the same response pattern elicited by ambiguous words out of context (Simpson & Burgess, 1985; Simpson & Foster, 1986). The most salient (frequent) sense was accessed faster. The less frequent sense was accessed after a short delay (of 300 milliseconds) in parallel to the more salient (frequent) sense. However, after 700 milliseconds delay, only the salient meaning was facilitated. In contrast, when the context was biased toward *either* meaning, only that meaning showed facilitation, regardless of degree of salience. Simpson and Krueger's findings are consistent with the selective access model. However, it is also possible that self-paced reading aloud is a slow enough process to allow for post-access decisions to take place by the time the participant reaches the end of the sentence context. (For different findings related to context effect on pronunciation of homographs—on words that have same spelling but distinct meanings and sounds—see Carpenter & Daneman, 1981.)

A most interesting challenge to the context-independent modular view comes from studies showing that findings that lexical access is exhaustive and impervious to context effects (Onifer & Swinney, 1981; Swinney 1979) attest, in fact, to backward priming (Kiger & Glass, 1983; Koriat, 1981). Backward priming may occur when (visual) test words are presented simultaneously with (auditory) primes, particularly when the task requires depth of processing, as in the case of a lexical decision task (employed by Onifer & Swinney, 1981; Swinney, 1979) but not in a naming task (employed by Seidenberg et al., 1982; for a more recent review and findings, see Chwilla, Hagoort, & Brown, 1998). Given the time course of echoic memory and of the processing of the auditory stimulus itself, the visual target (spy) may well be available simultaneously with the mental representation of the ambiguous word-prime (*bug*) while *bug* itself is still being processed (Glucksberg et al., 1986: 325). Thus, when the test word related to the less salient meaning of the ambiguous word is presented, it may activate this sense through backward priming and foster an illusion of context-independent, multiple access of the various meanings of an ambiguous word. It is possible, then, that findings attesting to multiple access in cross-modal studies are a result of a task-related artifact.

Following Gildea and Glucksberg (1984), Glucksberg et al. (1986) attempted to control for backward priming. On the assumption that nonwords cannot backward prime, Glucksberg et al. used misspelled words as probes in a replication of Onifer and Swinney (1981, experiment 2). These misspelled test words were similar to potentially correct test words. For example, instead of 'weigh' and 'fish', the visual strings 'weign' and 'fisch' were used as probes for the (auditory) ambiguous *scale* in the sentence context *John put the heavy bag on the scale*. They found that, when controlled for backward priming, the same contexts that gave rise to multiple access in Onifer and Swinney's study elicited responses supporting a selective access model: for both the more and the less salient senses of the ambiguous words, only the contextually appropriate meaning was activated. These context effects were not obtained when the context was neutral, thus unrelated to the visual lexical decision items.

Burgess, Tanenhaus, and Seidenberg (1989) questioned Glucksberg et al.'s (1986) findings. On the assumption that participants rely heavily on contextual information when they must distinguish between words and word-like probes (Forster, 1981; Stanovich & West, 1983), Burgess et al. set out to show that the misspelled test words in Glucksberg et al.'s studies were sensitive only to contextual information and therefore failed to test for priming of ambiguous words. Instead of attesting to selective access of a single, contextually appropriate sense of an ambiguous word in a context biasing one of its meanings, Glucksberg et al., they contend, attested to the effect of context alone on the related meaning of the test words.

In a series of experiments, Burgess et al. (1989) showed, first, that the nonword methodology cannot diagnose initial activation of word senses. In the absence of context, ambiguous words did not prime any meaning of the word-like test words used by Glucksberg et al., not even when primes were presented auditorily and test words visually. In contrast, they primed the words from which these nonwords were derived. Second, and more important, Glucksberg et al.'s findings were replicated in the absence of the ambiguous word primes from the sentence contexts (e.g., example 3), suggesting that their findings were a function of the sentence context and the congruence of the word-like test words rather than a result of ambiguous words priming contextually related nonwords. In light of their findings, Burgess et al. concluded that Glucksberg et al.'s findings cannot support a selective access model.

(3)   Before he started his diet he had been afraid to get on a * ladder (replaces *scale*)
       but now he was pleased to see that dieting had been worth it and he was thinner.
       Test words: weign-winge
       (* indicates the point at which the test-word was presented).

Burgess et al. (1989) also noted that Seidenberg et al.'s (1982) findings, seemingly supporting the selective access view, derive from relationships among lexical items represented within the lexical module (Forster, 1979) and do not challenge the modular hypothesis. Although at this point, the issue of backward priming remains unresolved, evidence from eye tracking (discussed in section 1.6 in this chapter) may help rule it out.

Recently, however, Vu et al. (1998, 2000) and Martin et al. (1999) provided evidence in support of a constraint-based, context-sensitive model of lexical ambiguity resolution. Manipulating strength of context, Vu and his colleagues showed that when contextual information was weighted in favor of one of the meanings of an ambiguous word, it inhibited activation of contextually incompatible meanings, regardless of salience. This effect increased as the strength of context increased. Thus, in *The biologist wounded the bat*, the salience-related sense ('wooden') did not reach sufficient levels of activation. In contrast, the less salient ('fly') meaning of *bat* seemed to be selectively activated. Vu et al. reject the possible criticism that the ambiguous words they used are somewhat balanced (having multiple meanings which are symmetrically salient, such as *bug*) rather than polar (having multiple meanings that are asymmetrically salient so that one meaning is more salient than the other(s), as in the case of *bank*). Indeed, studies focusing on balanced ambiguities reported similar findings (see Rayner and colleagues, discussed later in this chapter). However, according to Vu et al., Rayner, Pacht, and Duffy's (1994) studies employed weakly biased contexts (but see sections 1.3 and 1.4 in this chapter).

In the studies reported in Martin et al. (1999), both polarity and strength of context were manipulated. Using self-paced reading, which, according to the researchers, is as ecologically valid as eye tracking (used by Rayner et al., 1994), Martin et al. show that when biased toward the less salient meaning, weak contexts indeed did not inhibit highly salient meanings but, rather, allowed for the interference of the salient meaning in the activation of the less salient meaning, resulting in slowing down processes (known as "the subordinate bias effect"; cf. Rayner et al., 1994). However, strongly biased contexts activated both less salient and salient meanings exclusively.

Although they are consistent with a selective view of lexical access, Vu et al.'s and Martin et al.'s findings may have an alternative explanation. It is possible that, as suggested by Peleg (2002), Peleg, Giora, and Fein (2001, in press), and Giora, Peleg, and Fein (2001), a strong sentence context has predictive effects to the extent that it avails the meaning of the last word of a clause or a sentence even before that verbal stimulus is encountered (for a somewhat similar view, see Rayner et al., 1999). In other words, it is possible that the central system mechanism of guessing (Fodor, 1983: 75), which according to Peleg is best operative at the end of segments, may avail the compatible meaning independently of the processes occurring inside the lexicon. Indeed, in Peleg et al. (2001, in press), we replicated Vu et al.'s findings in the absence of the last target word, showing that it was *not* the target (ambiguous) word (in context) that primed the probes but rather the context alone.

Specifically, in Peleg et al., we used Vu et al.'s (1998) materials. However, rather than presenting the probe immediately after the target, which appeared in sentence final position (as did Vu et al.), we presented it immediately before that target. For instance, in *The biologist wounded the* bat*, the probe was displayed at * rather than immediately after *bat*. In this way, we were able to examine the effect of context alone on the probe's levels of activation. Sixty native speakers of English were engaged in a lexical decision task. Results indeed replicated those of Vu et al.'s, demonstrating that Vu et al.'s findings need not testify that strong contextual information affects ambiguity resolution by inducing interlexical processes. Instead, they show that the "priming" effects may have been produced by context alone.

Moreover, in Peleg et al. (2001, in press) we were able to show when the integrative, guessing mechanism may be less or more effective. We demonstrated that in a position that favors contextual information, lexical effects might be masked. However, in a position that does not, lexical effects are just as visible as context effects. Thus, when target words were placed at the beginning of a new sentence, a position that does not favor contextual information because this is where we start building a new substructure (Gernsbacher, 1990), salient but contextually incompatible meanings ('criminal') were as available as nonsalient but contextually compatible meanings ('kids'), even though the preceding context was strongly biased in favor of the nonsalient meaning (*Sarit's sons and mine went on fighting continuously. Sarit said to me: These **delinquents**[2] won't let us have a moment of peace*). However, where the predictive mechanism could be more effective, as when target words were placed at the end of sentences and probed immediately afterwards (*Sarit's sons and mine went on fighting continuously. Sarit said to me: A moment of peace won't let us have these **delinquents***), the nonsalient but contextually compatible meanings ('kids') were somewhat more accessible than those of the salient but contextually incompatible meanings ('criminal'). Importantly, however, despite contextual information to the contrary, salient but contextually incompatible meanings were never inhibited.

These results attest to the independence of the two mechanisms. They show that context effects can occur independently of the relevant lexical stimuli. They further show that salience effects are equally independent of the contextual mechanism. Specifically, sentence initial position, which is less sensitive than sentence final position to contextual effects induced by prior discourse, allowed both contextual and lexical effects to be similarly visible. While context effects could not be attributed to the lexical stimulus, being new information, neither could the lexical effects be driven by context, being contextually inappropriate.

In Giora, Peleg, and Fein (2001), we were further able to tease apart the two mechanisms. This time, we tested the effect of context on salient and less salient meanings. Our materials included those in Vu et al. (2000). Indeed, when targets (*bulb*) were placed in sentence final position (*The gardener dug a hole. She inserted the **bulb***) and probed immediately afterward, we replicated Vu et al.'s findings: appropriate though less salient meanings ('plant') of target (ambiguous) words (*bulb*) were facilitated by a strong and supportive context. In contrast, inappropriate though salient meanings ('light') were not. However, as before, when placed in sentence initial position (*The gardener dug a hole. The **bulb** was inserted*) and probed immediately afterward, both appropriate (less salient) and inappropriate (salient) meanings of target (ambiguous) words were similarly available, demonstrating that in sentence initial position, where a biased context is not as fast in predicting the appropriate meaning, salient but inappropriate meanings are just as available as appropriate ones.

To show that, contrary to Vu et al.'s and our findings, salient but inappropriate meanings do get accessed when the verbal stimulus is encountered, even in sentence final position, we ran another experiment. This time, however, we compared a target discourse involving an ambiguous word whose less salient meaning was intended (*The gardener dug a hole. She inserted the **bulb***) with a control discourse that contained an appropriate target (*The gardener dug a hole. She inserted the **flower***). We probed both sentences for the salient but inappropriate meaning ('light') of the ambiguous word (*bulb*). Results indeed show that, compared to the control sentence, the salient meaning ('light') of the ambiguous target (*bulb*) was activated in the target sentence. Such findings show that, although salience effects were invisible and probably masked in previous experiments, they were nevertheless operative even in sentence final position.

These findings are consistent with the encapsulation hypothesis and disconfirm the interactionist, direct access view. They support the view that central system, general cognitive mechanisms operate in parallel to lexical processes and avail cloze probable output without interacting with lexical processes. They further demonstrate the conditions under which effects of a specific context may coincide, precede, or follow lexical effects. Indeed, such views can account for conflicting findings in Gibbs (1990) and Onishi and Murphy (1993). In the studies reported in Gibbs (1990), metaphoric targets took longer to read than literal targets when the targets were placed in sentence initial position (followed by a biasing context), but these differences disappeared when these targets were placed in sentence noninitial position (Onishi & Murphy, 1993; see also Dopkins, Morris, & Rayner, 1992). Such a view can also account for the findings in Van Petten and Kutas (1991), in which ambiguous words (*bug*) were initially accessed in accordance with contextual bias, followed by an exhaustive stage, with a later stage of contextually compatible meanings only. According to the graded salience hypothesis, the effects of a rich context can be fast enough to avail the appropriate meaning on their own accord, without penetrating lexical access. Then, when the lexical stimulus is encountered, exhaustive access occurs, followed by a selective, fine-tuning stage in which irrelevant meanings are dampened. In the presence of inappropriate meanings, it makes more sense to assume two independent mechanisms, top-down and bottom-up, that run in parallel without affecting each other initially than to assume a single interactionist mechanism that penetrates the lexicon but, at the same time, lets the lexicon have "a mind of its own" (Bates, 1999). Note also that it is not even the case that the contextually appropriate meaning is always activated before the inappropriate one (Gibbs, 1990; Giora & Fein, 1999a,c; Giora, Fein, & Schwartz, 1998; Giora, Peleg, & Fein, 2001; Hillert & Swinney, 2001; Peleg et al., 2001, in press).

It should be noted further that findings attesting to the subordinate bias effect (Rayner et al., 1994) cannot be related to weakness of contextual information as suggested by Vu and his colleagues. Contra Vu et al.'s and Martin et al.'s criticism, the contexts used in Rayner et al. (1994) were strongly rather than weakly biased. In contrast, in a series of studies, Rayner and his colleagues (Binder & Rayner, 1998, 1999; Rayner, Binder, & Duffy, 1999) demonstrated that some of the items used by Vu and Martin and their colleagues were problematic. Once these items were removed, results attested to the subordinate bias effect, so much so that even in a strongly biased context, salient meanings were not inhibited. Importantly, Wiley and Rayner (2000) showed that when context was biased in favor of the less frequent but familiar meaning of an ambiguous word, that meaning was accessed first (eliminating the subordinate bias effect). Future research will have to look more carefully into effects on comprehension of weighted contextual information, polar ambiguities, and location in the sentence context.

1.3 Ordered Access: When Salient Meanings Are Accessed First

The graded salience hypothesis is partly consistent with a more moderate version of the modular view according to which access is autonomous and exhaustive but sensitive to salience: more salient meanings are accessed first, faster than less salient meanings, regardless of contextual bias (for frequency effects in spoken and printed word recognition, see Bradley & Forster, 1987; for frequency effect on access of ambiguous words out of context and in a neutral context, see Simpson, 1981; Simpson & Burgess, 1985; Simpson & Foster, 1986; Simpson & Krueger, 1991; see also Swinney & Prather, 1989). This salient-first model of lexical access has been supported by Beauvillain and Grainger (1987, concerning interlexical homographs—that is, words that have two distinct meanings in two languages); Duffy et al. (1988); Li and Yip (1996, who showed that when the test word was presented at onset of the homophone, frequency was the main factor in determining subjects response speed; the effect was stronger for the unbiased context); Rayner and Frazier (1989); Rayner and Morris (1991); Sereno, Pacht, and Rayner (1992); and Tabossi (1988).

Using on-line gaze duration measures, Rayner and his colleagues found that participants gazed at unbalanced (polar) ambiguous words as long as they gazed at unambiguous control words, regardless of whether the disambiguating context followed or preceded the ambiguous word. Such findings suggest that only one meaning of the ambiguous word—presumably the more salient one—was computed initially, regardless of contextual information. In contrast, balanced ambiguities were gazed at longer (than unambiguous controls) when followed than when preceded by a disambiguating context.

The shorter gaze duration induced by balanced ambiguous words (*match*) preceded by a disambiguating context, which suggests that the homograph is perceived as unambiguous, may be explained by inhibition of contextually inappropriate meanings. Alternatively, it may be explained by context effects availing the appropriate meaning even before lexical access takes place (see Peleg et al., 2001). When biased in favor of one of similarly salient meanings placed in sentence final position, context may avail that meaning immediately, even before the target is encountered. Consequently, the coincidence of salience and contextual fit induces an impression of inhibition of contextually inappropriate meanings (Gernsbacher & Robertson, 1999). Indeed, Binder and Morris (1995) have shown that the unselected meaning of a balanced ambiguous word was not less accessible on a later encounter than if the word had not been previously encountered. Gaze duration on the target word (*club*) did not differ between the same meaning with prior ambiguous word condition (4a) and different meaning with prior control word condition (4b). That is, prior instantiation of the 'bar' meaning of *club* did not affect the availability of its 'rod' meaning:

(4)   a. *Same meaning*

There was a lot of excitement at the bars downtown. Crowds of people were gathered outside the (club/home) on the street. It appeared that someone had been hurt in the *club* that night. The police had been called.

b. *Different meaning*

There was a lot of excitement at the bars downtown. Crowds of people were gathered outside the (club/home) on the street. An hour earlier, a man was struck on the head with a *club* and robbed. The police had been called.

(The first instance of the ambiguous word or its matched control word is in parentheses. The target word is in the third sentence and is italicized.)

But, as shown by Gernsbacher and Robertson (1999), it is possible that, contrary to appearances, the unselected meanings in Binder and Morris's study were in fact suppressed, but that suppression is short-lived and could, therefore, be invisible a couple of sentences later. According to Gernsbacher and Robertson, the costs incurred by suppressing an irrelevant meaning of a homograph are immediate. When prime sentences precede the targets by five sentences, however, participants can still reap a reliable benefit due to enhancement but they do not incur a reliable cost (measured by either their response time or error rate).

There is ample evidence showing that contextual information does not inhibit salient meanings, as assumed by the graded salience hypothesis. For instance, findings in Garrod and Terras (2000) demonstrate that even predictive contexts do not block salient meanings. Using eye tracking, Garrod and Terras showed that contexts predictive of the less salient meaning nevertheless facilitated a salient associate initially before facilitating the compatible, less salient meaning. For instance, in the context of *writing on a blackboard*, 'pen' (a salient associate of *writing*) was facilitated before the compatible but less salient 'chalk' was. Similarly, when prior context was heavily biased in favor of the less salient meaning of an ambiguous word that was also made explicit, gaze duration upon its later encounter was longer—as when encountering a balanced ambiguous word in an unbiased context (Rayner et al., 1994). On one interpretation, contextual information increased the level of activation of the less salient meaning, but not sufficiently enough to override the activation of the salient meaning. Alternatively, it is possible that the more salient meaning was accessed first and rejected as contextually inappropriate, allowing the less salient meaning to reach sufficient levels of activation. These findings thus show that even when context is supportive of the less salient meaning, salient information cannot be bypassed (see also Pacht & Rayner, 1993; Tabossi, 1988).

Findings reflecting individual differences and developmental aspects further support the ordered access view. Miyake, Just, and Carpenter (1994) found that for low-span readers, difficulty in ambiguity resolution varied with the degree of salience of the various interpretations. Looking into individual differences in lexical ambiguity resolution, they found that the degree of salience (frequency) of the various meanings of a target homograph induces different processing mechanisms in both high- and low-span individuals. High-span individuals retained multiple interpretations in neutral context, even when one of the interpretations was more highly activated because it was more frequent. Low-span individuals showed a larger effect of ambiguity, suggesting that they had only the more salient (frequent) interpretation available ('wrestler' in *Since Ken liked the boxer, he took a bus to the nearest pet store to buy the animal*). Low-span individuals, who can retain only one meaning, activated only the more salient interpretation. Swinney and Prather (1989) found similar evidence for children under 4.8 years of age who activated only the salient (frequent) meaning, regardless of contextual appropriateness. A similar pattern of exclusive activation of the salient meaning was found for people with Broca aphasia (Swinney, Zurif, & Nicol, 1989).

1.4 Reordered Access: When Context and Salience Affect Speed of Access

According to the hybrid reordered access model (Duffy et al., 1988; Kawamoto, 1993), both salience (frequency, 'dominance') and contextual information affect lexical access. However, in most of the cases, salient meanings are those mostly affected by contextual information when contextually compatible, yet they are also those most resistant to context effects when they are not. For instance, Carpenter and Daneman (1981) found that context was more effective in speeding up response when the more salient meaning was intended. Only when the context was heavily biased in favor of the less salient meaning did speed of response to the less salient meaning slightly increase. However, the level of activation of the less salient meaning did not reach that of the salient meaning (see also Rayner et al., 1994; Tabossi, 1988). In Kawamoto's (1988, 1993) simulations, the proportion of each sense (regardless of meaning salience) was determined by the bias strength of the context: the proportion of contextually appropriate responses increased as the strength of the context increased. However, the salient senses were always more affected. Duffy et al. (1988) showed that a neutral context allowed for both meanings of a balanced ambiguous word (homograph) to become available. When the homograph was unbalanced, the salient (dominant) meaning became available much earlier. In a biased context, however, the contextually compatible meaning of a balanced homograph was made available first. However, if the homograph was unbalanced and the context was biased in favor of the less salient meaning, access of that meaning was speeded up and reached the level of activation of the salient meaning, resulting in a competition between the two.

In sum, the evidence accumulated so far supports the graded salience hypothesis (Giora, 1997b; chapter 2 in this volume). It demonstrates that although contextual information may affect the availability of both salient and less salient meanings, it does not inhibit activation of salient senses. Salient meanings are not preempted.

1.5 Hemispheric Perspective

Research into hemispheres' role in resolving lexical ambiguity alludes to the psychological reality of the graded salience hypothesis. Although both hemispheres contribute to linguistic processes, their contributions vary at times (Burgess & Simpson, 1988a,b). For example, even though both hemispheres may be involved in processing the salient and less salient information initially (Faust & Chiarello, 1998), it is in the right hemisphere that the less salient meaning is retained (the 'riverside' meaning of *bank,* as shown by Chiarello, 1998; Faust & Chiarello, 1998; Faust & Kahane, 2002; and Koivisto, 1997; see also Bottini et al., 1994; Burgess & Simpson, 1988a; Sundermeier, Marsolek, van den Broek, & Virtue, 2002). This is also true of the less salient associate (*throw*) of a word (*hammer*) compared to its more salient (*pound*) associate (Abdullaev & Posner, 1997).

Notwithstanding the hemispheres' division of labor, research has attested that, across the board, salient meanings are not bypassed, not even when context biases interpretation toward the less salient meaning. For instance, in Titone (1998), at offset of the sentence-final homonym, priming in both hemispheres was found for salient (frequent/dominant) meanings of ambiguous words embedded in neutral sentence contexts. Moreover, priming at offset was found in both hemispheres for salient and less salient meanings of ambiguous words embedded in sentence contexts biased toward a central feature of the less salient meaning. In addition, priming at offset was found in the left hemisphere for the salient meaning of ambiguous words and in the right hemisphere for the less salient meaning of these words, when the contexts were biased toward a peripheral feature of the less salient meaning. These findings attest to the psychological reality of the graded salience hypothesis. They are consistent with the view that whatever the contextual bias, salient meanings are always activated, albeit not always in both hemispheres.

Faust and Chiarello (1998) allow us an insight into the temporal aspects of processing salient and less salient meanings. They show that, 450 milliseconds after offset of the target word (at stimulus onset asynchrony [SOA] of 900 milliseconds), the contextually incompatible meanings are undergoing suppression in the left but not in the right hemisphere. In their study, facilitation was found for contextually compatible meanings in the left hemisphere, whereas in the right hemisphere, related test words were facilitated regardless of contextual bias or salience. While both hemispheres are involved in automatic processing of multiple meanings, these findings suggest left hemisphere sensitivity to contextual information (see also Chiarello, 1991; Faust & Gernsbacher, 1995; Faust & Kahane, 2002). In a number of studies, the left hemisphere was found to specialize in selecting a single contextually appropriate meaning. Although it also operates on a word-by-word basis, the left hemisphere is more adept than the right hemisphere at utilizing higher level information. In contrast, the right hemisphere retains multiple meanings and benefits less from contextual information. However, the presence of a word semantically related to the test word diminishes the difference between the hemispheres (Faust, 1998).

Sensitivity to the salient meaning was found in the left hemisphere (Sundermeier, Marsolek, van den Broek, & Virtue, 2002) in which the less salient meaning was suppressed. As mentioned earlier, however, this meaning was retained in the right hemisphere (Burgess & Simpson, 1988b; see also Beeman, Friedman, Grafman, Perez, Diamond, & Lindsey, 1994; Titone, 1998). Neutral sentence contexts—for example, *Jane had a bad day when she broke her heel*, in which *heel* is ambiguous between shoe and foot heel—activated the salient meaning in both hemispheres, with few less salient meanings in both but with higher scores for the right hemisphere (Zaidel, Zaidel, Oxbury, & Oxbury, 1995). These findings lend support to the hypothesis that salient meanings are not filtered out.

1.6 Conclusions

Despite ample evidence favoring the stronger version of the modular view, most of the evidence favoring a salience-sensitive access comes from a more a natural measure: eye tracking is an unintrusive, on-line methodology that does not interfere with the comprehension process (see Rayner & Sereno, 1994). Nor can eye tracking be affected by backward priming. Though it is an implicit measure—directly tapping processes while being obscure as to which meanings are being processed—it can easily be augmented, in this respect, by findings from lexical decision and naming tasks. Taken together, these findings strongly support the graded salience hypothesis, which assumes that processing involves (at least) two distinct mechanisms that run in parallel: an exhaustive but salience-sensitive mechanism that is receptive to linguistic information but impervious to context effects, and a predictive, integrative mechanism that is sensitive to linguistic and nonlinguistic contextual information and interacts with lexical outputs.

2. Salience and Syntactic Ambiguity Resolution

Recent research into syntactic ambiguity suggests that (among other influential "constraints"), some syntactic ambiguity resolution hinges on lexical ambiguity, particularly on the ambiguous (grammatical) information associated with the verb.[3] While early accounts explained the data by reference to tree-diagrammatic memory representations only, more recent accounts also allude to the role lexical salience has in syntactic ambiguity resolution (Trueswell, 1996). They propose that lexical information may also account for the data (Mitchell, 1994).

Accounting for the data in terms of tree-diagrammatic memory representations has been dubbed the "garden path model." According to this model, the parser's initial analysis is based on only the structural properties of the linguistic input. It activates the minimal/simpler analysis first, with no access to contextual or lexical information, with back-up revision as a later monitoring stage. Initially the syntactic processor or parser constructs a single parse. If it is compatible with more than one analysis, the processing is determined by *minimal attachment*, which dictates that incoming material be attached "into the phrase marker being constructed using the fewest nodes consistent with the well-formedness rules of the language under analysis" so that the simplest structure may be pursued (Frazier, 1978: 24). When alternative structures are equally simple, *late closure* would operate, attaching "incoming material into the phrase or clause currently being parsed" so that only a single analysis may be pursued (Frazier, 1978: 33). Hence the difficulty in processing ambiguous strings which require accessing the more complex alternative (thereby misleading the processor down the 'garden path'). For example, the ambiguous string in example (5) is usually interpreted with *to Mary* as the goal associated with reading rather than as a modifier of *the letter*. The second *to*-phrase in the unambiguous example (6) usually results in longer reading times, since it requires the more complex analysis of *to Mary* (Ferreira & Clifton, 1986; Fodor, 1990; Frazier, 1987a,b, 1990; Frazier & Clifton, 1996; Frazier & Rayner, 1987; Rayner, Carlson, & Frazier, 1983; Rayner, Garrod, & Perfetti, 1992):

(5)   John is reading the letter to Mary.
(6)   John is reading the letter to Mary to Bill.

The hypothesis that initial parsing is based exclusively on tree structural considerations has been questioned by findings attesting that different languages show different structural preferences (Carreiras, 1992). According to

Pritchett's (1988, 1991) principle-based theory, however, these findings are accountable by linguistic principles.

Additionally, it has been proposed that processing syntactic information is affected by the salience (frequency) of the lexical information involved (MacDonald, 1994, 1999; Pearlmutter & MacDonald, 1992; Tabossi, Spivey-Knowlton, McRae, & Tanenhaus, 1994; Tanenhaus, Garnsey, & Boland, 1990; Trueswell, Tanenhaus, & Kello, 1993; and more recently McRae, Ferretti, & Amyote, 1997; and McRae, Spivey-Knowlton, & Tanenhaus 1998). According to these proposals, dubbed "constraint-based" models, comprehension is achieved through parallel satisfaction of multiple probabilistic constraints, including constraints from lexical representations. According to constraint-based models such as those in MacDonald (1994) and MacDonald, Pearlmutter, and Seidenberg (1994), the mental lexicon accommodates extensive grammatical information, including tense, finiteness, voice, number, person, gender, morphological information, argument structure, and thematic structure. Constraint satisfaction models (Boland, Tanenhaus, & Garnsey, 1990; Juliano & Tanenhaus, 1993, 1994; Merlo, 1994; Spivey-Knowlton & Sedivy, 1995; Tabossi et al., 1994; Tanenhaus & Trueswell, 1995; Trueswell, Tanenhaus, & Garnsey, 1994) suggest that the parser may be affected by nonstructural factors such as verb meaning frequency, which may affect the evaluation of the alternative structural representation of ambiguous sentence (Ni, Crain, & Shankweiler, 1996).

For instance, Tanenhaus et al. (1990) showed that comprehenders do not wait until the end of the sentence to apply the correct parsing.[4] Rather they access combinatory information immediately upon encountering the verb (see also McRae et al., 1998). MacDonald (1994) and MacDonald et al. (1994) found that difficulty in ambiguity resolution varies with the strength (i.e., degree of salience) of the alternative interpretations available (on how syntactic ambiguity depends on the availability of the competing lexical alternatives of a morphologically ambiguous word, see MacDonald, Just, & Carpenter, 1992; Pearlmutter & MacDonald, 1995; Trueswell, 1996; Trueswell, Tanenhaus, & Garnsey, 1994). On such analysis, garden path effects, allegedly a result of minimal attachment, receive an alternative explanation. Garden path sentences such as Bever's, (1970) *The horse raced past the barn fell* are viewed as more difficult to process than a similar (main verb reduced relative) structure such as *The former mental patients heard here sound unusually sane,* because of the varying degrees of frequency of rival interpretations. While the more frequent interpretation of *hear* is transitive, its rival, less salient intransitive and sentential complement interpretations are weaker competitors. *Race,* by contrast, assumes an intransitive interpretation more often. Hence the strong interference of the more salient interpretation (the intransitive reading) with the less salient transitive interpretation proposed by Bever's sentence (MacDonald, 1994).[5]

More recent findings can also be examined along the lines suggested by constraints satisfaction models. These findings show that, contra the syntactic-based, garden path model which predicts processing difficulties at a delayed stage down the garden path, processing difficulties occurred early on (McRae et al., 1998). According to the constraint-based account, information from various sources, both syntactic (main clause interpretation) and conceptual (thematic roles), should affect processing as early in the course of sentence comprehension as it becomes available. McRae et al. quantified the strength of a number of constraints (frequency of main clause versus reduced relative interpretation, frequency of passive versus active voice interpretation, and goodness of thematic roles—that is, whether a noun phrase is a good agent or a good patient) and 'by' bias. They demonstrated that when the weight of the constraints favored one interpretation, its early effects were pronounced. For example, a sentence with (1) a prototypical agent such as *The cop* in *The cop arrested by the detective was guilty of taking bribes,* (2) a main clause interpretation bias, and (3) a frequent passive voice verb interpretation elicited increasing reading times following the *by* constituent. In contrast, a similar sentence with a less prototypical agent, one that better fits a patient role, such as *The crook* in *The crook arrested by the detective was guilty of taking bribes,* induced decreased reading times following the *by* constituent. Such patterns suggest that initial processing was affected by nonlexical information interacting with the lexicon very early on. They further suggest that accounts based on a single factor may be deficient.[6]

Pickering, Traxler, & Crocker (2000), too, challenge both the modular and the frequency based models. They introduce, instead, the testability principle (termed the "informativity principle"), according to which the preferred parsing is the one for which the parser is likely to receive good evidence quickly. The rationale is that "an efficient parser need not always adopt the most likely analysis immediately: it may be better to favor a somewhat less likely analysis that can be abandoned quickly and straightforwardly over a somewhat more likely analysis that cannot be abandoned without great reprocessing difficulty" (p. 468). Thus, while an object analysis of *realize* (*The young athlete realized her potential*) would be a less likely analysis, it would nonetheless be a highly testable analysis compared to a more likely sentential-complement analysis (*The young athlete realized her potential one day might make her a world-class sprinter*). That is, if the parser encounters objects such as *potential* or *dreams* following *realize,* the object analysis seems very likely. However, if it encounters *exercises* (*The young athlete realized her exercises one day might make her a world-class sprinter*), then the object analysis is impossible but can be easily abandoned. By contrast, adopting the frequent-first analysis may be highly costly, since rejecting a highly probably candidate is effortful. Using eye tracking, Pickering et al. show that readers favor the testable analysis even though they do not rule out the possibility that the more frequent analyses also play a role during initial processing. Only, they argue, the effect of the more frequent analyses is not strong enough to allow for an exclusive retrieval of the most frequent analysis. They conclude, then, that "the processor obeys the principle of informativity, under which initial selection of analyses is dependent both on how frequent an analysis is and how testable it is" (p. 471).

Another alternative to the modular view is Just and Carpenter's (1992) and MacDonald et al.'s (1992) working memory constraints hypothesis (see also Miyake, Just, & Carpenter, 1994). According to this hypothesis, garden path effects may be a result of limited working memory capacity, which constrains the amount of contextual information entertainable by low-span readers. Accordingly, high-span readers should not show garden path effects while reading sentences such as *The evidence examined by the lawyer shocked the jury* compared to *The defendant examined by the lawyer shocked the jury.* High-span comprehenders have enough resources to allow for contextual information (about the inanimacy of the head noun) to be maintained and affect syntactic ambiguity resolution. In contrast, low-span readers should show garden path effects under these circumstances, because their working memory capacity is too limited to entertain nonsyntactic information (as shown by Just & Carpenter's, 1992 rerun of Ferreira & Clifton, 1986). According to this proposal, then, garden path effects are a function of limited working memory resources, which do not allow for the interaction of contextual and syntactic information when the ambiguous word is encountered.

According to MacDonald et al. (1992), however, the garden path effects shown by low-span but not by high-span comprehenders is a result of low-span comprehenders' inability to entertain multiple syntactic representations. When a sentence is biased toward the less frequent syntactic representation (as in *The experienced soldiers warned about the dangers conducted the midnight raid*), it takes low-span comprehenders longer to read than when it is not (as in *The experienced soldiers warned about the dangers before the midnight raid*). Notwithstanding, a more parsimonious explanation is in order here. Consistent with findings regarding lexical ambiguity of nouns, it seems more plausible to assume that low-span comprehenders have difficulties either activating or retaining multiple salient and less salient interpretations of the ambiguous verb, rather than multiple structures, as shown by Miyake et al. (1994; see earlier).

There is, then, some evidence suggesting that, at least in part, syntactic ambiguity resolution is a function of meaning salience. Still, to validate the salience-based accounts, substantial research in which one manipulates relevant variables such as frequency of occurrence or familiarity is in order. For initiations, see Burgess and Lund (1997); Carroll and Rooth (1998); Hindle and Rooth (1993); Jurafsky (1996); Landauer (1999); Landauer and Dumais (1997); Landauer, Foltz, and Laham (1998); and Lund, Burgess, and Atchley (1995).

In sum, most of the findings, particularly from lexical ambiguity resolution but also from syntactic ambiguity resolution, are consistent with the hypothesis that salient information is a major factor in language comprehension and may not be sieved out even when it is contextually inappropriate. Recent studies (Martin et al. 1999; McRae et al., 1998; Vu et al., 1998, 2000), however, suggest that multiply constrained contextual information favoring one sense of a polar ambiguity has inhibitory effects, so that only that meaning is activated (but see Giora, Peleg, & Fein, 2001; Peleg et al., 2001, in press). More research, however, is needed to allow for balanced designs in which strength of context and strength of polarity of ambiguities are more evenly weighed against each other.

3. Concluding Remarks

To what extent is the graded salience hypothesis related to the models of lexical access delineated in this chapter? Assuming that salient information is accessed autonomously, irrespective of contextual information, the graded salience hypothesis is inconsistent with the selective access model, according to which meaning activation is a function of higher level information interacting with lower level lexical processes and allowing for the inhibition of salient (but contextually inappropriate) meanings. As shown, in fact, most of the evidence supporting an interactionist view attests to coincidence of meaning salience and context fit (Tabossi, 1988). When context seems to selectively access contextually appropriate and less salient information (Martin et al., 1999; Vu et al. 1998, 2000), it has been shown to be driven by contextual expectations before encountering the relevant stimuli (Peleg et al., 2001, in press; see also Rayner et al., 1999). Indeed, the graded salience hypothesis predicts that when meanings of considerably low salience are intended, having to compete with highly salient meanings, multiconstrained contextual information favoring the low salience meaning will not sieve out salient information (see also Binder & Rayner, 1998, 1999). More research is needed to test this prediction (but see findings from figurative language comprehension in the following chapters).

The assumption that access of salient information is context resistant is akin to the assumptions of the modular model. However, whereas the strong, traditional version of the modular view assumes exhaustive access that is insensitive to salience, the graded salience hypothesis assumes a salience-sensitive order of activation: given a neutral context, more salient information is accessed faster than less salient information, as assumed by the ordered access version of the modular model. Note that the graded salience hypothesis is agnostic with regard to the mode or location of stored information. It only assumes that salient information is always accessed and cannot be preempted by contextual information.

Although the graded salience hypothesis does not allow contextual information to deactivate salient information before it is accessed, this hypothesis does allow contextual information to avail (both salient and less salient) information, as assumed by the reordered access model. The graded salience hypothesis is thus partly compatible with the reordered access view, although it precludes the possibility of predictive contextual information that affects lexical accessing. Contextual information can be predictive to the extent that it can make compatible information available even before the target word is processed, yet without interacting with lexical accessing (Giora, Peleg, & Fein, 2001; Peleg et al., 2001, in press; see also Fodor, 1983: 78).

Context could also make available the *referent* or concept represented by an expression without facilitating the *sense* of that constituent. For example, in a context describing a babysitter losing control over the children she is looking after to the point where she threatens to punish them, the topic of the next sentence (the kids) may be accessible: *Regardless of the danger, the troops marched on.* The sense of the referring expression (*the troops*) might not (as shown by Janus & Bever, 1985; Peleg et al., 2001, in press).

Note, though, that some predictive effects are also accommodated by the modularity-based account, which allows contextual information to prime lexical items via intralexical processes. Indeed, where contextual information has been shown to speedily avail less salient meanings, this effect could be partially attributed to intralexical processes: context was either highly informative, making explicit features of the less salient meaning (Tabossi, 1988), or it manifested the word itself biased toward its less salient meaning (Rayner et al., 1994). These processes may be categorized as alluding to effects occurring within the lexicon.

According to the graded salience hypothesis, however, but contra the modular view (or at least on how it is interpreted; Swinney, 1979), contextually inappropriate information need not necessarily be dispensed with. The graded salience hypothesis is augmented by functional assumptions, which predict suppression and retention of contextually incompatible meanings, depending on the role such information plays in constructing the appropriate interpretation. For instance, since the salient, contextually incompatible literal meaning of metaphors and ironies is functional in constructing the figurative meaning (Giora, 1995, 1997b), it is retained for further elaboration (see Giora & Fein, 1999a,b,c; Giora et al., 1998; Williams, 1992; chapters 4–5 in this volume). When they do not partake in the interpretation of the intended meaning, as in the case of some jokes' punch lines, and might be disruptive, they are discarded (Gernsbacher & Robertson, 1995; Giora, 1991; chapter 6 in this volume). Suppression of apparently incompatible meanings, then, is not automatic.

Assuming such functional view of interpretation implies that automatic access of salient information is a "rational" process, after all. It avails information that might be intended, affecting seamless integration with context; it avails information that might be used in spite of contextual misfit; it avails information deemed necessary for deliberate manipulations (such as humor). Contrary to appearances, then, the mind is neither "stupid" (Fodor, 1983) nor wasteful.

4

Irony

The following message was recently distributed on the Internet. Is it taken at face value? What are the processes involved in its interpretation?

(1)   *Disney Supports New Solution to Status of Jerusalem*
       Jerusalem, Israel (JFP)—April 1, 1998: For Immediate Release
            When U.S. peace negotiator Dennis Ross was asked by reporters, immediately following the conclusion of the grueling Hebron accord, where his next destination would be, the weary diplomat answered "I want to go to Disneyland." Most observers understood this to be nothing more than a wish for well-deserved relaxation from the exhausting demands of Middle East diplomacy.
            However, sources close to the Netanyahu government have now let it slip that Ross's words were actually a veiled hint at a possible solution to the next, most difficult stage, in the implementation of the peace process, the formidable discussions regarding the final status of Jerusalem. A potential breakthrough in the anticipated impasse may now have been reached as a result of an unexpected offer from the Disney corporation.
            Although all parties concerned insist that the final arrangements will have to be settled through direct negotiations between the involved parties, the preliminary details are as follows:
            The Old City of Jerusalem will be leased for an undetermined length of time to the Disney corporation, who will turn it into a religious theme park that will tentatively be called "Holy Land." The park will be subdivided into "Jewish Land," "Christian Land" and "Muslim Land," with the area of each coinciding roughly with the extent of Old Jerusalem's present religious "quarters."

Precise blueprints for the park have of course not been finalised, but the Disney planners, speaking off the record, were visibly enthusiastic about the potential for a series of mechanical rides and roller coasters based on appropriate themes. "We have already produced outlines of a simulation in which visitors, driving along on tracks, will retrace the steps of the High Priest through the ancient Temple, culminating in a special surprise in the Holy of Holies." A similar ride has been devised for the Via Dolorosa, following the stations of the cross. The greatest excitement is being generated by the projected "Muhammad's Night Journey" ride which will be based on the Muslim prophet's ascent on the steed Buraq through the heavens from the Al-Aqsa mosque. [See appendix to this chapter for the rest of the text.]

Given the context in which this discourse is quoted (i.e., a chapter on irony), could the more salient (literal) interpretation escape our notice even under these circumstances? What function might the activated literal meaning (of the constituents that make up the above discourse) have in interpreting this piece? This first of April hoax laments the standstill in the so-called peace process in the Middle East, alluding to the intractability of the real political situation by featuring fictional absurdity that is far more feasible than the absurdities of real politics. How do we arrive at such an interpretation? Would a less elaborate irony be processed differently?

The various theories of irony reviewed in this chapter would come up with different proposals as to how we process irony. Note that with the exception of the graded salience hypothesis, however, they all deal with less familiar, nonconventional language without acknowledging it, entirely failing to directly and explicitly address salient versus less or nonsalient meanings.

1.   Theories of Irony Comprehension

The theories discussed here can be classified as consonant with either the interactionist, direct access view or the modular view (chapters 1–3).[4] Table 4.1 (see p. 73) summarizes the predictions of the various theories regarding processing of irony. In what follows, reference to "ironies" or "ironic" statements should be taken as a shortcut to utterances that are embedded in irony-inducing contexts. The same holds for their "literal" interpretation, which is, likewise, a consequence of these same utterances being embedded in literally biasing contexts.

1.1   The Interaction-Based, Direct Access View

Recall that the interactionist, direct access view assumes that a strong context governs processing and thus significantly affects lexical processes very early on (see chapter 3). Consequently, in a rich and supportive context, irony comprehension need not involve a contextually incompatible (e.g., literal) stage at all. Rather, context should activate the ironic—contextually appropriate—interpretation exclusively so that only the ironic meaning becomes available for further processes. In a strong context, then, irony comprehension should proceed seamlessly.[2]

According to this view, understanding familiar and less or unfamiliar ironies should not involve different processes. Neither should literal and irony interpretations. Proponents of this view, then, assume equivalent initial processes for both familiar and unfamiliar ironies on the one hand and irony and its literal interpretation on the other.

Indeed, for proponents of the direct access view, the first lexical access stage is also the end product of the comprehension process (but see the allusional pretense theory later in this chapter for a different view).[3] Since the direct access approach assumes that contextual information interacts with lexical processes very early on, the first step—the one that taps the contextually appropriate meaning directly—is the only step. Irony, as well as nonironic language, involves one process upon which the compatible meaning is the only one activated and integrated with contextual information. According to the direct access view, then, rich ecology results in equivalent processes for both literal and nonliteral language, regardless of salience. In a literally biasing context, only the literal meaning is retrieved; in an irony-inducing context, only the ironic meaning is processed (Gibbs, 1986a,b, 1994; Sperber & Wilson, 1986/1995; see also chapter 8 in this volume).

It should be noted, however, that even though Gibbs (1994, 2002) posits similar processes for literal and nonliteral utterances, he nevertheless proposes that the direct access view applies to nonliteral language only: "An alternative view of figurative language use suggests that people can comprehend the intended meanings of many nonliteral utterances directly if these are seen in realistic social contexts (Gibbs, 1994). The *direct access view* simply claims that listeners need not automatically analyze the *complete* literal meanings of linguistic expressions before accessing pragmatic knowledge to figure out what speakers mean to communicate" (Gibbs, 2002: 459–460; emphasis in the original). The insistence upon full propositionality does not preclude accessing incompatible word meanings (Gibbs, 1984).

1.1.1 The Echoic Mention View

The relevance theoretic account of irony (Jorgensen, Miller, & Sperber 1984; Sperber 1984; Sperber & Wilson 1981, 1986/1995; Wilson & Sperber 1992) is consistent with some aspects of the direct access, processing-equivalence hypothesis. Basically, it assumes that both literal and nonliteral utterances are processed along similar patterns (for a different possible interpretation of the relevance theoretic account, see Curcó, 1997, 2000; Giora, 1998c; Yus, 1998, 2001). According to Sperber and Wilson, context is generally not fixed in advance but is constructed as part of the interpretation process. This construction is governed by the same general principles that affect the recovery of explicit and implicit content. Thus, interpretation of utterances is context dependent: it is significantly affected by the contextual information brought to bear. As a result, processing an "echoic interpretive use in which the communicator dissociates herself from the opinion echoed with accompanying ridicule or scorn" (Wilson & Sperber 1992: 75) need not differ from processing a similar utterance in which the communicator endorses the opinion echoed. Both should involve equivalent processes, as illustrated by the following examples (cited in Sperber & Wilson 1986/1995: 239):

(2)   a. He: It's a lovely day for a picnic.
        [They go for a picnic and the sun shines.]
      b. She (*happily*): It's a lovely day for a picnic, indeed.

(3)   a. He: It's a lovely day for a picnic.
        [They go for a picnic and it rains.]
      b. She (*sarcastically*): It's a lovely day for a picnic, indeed.

Sperber and Wilson say that "in both (2b) and (3b) there is an echoic allusion to be picked up. In the circumstances described, it is clear that the speaker of (2b) endorses the opinion echoed, whereas the speaker of (3b) rejects it with scorn. These utterances are interpreted on exactly similar patterns; the only difference is in the attitudes they express" (1986/1995: 239). With context guiding the interpretation process, the different meanings are tapped directly; no revision or sequential processes are required. (For a different view, see Smith & Wilson, 1992. For a critique of the conflicting views prevalent in the relevance theoretic accounts regarding processing literal and figurative language and the possibility of reconciling the discrepancy, see Giora, 1997a, 1998a,c.)

Experiments conducted to test the echoic mention theory attempted to show that echoic irony is understood faster than nonechoic irony. Findings (particularly by Gibbs, 1986b, but see also Jorgensen et al., 1984) showed that ironies with an explicit echo were read faster than ironies with an implicit echo. For instance, in the echoic story (4), the irony (*This sure is an exciting life*) alludes to a prior remark ("Navy was not just a job, but an adventure"), while the nonechoic version lacks such a prior mention:

(4)   *Echoic story*
      Gus just graduated from high school and he didn't know what to do. One day he saw an ad about the Navy. It said that the Navy was not just a job, but an adventure. So Gus joined up. Soon he was aboard a ship doing all sorts of boring things. One day as he was peeling potatoes he said to his buddy,
        "This sure is an exciting life."

      Nonechoic story
      Gus just graduated from high school and he didn't know what to do. So, Gus went out and joined the Navy. Soon he was aboard a ship doing all sorts of boring things. One day as he was peeling potatoes he said to his buddy,
        "This sure is an exciting life."

Participants, indeed, took longer to read nonechoic than echoic ironies and rated them lower in sarcasm. However, this is precisely the kind of finding that would support a modular-based view (rather than a direct access view) according to which the salient, literal ('adventurous') meaning of less familiar irony (*exciting*) must be involved in irony comprehension. If the salient, literal meaning ('adventurous') of irony is indeed involved when it is encountered (*exciting*), a prior mention of that meaning or its associate should prime it—that is, facilitate its processing when it is encountered again. In contrast, nonechoic utterances, being newly introduced, do not contain that freshly enhanced information. Therefore, they should take longer to read: both their literal and nonliteral meanings should be searched anew. In other words, if processing irony does not require activating the literal meaning of its components, priming those irrelevant meanings should result in slower reading times for echoic ironies.

1.1.2   *The Allusional Pretense View*

Kumon-Nakamura, Glucksberg, and Brown (1995) proposed a more general theory of discourse irony (than the echoic mention and the Gricean models; see section 1.2.1 in this chapter). According to the allusional pretense view, irony alludes to or reminds the addressee of what should have been—of an expectation or a norm that went wrong (see also Kreuz & Glucksberg, 1989). To enable the addressee to appreciate the allusion, irony involves pragmatic insincerity, which allows various speech-acts to be ironic; note that on the Gricean account, which posits a breach of the quality or truthfulness maxim, irony is restricted to assertions only. For example, when a car driver says *I just love people who signal when turning* when the car ahead of her makes a turn without signaling, the speaker alludes to a social norm or expectation to signal upon turning, while simultaneously pretending to compliment the errant driver. Such a view of irony, which posits pragmatic insincerity, assumes that irony comprehension involves activating the linguistic meaning of what is said in order to assess its (in)sincerity and derive the ironic (or literal) interpretation (see also Glucksberg, 1995). It therefore does not assume the precedence of the literal interpretation, since initial comprehension does not involve an assumption about the speaker's sincerity. Rather, in any given situation, there is a decision to be made whether what is said is intended sincerely (i.e., literally) or insincerely (i.e., ironically). In this way, ironic and literal interpretations involve equivalent processes but result in different products.

1.2   The Modular-Based View

According to the modular view of lexical access (Fodor, 1983; Swinney, 1979; chapter 3 in this volume), *all* the meanings of a word are accessed automatically, regardless of contextual information. Adjustment to contextual information occurs later on and results in selecting the appropriate meaning and suppressing of contextually inappropriate meanings. Irony research consistent with some aspects of the modular-based approach (Attardo, 2000; Dews & Winner,

1997; Giora, 1995, 1998b; Giora & Fein, 1999a; Giora, Fein, & Schwartz, 1998; Grice, 1975; Searle, 1979) assumes an automatic initial access phase that is impervious to context effect. With the exception of the graded salience hypothesis (Giora and colleagues), the various modular-based views assume that the meaning activated initially is the contextually incompatible literal meaning. With the exception of the standard pragmatic model (Grice, 1975; Searle, 1979), the various views are not committed to an initial processing of the compositional meaning of the sentence. These views vary, however, as to whether the meaning activated initially should be suppressed as irrelevant and as disrupting irony comprehension or whether it should be retained for further processes.

1.2.1   The Standard Pragmatic Model

According to the traditional view, dubbed "the standard pragmatic model" (notably, Grice, 1975; Searle, 1979), understanding nonliteral language involves activating the literal compositional meaning of the utterance first, with a following stage of monitoring and adjustment. Thus, if I say *What a lovely day for a picnic* on a stormy day, my addressee would first compute the literal meaning of the statement, reject it as the intended meaning and replace it with an alternative, contextually appropriate interpretation. According to the standard pragmatic model, then, understanding nonliteral language involves a sequential process. The first stage is literal and obligatory, and the second is nonliteral and optional. In Grice's (1975) terms, the initial process involves a breach of a norm (primarily the quality maxim). According to Attardo (2000, 2001), the violation should be minimally disruptive, although perceivable as disturbing contextual appropriateness. The overt, least disruptive violation is a signal for the addressee to reject the literal meaning as the intended meaning and derive the speaker's intention (dubbed "[particularized] conversational implicature"). In contrast, literal language involves initially just one process. Therefore, understanding literal and nonliteral language should differ, with nonliteral language requiring a double take. Longer reading times found for utterances embedded in ironically versus literally biasing contexts support the standard pragmatic model (Giora et al., 1998; Schwoebel, Dews, Winner, & Srinivas, 2000).

Consistent with the modular view (which proposes that the contextually inappropriate meanings activated during the first initial access phase should be discarded subsequently), the standard pragmatic model assumes that the contextually incompatible literal meaning of irony should be suppressed and replaced by a contextually compatible ironic meaning. Thus, *What a **lovely** day for a picnic* said on a stormy day is rejected as contextually incompatible and replaced by its approximate opposite: *What a **lousy** day for a picnic*. In this view, then, irony comprehension involves a suppression process at the second integration phase. It therefore differs from processing its literal interpretation. This suppression hypothesis, however, has not gained empirical support (see Giora et al., 1998, and later).

1.2.2   *The Relevant Inappropriateness Assumption*

Attardo (1998, 2000, 2001) provides a more general account of irony by going beyond the rule violation condition posited by Grice (1975). According to Attardo, irony need not violate any maxim. Rather, while assuming the maxim of relevance for the second, integration phase, it should breach contextual appropriateness ostensibly at the initial phase, so that the comprehender may detect the intended violation and derive the ironic interpretation. For example, when, in a drought-stricken area, one farmer says to another *Don't you just love a nice spring rain?* the utterance may be true, yet inappropriate, given the situation of utterance (it is not raining). According to Attardo, violation of contextual appropriateness includes violation of both sincerity and cultural norms or expectations (assumed necessary for irony interpretation by the allusional pretense, see above) and more (e.g., deictic inappropriateness).

1.2.3   *The Joint Pretense View*

The joint pretense view (Clark, 1996; Clark & Carlson, 1982; Clark & Gerrig, 1984) is inspired by the Gricean view (Grice, 1978). It assumes a speaker who pretends "to be an injudicious person speaking to an uninitiated audience; the speaker intends the addressee of the irony to discover the pretense and thereby see his or her attitude toward the speaker, the audience, and the utterance" (Clark & Gerrig, 1984: 12). (For a similar view, see Boulton as quoted in Booth, 1974: 105.) By saying *What a lovely day for a picnic* on a stormy day, the ironist assumes the identity of another speaker addressing a gullible audience. The present addressee, however, is supposed to take delight in recognizing both the pretense and the intended attitude of ridicule toward the pretending speaker, the audience, and the utterance. According to Clark (1996: 368), joint pretense is conceived of as a staged communicative act (see also Haiman, 1998; Kotthoff, 1998) where the actual speaker is also an implied speaker performing a sincere communicative act toward an implied addressee, who is also the actual addressee. Both actual participants are intended to "mutually appreciate the salient contrasts between the demonstrated and actual situations" (p. 368), so that, if asked, the actual speaker would deny meaning for the actual addressee what the implied speaker means for the implied addressee.

According to this view, irony is a two-layered act of communication in which the salient literal meaning is activated and retained by both the speaker and the addressee, who reject it as the intended meaning even though they pretend otherwise.

Although this double-layered approach is inspired by Grice (1978), it is not quite clear whether it assumes a sequential or a parallel initial access. On the face of it, joint pretense seems to assume simultaneous activation of both the feigned literal and the intended ironic meaning of the utterance. Both the speaker and the addressee simultaneously assume their double roles: implied and actual. While this may be true, a close examination of the examples here suggests an alternative possibility of a sequential process, whereupon the literal interpretation precedes the intended interpretation. For instance, in a videotaped conversation (analyzed by Coates 1992, as cited in Clark, 1996: 367), the addressee seems to lag behind the speaker in joining in in the pretense.

In the conversation, two strangers, Susan and Ellen, are discussing a meal they will prepare of food they hate. Upon speculating who they would invite to it, Susan remembers someone she could invite:

(5)   Susan: Ahh. Okay. Th- the sergeant that I know who was really nasty. He didn't want any women on his course so he did his best to get them off. [At "on" Susan begins nodding to mean 'you understand the situation', and at "so" Ellen begins a face of disapproval of the sergeant.]
Ellen: Ah. Okay. [At "okay," Ellen begins nodding.]
Susan: **yes to thank him for all of his help in training**. [Over "thank" Susan raises her brow to signal "not really"; over "of his help in" she raises her brow to signal "unhelpful"; at the end, she laughs and smiles in humor. Meanwhile, over "of his help in train-" **Ellen smiles to signal understanding**.]

Note that Ellen smiles to signal understanding rather late in the course of Susan's turn—on the second half of the utterance, *after* the first ironic clause "to thank him" occurs, which is also marked as ironic by the speaker's raised brow. This example, then, suggests the possibility of a serial process, upon which the literal meaning is activated initially, only to be followed by the ironic interpretation. Although the joint pretense view does not make explicit its predictions as to whether or not the integration phase should involve suppression, it seems safe to assume that, given the double layered approach, the integration phase should involve retention of the contextually incompatible literal meaning.

1.2.4 The Tinge Hypothesis

On the tinge hypothesis (Dews, Kaplan, & Winner, 1995; Dews & Winner, 1995, 1997, 1999), irony is used to mute the intended negative criticism. The positive literal meaning of irony (*That was really funny* said on a mean joke) tinges the addressee's perception of the intended meaning. Similarly, the negative literal meaning of ironic compliments (*It's a tough life* said to someone on vacation) mitigates the positively intended meaning. Dews and Winner and their colleagues assume that the contextually incompatible, literal meaning of ironic remarks is processed at some level and interferes with the intended meaning. Following Long and Graesser (1988), they propose a dual-process model "in which comprehension may occur after the recognition of an incongruity or simultaneously" (Dews & Winner, 1997: 405). According to the tinge hypothesis, then, the literal meaning of irony is activated initially, either before or alongside the ironic meaning, and is retained in order to dilute the implicit criticism or compliment. Using a Stroop-like interference paradigm (Stroop, 1935), Dews and Winner tested this hypothesis. They asked subjects to judge the intended (rather than the literal) meaning of ironic utterances and recorded their responses. If utterances are shown to take longer to be judged as positive or negative relative to their literal interpretations, this suggests that the contextually incompatible, literal meaning is accessed automatically, interferes with the process, and slows it down. Consistent with the tinge hypothesis, ironies such as *What a lovely day for a picnic* were judged as less aggressive than their literal counterpart *What a lousy day for a picnic* and took longer to be judged as positive or negative relative to their literal interpretations. Dews and Winner concluded that, unlike literal language, irony comprehension involves an obligatory, contextually incompatible, literal phase (Dews et al., 1995; Dews & Winner, 1997; Winner, 1988).[4]

1.3 The Graded Salience Hypothesis

Before considering the assumptions and predictions of the graded salience hypothesis (Giora, 1997b; chapters 2–3 in this volume), let me first outline the comprehension model underlying this view (see also chapter 2, section 6). The following analyses assume a bipartite view of utterance comprehension, including an initial phase, involving meanings accessed directly or made available by a strong prior context (Giora, Peleg, & Fein, 2001; Peleg, Giora, & Fein, 2001, in press; 3) and an immediately subsequent phase of integration of activated information with contextual information (see also Attardo, 1998, 2000; and the "construction-integration" model, Kintsch, 1998). Note that the second, integration phase need not wait until lexical access of each and every component of the utterance has been accomplished before it becomes involved in the process. Rather, integration is attempted immediately after a word's meaning has been made available and is either retained, integrated, or suppressed as incompatible.

While the graded salience hypothesis has predictions regarding the first phase, the indirect negation view (Giora, 1995) supplements it with regard to the second, integration phase (the retention hypothesis; see chapters 2 and 5 in this volume).

1.3.1 Initial Phase

Initial processing may be affected by both lexical and contextual processes. It may involve meanings availed via a direct look up in the mental lexicon (including meanings primed via intralexical processes; Fodor, 1983; chapter 3 in this volume), as well as interpretations made available by the guessing and predictive mechanism (chapters 2–3 in this volume). Because lexical access is ordered—that is, sensitive to degree of salience—it may include more than one stage, depending on contextual fit. Thus, if initial output accidentally results in contextual fit, integration processes may be speedy. If it does not, however, further processes might ensue, either boosting the next available meaning or triggering inferencing. The assumption is that comprehension at the initial phase involves simultaneously activating any information available, bottom up (lexical access) as well as top down (world knowledge, contextual information), with bottom-up processes being automatic. Crucial, however, is the assumption that salient meanings would always be activated when the linguistic stimulus is encountered.

As illustration, consider the processes involved initially in trying to make sense of *What a lovely day for a picnic* said on a stormy day. According to this bipartite view, upon encounter, the processor would automatically retrieve the salient (literal) meaning of *lovely* ('nice') from the mental lexicon. Contextual information would result in a different output. Since this process will not achieve contextual fit, the accidental mismatch will most probably not terminate processing. If the phrase is said on a sunny day, however, the automatically retrieved, lexicalized meaning will accidentally achieve a contextual fit, rendering extra processes unnecessary. Initial processes of ironic and nonironic language are, then, the same: they evoke salient information initially, which, in the case of ironic but not literal language, is contextually incompatible.

1.3.1.1 PREDICTIONS   We can make some predictions about familiar versus less or unfamiliar ironies.

The graded salience hypothesis (Giora, 1997b, 1999b; see also chapters 2–3 in this volume) has different predictions about familiar and (less or) unfamiliar ironies with respect to initial processes. While familiar ironies have stored ironic interpretations that might be retrieved directly, unfamiliar ironies depend on context for their interpretation. That is, they would be ironies only insofar as they are embedded in a context that invites an ironic interpretation.

Recall that according to the graded salience hypothesis, salient meanings should be processed automatically, regardless of contextual bias. This implies that in a context inviting an ironic interpretation ('a stormy day'), processing a less or unfamiliar irony such as *What a lovely day for a picnic* would activate the salient, albeit contextually incompatible, literal meaning ('nice') of the key word *lovely* automatically. In most cases (unless the context is highly predictive and the critical word is in final position; Giora, Peleg, & Fein, 2001; Peleg et al., 2001, in press), the salient meaning would be accessed before the nonsalient, contextually compatible, ironic meaning ('lousy') is derived. In contrast, processing familiar ironies (*big deal; tell me about it*), whose literal and ironic meanings are both salient (i.e., listed in the mental lexicon and foremost on our mind), would activate initially both their contextually incompatible literal meaning ('great'; 'inform') and their contextually compatible ironic interpretation ('minor'; 'known').[5] Although both familiar and unfamiliar ironies activate their salient meaning automatically, this meaning is contextually appropriate only in the case of familiar irony. Unfamiliar ironies will require additional processes of adjustment to contextual information.

According to the graded salience hypothesis, interpreting familiar and even potentially unfamiliar ironic utterances literally should also induce different processes. Processing utterances such as *What a lovely day for a picnic* in a literally biasing context (a sunny day) should activate only their salient, contextually compatible, literal interpretation, which hinges on the literal meaning of the key word *lovely*. Processing familiar ironies such as *big deal, tell me about it* in a literally biasing context (when discussing an important achievement, or when someone is interested in the information), however, should automatically activate both their contextually compatible literal meaning ('great'; 'inform') and their contextually incompatible ironic meaning ('minor'; 'known') because both meanings are salient. Thus, it is only familiar ironies that are accessed via a contextually incompatible meaning when used literally. However, no adjustment processes are anticipated since the contextually compatible meaning is also available instantly on account of its salience.

We can also make some predictions about ironic versus literal interpretations of the same utterance. As can be deduced from the preceding discussion, the graded salience hypothesis assumes different processes for salient and nonsalient interpretations of the same utterance embedded in similarly strong and supportive contexts. For example, comprehending *What a lovely day for a picnic* on a stormy day is expected to involve a complex process upon which the salient, literal meaning of the key word would be activated automatically, would clash with contextual information, and would then get adjusted. In contrast, comprehending that same utterance in the literally biasing context (i.e., on a sunny day), would require no adjustment to contextual information since the salient meaning accessed initially is also contextually appropriate. If the contextual information is so predictive as to avail the appropriate interpretation before or upon encounter of the relevant lexical stimulus (*lovely*), lexical processes might be masked, though not aborted.

The predictions for familiar ironies are different. Because their ironic meaning is salient, they should be processed ironically automatically in both the ironically and the literally biasing context. Specifically, familiar ironies such as *big deal* and *tell me about it*, whose ironic and literal meanings are similarly salient, should be processed initially both ironically and literally in both types of context. Indeed, although the literal meaning is contextually incompatible in the irony-inducing context, and the ironic meaning is contextually incompatible in the literally biasing context, no adjustment process is required in either context since the contextually compatible meaning is available instantly. In addition, highly conventional ironies such as *wise guy*, which have a salient ironic meaning and a less salient literal meaning, should be processed ironically faster in both types of context.[6]

The graded salience hypothesis, then, agrees with the direct access view in that it deflates the traditional distinction between literal and nonliteral language. However, instead of assigning context an exclusive role in comprehension, it posits the familiarity continuum as a crucial factor in language comprehension (alongside contextual mechanisms). It further agrees with Gibbs's version of the direct access view in that it does not assume that processing of complete utterances is necessary before comprehenders begin making sense of them. Unlike Gibbs, however, the graded salience hypothesis does not limit this assumption to nonliteral language only. People recruit any available linguistic and pragmatic knowledge in comprehending any linguistic expression, regardless of literality, without waiting for the full expression or utterance to be processed first. In fact, in many cases, people do not even attempt a full comprehension of linguistic expressions (for evidence that speakers are not always after a full propositional meaning, see Ariel, 2002b).[7]

1.3.2 Subsequent Integration Phase

The second, contextual integration phase (which follows the initial phase immediately) may also involve a number of processes. Either the activated meanings are retained for further processes (and integrated into the current representation of the discourse), or they are actively suppressed as irrelevant or disruptive to utterance interpretation, or they decay, requiring no effort on the part of the processor. Recall that the graded salience hypothesis makes predictions only with regard to the initial phase. However, it is further supplemented by a functional principle (the retention hypothesis; see also Giora & Fein, 1999b,c and chapter 2 in this volume) which assumes that if an activated meaning is instrumental in constructing the interpretation in question it will be retained, regardless of contextual fit; if it is disruptive, it will be suppressed. Highly salient meanings may be difficult to suppress, however (for a similar view, see Morris & Binder, 2002). Indeed, the indirect negation view of irony, as well as the pretense and tinge hypotheses, assume that understanding irony involves retention of the salient, literal meaning.

1.3.2.1 PREDICTIONS   We can also make predictions of the indirect negation view. According to this view (Giora, 1995), irony is a form of negation that does not use an explicit negation marker. Often, an affirmative (*What a lovely day for a picnic* said on a stormy day) rather than a negative (*What a lousy day for a picnic* said on a sunny day) expression is used to implicate that a specific state of affairs is different or far from the state of affairs that is taken for granted, expected, or more desirable and that is made explicit by the expression. Such a view assumes that irony comprehension involves activating the salient, often literal meaning automatically.[8] However, it does not assume that the indirectly negated meaning is suppressed and replaced by its opposite, as suggested by the traditional account. Rather, irony entertains both the explicit and derived messages, so that the dissimilarity between them may be computed. By saying *What a lovely day for a picnic* on a stormy day, the ironist points out the extent to which the criticized object (*weather*) has fallen short of expectations, and is far from being 'lovely'. The indirect negation view thus predicts that the explicit, often literal meaning of irony activated initially would be retained for purposes of irony interpretation.

2. Empirical Findings

We have seen that the various theories reviewed so far vary with respect to their assumptions regarding initial comprehension and subsequent interpretation processes. In what follows, I specify the predictions of each model with regard to the various phases vis-à-vis the measures employed to test them (see table 4.1 for a summary) and present the findings concerning each of the theories. I begin by looking into initial processes, primarily the first lexical access phase, and then proceed to look into the subsequent integration phase.

TABLE 4.1 Predictions of the direct access views (echoic mention and allusional pretense), the Modular-based views (standard pragmatic model; relevant inappropriateness; joint pretense; tinge hypothesis), and the Salience-based view (Graded salience and indirect negation hypotheses).

Predictions	Comprehension and Integration		
	Direct access	Modular-based	Salience-based
1. Equal reading times of literals and nonliterals	x		
2. Faster response to appropriate probes	x		
3. Faster reading times in a rich context	x		x
4. Completion of appropriate word	x	x	
5. Spontaneous response only to appropriate word	x	x	
6. Predictions 1–5 true of more and less familiar ironies	x		
7. Different reading times for literals and nonliterals		x	
8. Faster response to literal probes at short intervals		x	
9. Faster response to ironic probes at long intervals		x	
10. No context effects		x	
11. Predictions 5–9 true of more and less familiar ironies		x	
12. Longer reading times for unfamiliar ironies vs. (more familiar) literals		x	x
13. Equal reading times for familiar ironies and their (familiar) literals.			x
13.1 Shorter reading times for highly familiar ironies than their literals.			x
14. Fast response times to salient-related probes at short intervals			x
15. Equal response times to salient and intended-related probes at long interval		x	x
16. Predictive context effects			x
17. Completion of ironic and literal probes		x	x
18. Spontaneous response to ironic and literal probes		x	x

2.1 Initial Processes

2.1.1 Less and Unfamiliar Irony

2.1.1.1 READING TIMES   Reading times of complete utterances have been criticized for being a crude measure, having the potential of masking the underlying processes. However, findings of different reading times of statements can suggest that different processes may be at work, as when same or similar statements elicit different reading times in different contexts.

According to the direct access view, since a strong context directs comprehension completely and would activate the contextually appropriate meaning exclusively, an utterance such as *What a lovely day for a picnic* should take equally long to read in both ironically and literally biasing contexts (prediction 1, table 4.1). In contrast, the literal-first, standard pragmatic model predicts that an utterance would take longer to read in an ironically than in a literally biasing context, since comprehension begins with a literal stage that should be revisited in a nonliteral irony-inducing context (prediction 7, table 4.1). According to the graded salience hypothesis, however, since the meaning of unfamiliar irony is not salient but context dependent, a nonsalient irony such as *What a lovely day for a picnic* will take longer to read in an ironically than in a literally biasing context (prediction 12, table 4.1). However, familiar ironies such as *Tell me about it*, whose ironic and literal meanings are coded in the mental lexicon, will take no longer to read in ironically than in literally biasing contexts (prediction 13, table 4.1). Highly familiar ironies, however, may have only one highly salient meaning—the ironic—and will, therefore, take longer to read in a literal than in an irony-inducing context (prediction 13.1, table 4.1).

In Giora et al. (1998) and Giora and Fein (1999a), we tested the predictions of the salience-based view vis-à-vis the standard pragmatic and direct access views. In Giora et al., we first showed that, contra the interactionist, direct access view, but as predicted by the salience-based view (Giora, 1995, 1997b), and partly along the lines suggested by the standard pragmatic model (Grice, 1975), utterances took longer to read when they were embedded in an irony than when they were in a literal-inducing context.

We used unfamiliar ironies such as *You are just in time* (see example 6) that were selected for the experiment on the basis of a familiarity pre-test and presented in Hebrew. In the familiarity pre-test, native speakers of Hebrew were presented context-less sentences. They were asked to act as lexicographers and write down the coded meaning(s) of the sentences. A sentence that received an ironic interpretation by more than half of the tested population was classified as "familiar irony." Sentences not reaching that threshold were classified as "unfamiliar irony." For each target sentence, two contexts, three to four sentences long, were prepared: one biased the target sentence toward the ironic interpretation (6a), and the other biased it toward the literal interpretation (6b). Some of the materials used were taken from the classical studies of irony (Gibbs, 1986b; Wilson & Sperber, 1992), and some were naturally occurring ironic texts for which literal counterparts were contrived.

(6) a. Anna is a great student, but she is very absent-minded. One day while I was well through my lecture, she suddenly showed up in the classroom. I said to her: "You are just in time."

b. Anna is a great student and very responsible. One day she called to tell me she did not know when she would be able to show up for my lecture. However, just as I was starting, she entered the classroom. I said to her: "You are just in time."

As predicted by the graded salience hypothesis and the indirect negation view, participants took longer to read the unfamiliar ironic targets than their literal counterparts.

These findings are consistent with the prediction of the modular-based views (Attardo, 1998, 2000, 2001; Grice, 1975; Searle, 1979) and with findings by Dews and Winner (1997) and Schwoebel et al. (2000), showing that ironic utterances took longer to be judged as positive or negative and longer to read than their literal counterparts. They are inconsistent with the echoic mention, joint pretense, and allusional pretense views, which predict equal reading times for literal and ironic utterances. They also stand in contrast to findings by Gibbs and his colleagues. For example, Gibbs (1986b) conducted a number of experiments that were interpreted as supportive of the direct access view. They showed that irony (sarcasm) did not take longer to read than its literal "counterpart." Gibbs used materials such as the following:

(7) a. Harry was building an addition to his house. He was working real hard putting in the foundation. His younger brother was supposed to help. But he never showed up. At the end of a long day, Harry's brother finally appeared. Harry said to his brother:
"You are a big help." [*Sarcastic target*]
"You are not helping me." [*Nonsarcastic target*]

b. Greg was having trouble with calculus. He had a big exam coming up and he was in trouble. Fortunately, his roommate tutored him on some of the basics. When they were done, Greg felt he'd learned a lot. "Well" he said to his roommate,
"You are a big help." [*Literal target*]
"Thanks for your help." [*Compliment target*]

Gibbs found that the difference between the reading times for the literal and the sarcastic (ironic) targets (*You are a big help*) was not significant. He further found that the nonsarcastic target (*You are not helping me*) took longer to read than the sarcastic target (*You are a big help*). In fact, the literal and nonsarcastic (nonironic) targets took longer to read than the sarcastic (*You are a big help*) and compliment (*Thanks for your help*) targets, with the compliment target being read significantly faster than any other target. In Giora (1995), I explained these findings in terms of discourse well-formedness. Given the conditions of discourse coherence (Giora, 1988, 1995; Grice, 1975), the literal and nonsarcastic text versions used in Gibbs (1986b) are the least well-formed of the four alternatives tested: their final (target) sentences add no new information to the discourse; they just state the obvious. The best versions in terms of informativity are, in fact, the compliment and sarcastic targets, which adduce information about attitudes.[9] The literally intended compliment version improves on the sarcastic version in that its literal meaning based on the salient meanings of its components is also the intended meaning, whereas the sarcastic target involves a salient (literal) meaning that is contextually incompatible and requires additional adjustment processes. Therefore, the sarcastic version took longer to read than the compliment version.

The sarcastic and compliment versions are indeed comparable in that they make up a pair of well-formed discourses that contrast thanking literally (the compliment target *Thanks for your help*) with thanking ironically (the sarcastic target *You are a big help*) and show that thanking ironically requires additional processing time. Gibbs explained these results differently, suggesting that "positively intended evaluative remarks are processed more quickly than negatively evaluative remarks, although it could simply mean that conventional phrases within the acknowledgments, such as 'thank you', facilitated processing for these targets" (1986b: 6).[10]

The same results are replicated in Gibbs's (1986b) experiment 3. In this experiment, Gibbs examined sarcastic remarks and their literal (nonsarcastic) counterparts in normative versus nonnormative contexts:

(8)   a. *Normative context*

Billy and Joe were long-time pals. But one time when Billy was away on a business trip, Joe slept with Billy's wife, Lynn. When Billy found out about it afterward, he was upset. He confronted Joe and said to him:

"You are a fine friend." [*Sarcastic target*]

"You are a terrible friend." [*Nonsarcastic target*]

b. *Nonnormative context*

Billy and Joe were long-time pals. One time Billy was in desperate need of money. His car had broken down and he needed $300 to fix it. So, he asked Joe for a loan. Joe said he could lend Billy the money. This made Billy happy and he said to Joe,

"You are a terrible friend." [*Sarcastic target*]

"You are a fine friend." [*Nonsarcastic target*]

Again, as predicted by the graded salience hypothesis and modular-based views, participants took longer to read sarcastic remarks such as *You are a fine friend* in normative texts than their nonsarcastic uses when presented in other nonnormative contexts. Similarly, participants took longer to read sarcastic remarks such as *You are a terrible friend* in nonnormative contexts than their nonsarcastic uses when presented in other normative contexts. Gibbs explained this by suggesting that positively intended evaluative remarks are processed faster than negatively evaluative remarks: "Literally saying something nice about someone is understood more rapidly than sarcastically saying something nice and more rapidly than saying something negative, whether literally or sarcastically" (1986b: 9). But Gibbs's findings further evince that literally saying something negative about someone (*You are a terrible friend*) is more rapidly understood than sarcastically saying something negative about someone (i.e., saying a positively intended remark such as *You are a terrible friend*). Therefore, the first explanation cannot hold. A more parsimonious explanation may be the one that suggests that nonsalient meanings induced by nonconventional instances of sarcasm or irony take longer to understand than salient meanings activated by more conventional (e.g., literal) uses of these instances.[11]

In sum, reading times of whole sentences support the salience-based view, according to which unfamiliar/nonsalient irony should involve a salient though contextually incompatible phase initially.

2.1.1.2 RESPONSE TIME TO RELATED AND UNRELATED CONCEPTS The time taken to make a decision whether a letter string makes up a word or a nonword may suggest whether a concept has been activated in the course of comprehension. Short response times to a test word indicate the high accessibility of its meaning. Longer response times suggest that the meaning is less accessible. If the probe (test word) is presented upon or immediately after displaying the key word in the target sentence (*lovely* in *What a lovely day for a picnic*), response times can be revealing as to which concepts or meanings are initially involved. When they are presented after a delay, response times can tell us which additional meanings become available. Although this measure may be highly revealing as to which meanings are involved in the process, it may nevertheless be unable to tease apart word-level from message-level interpretation (see chapter 2 in this volume).

The direct access view predicts that in a strongly supportive context, readers would always respond faster to the contextually appropriate probe since they activate only the contextually appropriate meaning (prediction 2, table 4.1). Thus, in a literally biasing context (sunny day), the contextually compatible, literally related probe ('nice') would invoke a faster response than the ironically related probe (following *What a lovely day for a picnic*). Similarly, in an ironically biasing context (a stormy day), the contextually compatible, ironically related probe ('lousy') would invoke a faster response than the literally related probe.

In contrast, the standard pragmatic model assumes that, if measured immediately, even in a highly supportive ironic context, readers would respond faster to the literally related probe because they always activate the literal meaning of irony first and the implicated ironic meaning second (prediction 8, table 4.1).

According to the graded salience hypothesis, readers will respond faster to probes related to salient than to less or nonsalient meanings (prediction 14, table 4.1; but for more specific restrictions when highly predictive contexts are involved, see Giora, Peleg, & Fein, 2001 and Peleg et al., 2001, in press). Regarding less or unfamiliar ironies, this response should (often) be true of the literal meaning because this meaning is the only one coded in the mental lexicon. The ironically related probe ('lousy') will take longer to respond to and will benefit from extra processing time. Similarly, in the literally biasing context, the probe related to the salient (literal) meaning will be responded to faster; however, response times to literally and ironically related probes of familiar ironies will not differ. Given their similar salience, comprehenders would activate both their literal and ironic meanings initially in both types of contexts. Consequently, tapping the appropriate meaning should not benefit from extra processing time.

In Giora et al. (1998), we tested these hypotheses. We measured response times to literally and ironically related probes using interstimulus intervals (ISI) of 150 and 1000 milliseconds. Such different delays, we assumed, should be revealing about the temporal aspects of irony comprehension. In one of the experiments, participants read texts (such as example 6 here) at their natural speed. After the target sentence has been read, the screen went blank for an interstimulus interval of either 150 or 1000 milliseconds, and a letter string was displayed. The letter strings made up words that were either literally (*punctual*) or ironically (*late*) related to the target sentences, or were (scrambled) nonwords (*atle*). Participants had to make lexical decisions as to whether the probes were words or nonwords by pressing a "yes" or "no" key.

As predicted by the graded salience hypothesis, participants were faster to respond to the salient-related than to the nonsalient-related test words. In the literally biasing context, they responded faster to the contextually compatible literal probe (*punctual*) than to the ironically related probe (*late*). Similarly, in the ironically biasing context, they responded faster to the contextually incompatible literal probe (*punctual*) than to the contextually compatible ironic probe (*late*). That is, they always responded faster to the salient (literally related) probe, irrespective of type of context (see figure 4.1). This pattern of response held for interstimulus intervals of both 150 and 1000 milliseconds, as illustrated by the top and bottom panels of figure 4.2.

While in the literally biasing context, participants' response time did not vary, no matter whether they had an interstimulus interval of 150 or of 1000 milliseconds, the ironically biasing context elicited a different pattern of response. In the ironically biasing context, participants took much longer to respond when the interstimulus interval was 150 milliseconds than when it was 1000 milliseconds (see figure 4.3).

These findings were replicated in Giora and Fein (1999a), where the same set of less and unfamiliar ironies was tested with new participants. Again, at the short delay condition (150 milliseconds after offset of the target sentences), participants were faster to respond to the salient-related (literal) than to the nonsalient-related (ironic) test words, regardless of context. In the literally biasing context, they responded faster to the contextually compatible, literally related probe than to the contextually incompatible, ironically related probe. Similarly, in the ironically biasing context, they responded faster to the contextually incompatible, literally related probe than to the contextually compatible, ironic probe.

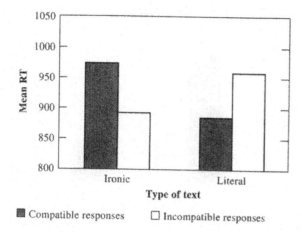

Figure 4.1 Mean response time (RT) (in milliseconds) to compatible and incompatible probes related to **less familiar ironies** embedded in ironically and literally biasing texts.

However, after a 1000 milliseconds delay, contextual information affected the processing of less and unfamiliar ironies, and participants no longer responded faster to the salient-related test words in those contexts. In contrast, the same comparison performed on results obtained from the literally biasing context revealed that in this context, literally related test words were still processed faster than ironically related test words (see figure 4.4).

To control for the possibility that the results were obtained due to context effects, we repeated the same experiment, this time displaying only the contexts, without the target sentences. Indeed, when participants were presented the contexts without the target sentences, the results obtained in the previous experiment were not replicated. In the absence of target sentences, test words were responded to similarly fast, irrespective of contextual bias. Moreover, they were responded to more slowly than when the targets were present (as in the previous experiment). These results eliminate the possibility that the findings were affected by contextual information rather than by the targets themselves (albeit in context).

In all, these findings support the graded salience hypothesis (Giora, 1997b and chapter 2 in this volume), the indirect negation view (Giora, 1995), the standard pragmatic model (Grice, 1975), and the relevant inappropriateness view (Attardo, 1998, 2000, 2001), and they disconfirm the processing-equivalence hypothesis inspired by the direct access view (Gibbs, 1986a,b; Sperber & Wilson, 1986/1995). They show that irony comprehension involves activation of the salient (literal) meaning initially, regardless of context. Moreover, finding that in the irony-inviting contexts response to the literally related probes was faster than to the ironically related probes even when comprehenders enjoyed extra processing time (at an ISI of 1000 milliseconds) suggests that comprehen-

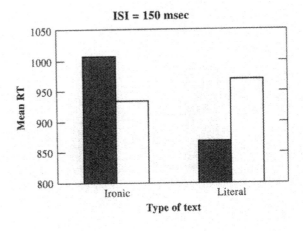

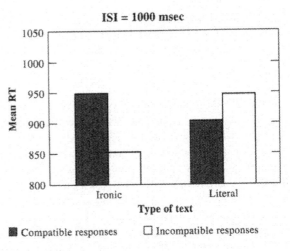

■ Compatible responses   □ Incompatible responses

Figure 4.2 Mean response time (in milliseconds) to compatible and incompatible probes related to **less familiar ironies** embedded in ironically and literally biasing texts, for interstimulus intervals (ISIs) of 150 msec (top panel) and 1000 msec (bottom panel).

ders might have first computed the literal meaning of the statement as a whole before attempting to derive the ironic interpretation.

Irony comprehension, then, involves a contextually inappropriate phase. Derivation of the nonsalient, ironic meaning of unfamiliar irony requires additional time, compared to that consumed by the activation of the salient, literal meaning of the same utterance (cf. section 1.3.1.1). Taken together, these findings contest the direct access view, which predicts that only contextually compatible meanings would be involved in comprehension, regardless of salience. Instead, these findings show that it was always the salient rather than the compatible meaning that was processed faster, regardless of context.

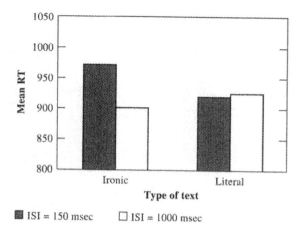

Figure 4.3 Mean response time (in milliseconds) to probes related to **less familiar ironies** embedded in ironically and literally biasing texts, for interstimulus intervals (ISIs) of 150 and 1000 msec.

2.1.2 Familiar versus Less Familiar Irony

To further validate the graded salience hypothesis, it is also necessary to show that familiar ironies are processed differently than unfamiliar ironies. Recall that the graded salience hypothesis has different predictions regarding processing familiar and less familiar instances of language. Because less familiar ironies have (usually) only one salient meaning—the literal meaning (relying on the salient/literal interpretation of the words that make it up)—they should be initially processed only literally, in both literally and ironically biasing contexts (as shown in the preceding discussion).[12] Ironically biasing contexts should affect their processing only at a later stage, at which the ironic meaning would be derived. In contrast, familiar ironies should be initially processed both literally and ironically (predictions 13–14, table 4.1 and see section 1.3.1.1), regardless of context, because both their literal and ironic meanings are coded in the mental lexicon.

In Giora and Fein (1999a), we provided evidence supporting the graded salience hypothesis. In this study, participants were presented Hebrew familiar ironies such as *Very funny*, embedded in either a literally or an ironically biasing context:

(9) a. Iris was walking on her own in the dark alley, when all of a sudden a hand was laid on her back. Startled, she turned around to find out that the hand was her young brother's who had sneaked behind her to frighten her. She said to him: "Very funny."

   b. Tal and Ortal, the twins, wanted to go to the movies. Their mother recommended a movie she had seen shortly before. When they came home, she was

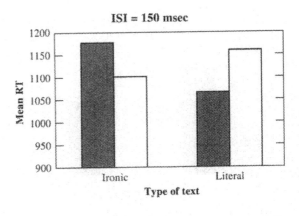

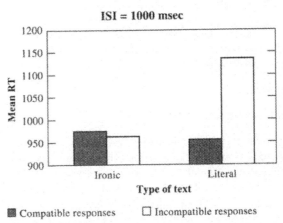

■ Compatible responses   □ Incompatible responses

Figure 4.4 Mean response time (in milliseconds) to compatible and incompatible probes related to **less familiar ironies** embedded in ironically and literally biasing contexts, for interstimulus intervals (ISIs) of 150 msec (top panel) and 1000 msec. (bottom panel)

eager to know how they found the movie. They both agreed:
"Very funny."

Participants read the texts at their own natural speed. When the last target sentence was read, the screen went blank for an interstimulus interval of either 150 or 1000 milliseconds. Response time to ironically related (*annoying*) and literally related (*amusing*) test words displayed under these interstimulus intervals was measured.

As predicted, familiar ironies and their literal counterparts were processed similarly under both time constraints. Figure 4.5 illustrates the similarity between contextually compatible and incompatible responses in all the conditions. Given the coded, salient status of both literal and ironic meanings of familiar ironies, they were both activated initially, regardless of contextual bias. Recall, however, that unfamiliar ironies elicited a different response pattern (see figure 4.4).

Taken together, findings of reading times and response times from familiar and unfamiliar ironies support the graded salience hypothesis and contest the direct access view. They show that salient meanings are always processed initially, regardless of contextual information. The salient (literal) meaning of familiar and less or unfamiliar ironies was instantly available in the ironically biasing context, even though it was incompatible with contextual information. Further, familiar ironies facilitated their salient albeit contextually incompatible (ironic) meaning in the literally biasing contexts. These findings are consistent with the view that contextual information is ineffective in blocking salient though incompatible meanings. In our studies, salient information was accessed directly. When it did not reach contextual fit, it was revisited and redressed. Direct access, then, is not necessarily a function of context monitoring access of contextually appropriate meanings (as assumed by Gibbs, 1994; Glucksberg, Kreuz, & Rho, 1986; Vu, Kellas, Metcalf, & Herman, 2000; Vu, Kellas, & Paul, 1998). Rather, direct access may be a function of meaning salience (as also assumed by Horton & Keysar, 1996; Keysar, Barr, & Horton, 1998; Keysar, Barr, Balin, & Paek, 1998; Keysar, Shen, Glucksberg, & Horton, 2000).

2.1.2.1 MOVING WINDOWS   Although measures such as reading times of complete sentences and lexical decisions following offset of target sentences may be highly revealing, they may not be as sensitive as more finely tuned online measures (see chapter 2 in this volume). To further validate the graded salience hypothesis, findings from more sensitive online measures should be obtained. Self-paced moving windows, in which participants advance a text word by word across the screen by pressing a key, is such a tool. It allows for the computation of reading latency for each item in the target sentence, for the space following the sentence, and for the sentence that follows (attesting to difficulties that may spill over downstream, thereby increasing reading times of the subsequent sentence; see chapter 2). Short reading times suggest that a meaning is processed directly. Longer reading times may allude to more complex processes. Such a procedure also bypasses the problem of word versus message meaning, dispensing with test words.

The direct access view predicts shorter reading times for the key nonliterally intended words of an utterance, for the space following these key words, and for the first words of the following sentence in an ironically and literally biasing context relative to a neutral context (predictions 1 and 3, table 4.1). In contrast, the standard pragmatic model predicts longer reading times for key words in utterances embedded in irony-inducing contexts, for the space following the key words, and for the first words of the following sentence relative to a literal context (predictions 7 and 10, table 4.1). Similarly, the graded salience hypothesis predicts longer reading times for key words of less and unfamiliar ironies, for the space following the key words, and for the first word of the following

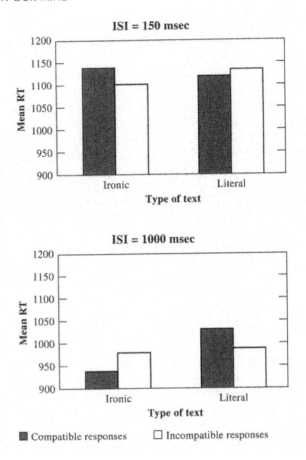

Figure 4.5 Mean response time (in milliseconds) to compatible and incompatible probes related to **familiar ironies**, in ironically and literally biasing contexts, for interstimulus intervals (ISIs) of 150 msec (top panel) and 1000 msec (bottom panel).

sentence than for the literal equivalents (prediction 12, table 4.1). Familiar ironies will not exhibit these differences, however (prediction 13, table 4.1). The graded salience hypothesis also allows for a supportive context to speed up processes, but not at the expense of blocking salient though incompatible meanings (prediction 16, table 4.1).

Studies by Ivanko and Pexman (2001), Pexman et al. (2000), and Schwoebel et al. (2000) may help test some of these predictions. Using self-paced moving windows, Pexman et al.'s participants read passages containing a nonliteral target sentence, which did not appear in text final position; these sentences were either familiar or unfamiliar instantiations of conceptual metaphors presented in the metaphoric form 'An X is a Y'. The contexts further varied in whether they included a high-irony, high-metaphor, neutral, or no occupation speaker, and whether they invited an ironic, metaphoric, or neutral interpretation. The following example illustrates a neutral (10a), a metaphor-inducing (10b), and an irony-inducing context (10c):

(10)   a. Jan and her cousin, a factory worker, were waiting in line at the supermarket checkout. About the cashier, the factory worker said: "Her mind is an active volcano." (An extra sentence follows here.)

b. Jan and her cousin, a factory worker, were waiting in line at the supermarket checkout. The cashier was working very efficiently. About the cashier, the factory worker said: "Her mind is an active volcano." (An extra sentence follows here.)

c. Jan and her cousin, a factory worker, were waiting in line at the supermarket checkout. The cashier was having difficulty counting change for the customer ahead of them in line. About the cashier, the factory worker said: "Her mind is an active volcano." (An extra sentence follows here.)

In accordance with the graded salience hypothesis, findings demonstrate that, although context has some facilitative effect, unfamiliar utterances (novel instances of irony and metaphor) took longer to read than familiar (metaphoric) utterances. Note that although only the metaphors were rated for degree of familiarity, their ironic uses were always nonsalient, since their interpretation was entirely dependent on the context. Specifically, all three conditions (10a–c) exhibited increased reading time at the last nonliteral word in the statement (relative to the baseline mean reading time for the first literal words in the statement). This finding suggests that processing the nonliteral meaning of the key word involved accessing the salient, contextually incompatible, literal meaning as well. However, the less familiar metaphor (10b) and irony (10c) exhibited shorter reading times at the last word than were observed in the neutral condition (10a), alluding to context effect in this location. Further, for unfamiliar ironical targets (10c), reading times at the space after the sentence were markedly slower than were found in the neutral condition but were similar to those found for unfamiliar metaphors in the metaphor condition. (For similar findings, see Gibbs, 1998a, and Colston & Gibbs, 2002, discussed in chapter 8 in this volume; for a discussion of the results relevant to metaphor interpretation see chapter 5). The difference that did emerge between the metaphor and its ironic interpretation was in the speed taken to read the last word in the 'X is a Y' item (e.g., *volcano*). This finding suggests that, for these items, recognizing the ironic sense involved both understanding the sentence (a positive metaphor) and how it is being used to convey negative information. In contrast, comprehending the metaphor involved only the first metaphoric process.

Thus, while for unfamiliar items, context speeded reading times at the last nonliteral word relative to the neutral context, all three conditions nevertheless exhibited spillover effects: reading time was longer at the space after the statement and for the processing of the first word of the next sentence, with longer reading times in the irony than in the metaphor condition.

Another comparison between salient and nonsalient language is offered by Schwoebel et al. (2000). In their study, processing both ironic praise (example 11) and ironic criticism (example 12) (induced by the first phrase in bold) was compared with processing their literal counterparts (induced by the second phrase in bold). Schwoebel et al. used a procedure similar to moving windows in which participants advanced a text phrase by phrase across the screen by pressing a key (see slashes in final target sentence in the examples):

(11) *Ironic praise*
      Sam complained to his mother that he had too much homework. He said it would take him the whole weekend. On Saturday morning, he started his work, and **was all done in one hour / by the end of the day he had finished less than half**. His mother said: Your workload/ is overwhelming/ this weekend.

(12) *Ironic criticism*
      A new professor was hired to teach philosophy. The professor was supposed to be really sharp. When Allen asked several questions, the professor offered **naive and ignorant / incisive and knowledgeable** answers. Allen said: That guy / is brilliant / at answering questions.

Results show that participants took longer to process the target phrase in the ironically than in the literally biasing contexts (although this difference was significant only for the ironic criticism targets and only by item analysis). Similar results were obtained by Ivanko and Pexman (2001), alluding to the complex processes involved in comprehending nonsalient language.

Evidence from fine-tuned online measures, then, is consistent with the graded salience hypothesis, indirect negation view, standard pragmatic model, relevant inappropriateness, and tinge hypothesis but contests some aspects of the direct access view. Findings from online measures are consistent with the view that unfamiliar irony is not processed directly, but avails its nonsalient ironic interpretation after the more salient literal and sometimes metaphoric interpretation has been activated. In accordance with the graded salience hypothesis, some of the evidence suggests that, in spite of its facilitative effects, contextual information, which is biased toward the ironic interpretation of the target sentence, does not block the salient but unintended meanings.

In sum, reading times and response times demonstrate that less familiar language (nonconventional irony) takes longer to process than more familiar language (literals, familiar ironies and metaphors) and may involve salient, though contextually incompatible meanings. Overall, reinterpretation of Gibbs's (1986b) findings (Giora, 1995; see also Dews & Winner, 1997, 1999) and new findings by Dews and Winner (1997), Giora and Fein, 1999a; Giora et al. (1998), Pexman et al. (2000), and Schwoebel et al. (2000) support a salience-based view of irony comprehension. They show that salient meanings are always processed initially, regardless of contextual bias, while nonsalient meanings lag behind.

2.2 Integration: The Retention Hypothesis

According to the retention hypothesis (see section 1.3.2 here; chapter 2, section 6.2; Giora & Fein, 1999c), a meaning activated initially is retained for further processes if it is instrumental in constructing the intended interpretation, regardless of contextual compatibility; it is suppressed if it interferes with the process. According to the indirect negation, the joint pretense, and the tinge hypotheses, the contextually incompatible (often literal) meaning of irony accessed initially should be retained for further processes because it is conducive to the interpretation of the ironic utterance. The indirect negation view assumes that the salient meaning of irony functions as a reference point relative to which the ironicized situation is assessed. The joint pretense assumes that the salient (literal) meaning is functional in the appreciation of the pretense. The tinge hypothesis assumes the retention of the salient (literal) meaning for the purposes of diluting or muting the criticism.

The direct access view, however, assumes that the integration phase should involve only contextually compatible meanings, since only compatible meanings have been tapped initially. Similarly, according to the standard pragmatic model, no contextually incompatible meanings are involved at the integration phase, since the contextually incompatible literal meaning activated initially has been suppressed and replaced by the contextually compatible ironic meaning.

2.2.1 Response Times

One way to test the retention hypothesis is to measure response time to contextually incompatible concepts in ironically biasing contexts after a long delay. Recall that in Giora and Fein (1999a), we measured response times to literally related probes after an interstimulus interval of 1000 milliseconds. After such a delay, it is contended, many meanings of lexical items that are contextually inappropriate are suppressed and, by some tests, are no longer available for comprehension (Gernsbacher, 1990; Swinney, 1979). Our findings from familiar and less or unfamiliar ironies demonstrate that, contra the direct access view (prediction 2, table 4.1) and the standard pragmatic model (prediction 9, table 4.1), but consistent with the indirect negation, the tinge and the joint pretense views, the salient (literal) meaning of irony activated automatically was not suppressed when the ironic meaning emerged, but remained active even after a long delay (prediction 15, table 4.1 and see bottom panel of figure 4.4).

In Giora et al. (1998), we tested the retention hypothesis in a longer delay condition. But even after an interstimulus interval of 2000 milliseconds, the literal meaning of the utterance embedded in the ironically biasing context was still as active. In contrast, the literal meaning of the same utterance embedded in the literally biasing context began to fade after such a delay (see figure 4.6).

Once comprehended and integrated, it was no longer required for further processes.

2.2.2 *Word Fragment Completion*

Another way to find out which meanings are retained in irony comprehension is to use an offline memory test such as a word fragment completion task. In a word fragment completion test, participants are asked to complete a fragmented word (b-tt-r) with the first word they can think of (*bitter; butter; better*). Some researchers take word fragment completion tests to be perceptual (data-driven) in nature, contending that it is greatly affected by manipulation of modality (visual or auditory; see Blaxton, 1989; Roediger & Blaxton, 1987) and symbolic form (word or picture; Weldon, Roediger & Challis, 1989). Others, however, have shown that these tests are also conceptually driven, being sensitive to both perceptual and semantic variables. Proponents of this view have shown that both cross-modal priming (Blaxton, 1989; Rajaram & Roediger, 1993; Roediger & Blaxton, 1987; Weldon, 1991) and semantic processing affect performance in this task (Bassili, Smith, & MacLeod, 1989; Challis & Brodbeck, 1992; Hirshman, Snodgrass, Mindes, & Feenan, 1990; Smith, 1991; Weldon, 1991). Notwithstanding, most studies in this area involved direct priming, in which participants were directly exposed to the to-be-tested stimulus (that is, presented with the word 'table' and tested later on 't-b-e'). Research in this area has shown that mere presentation of target-related words did not produce priming in a word fragment completion test (Mandler, Graf, & Kraft, 1986; Roediger & Challis, 1992). However, semantic processing during a study phase (like reading behavioral descriptions, reading short stories or poems, and category clustering) did produce indirect priming (Bassili, 1989;

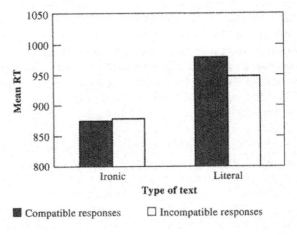

Figure 4.6 Mean response time (in milliseconds) to compatible and incompatible probes related to **less familiar ironies** embedded in ironically and literally biasing texts for an interstimulus interval (ISI) of 2000 msec.

Bassili & Smith, 1986; Mandler, Hamson, & Dorfman, 1990; Overson & Mandler, 1987; Richards & French, 1991; Whitney, Waring, & Zingmark, 1992).

In our studies (Giora & Fein, 1999b), we looked into such semantic priming in which the participant is exposed to a stimulus that is semantically related to the target (the word 'chair' and the test word 't-b-e'). We presented participants with short stories biased either toward the literal or toward the ironic interpretation of the last target sentence and tested completion of words related to either the literal or the ironic meaning of the target sentence. We expected to be able to detect priming, resulting in different patterns of response according to the bias of the context.

Our participants were children, aged 9–10.[13] They were presented Hebrew utterances such as *Moshe, I think you should eat something* in example (13), embedded in either ironically (13a) or literally (13b) biasing contexts comprising several sentences. They had to complete fragmented test words related either to the literal or to the ironic meaning of the target sentence. For instance, example (13) was followed by the fragmented test words (which in Hebrew correspond to *little* (li—le)—related to the literal meaning—and *stop* (s—p)—related to the ironic meaning of the utterance:

(13) a. After he had finished eating pizza, falafel, ice cream, wafers, and half of the cream cake his mother had baked for his brother Benjamin's birthday party, Moshe started eating coated peanuts. His mother said to him:
   "Moshe, I think you should eat something."

   b. At two o'clock in the afternoon, Moshe started doing his homework and getting prepared for his Bible test. When his mother came home from work at 8 p.m., Moshe was still seated at his desk, looking pale. His mother said to him:
   "Moshe, I think you should eat something."

Two pretests were performed, ruling out the possibility that any difference to be found later in the experiment would be a function of context effects or salience difference between the test words.

Recall that the direct access view and the standard pragmatic model anticipate that only contextually compatible meanings would be facilitated in both types of context (prediction 4, table 4.1). However, according to the indirect negation, tinge, and joint pretense hypotheses, later processes should facilitate both contextually compatible and incompatible meanings in the ironically biasing context (prediction 17, table 4.1). Specifically, participants should be able to complete literally and ironically related words in the ironically biased context condition, but only literally related words in the literally biased context condition.

As illustrated in figure 4.7, our findings show that, indeed, as predicted by the indirect negation, as well as by the tinge and pretense views, but contra the direct access and standard pragmatic models, the ironically biased targets facilitated both contextually compatible and incompatible-but-salient responses. In

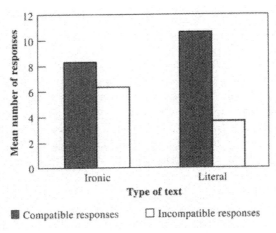

Figure 4.7 Mean number of compatible and incompatible responses to **less familiar** ironies embedded in ironically and literally biasing contexts.

contrast, the literally biased targets facilitated only the salient, literally related concepts. Such findings suggest that salient though incompatible meanings are retained when they are functional. Proponents of the direct access view could argue that the offline nature of the task might enable readers to contemplate the targets longer and evoke contextually incompatible meanings alongside compatible ones. Such criticism, however, cannot explain the whole picture: it is only in the irony-inducing context that salient but contextually incompatible meanings were made available when extra processing time was allowed. The literally biased targets did not induce such responses. Findings from word fragment completion task, then, show that salient meanings are neither filtered out nor suppressed, in spite of contextual information to the contrary. Rather, they are retained and sustain the ironic interpretation.

2.2.3 Spontaneous Response: Evidence from Text Production

Spontaneous responses to ironic utterances in naturally occurring conversations and written texts may further provide an insight into which meanings have been kept in the mind of the producer and the interlocutor. In the final analysis, what we are interested in is what happens outside the lab—that is, in the processes involved in spontaneous speech. Spontaneous speech would be particularly revealing because such discourse is less amenable than written discourse to control and revision. The claim, then, that information available to interlocutors has a major role in discourse comprehension and production must be particularly pertinent to such discourse. Of course, spontaneous talk is monitored (see Kaplan & Zaidel, 2001; Zaidel, 1987), and it involves error correction. However, given the time constraints imposed on face-to-face interaction, producing spontaneous speech must be more "error"-prone than producing written discourse, which is self-paced and can be revisited any time. To examine the extent to which contextually incompatible meanings are activated and manipulated in the course of discourse construction, spontaneous talk seems the natural environment to explore.

Indeed, spontaneous discourse may provide evidence reflecting the retention or availability of salient though contextually inappropriate meanings, if these meanings are perceived by interlocutors (the speaker included). For instance, if the salient, yet contextually incompatible, literal meaning of irony is focused on and reinstated in conversation—that is, if addressees respond to it—this would be evidence of its availability. Example 14 (from Drew, 1987, cited in Clark, 1998: 374) may serve to illustrate the point that salient (literal) meanings are retained in conversation even when they are contextually inappropriate. In this example, Gerald has just bought a new sports car and is late for a meeting:

(14)   Gerald: Hi, how are you?
        Martha: Well, you are late as usual.
        Gerald: eheh eheh eheh eheh.
        Lee: What's the matter, **couldn't you get your car started?**
        Gerald: **hehh That's right. I had to get it pushed, eheh eheh**

Gerald could have responded to Lee's ironic reprimand by addressing the ironic meaning (the reprimand)—that is, by saying "I'm sorry" or by coming up with a real explanation. Instead, he proceeded along the lines proposed by Lee, thereby elaborating on the tease—that is, on the salient, contextually incompatible (literal) meaning of the ironic utterance.

Responses to the literal meaning of irony attest to its availability that is assumed by the graded salience and indirect negation, joint pretense, and tinge hypotheses (prediction 18, table 4.1) but not by the direct access view. They also attest that, contra the standard pragmatic model (prediction 5, table 4.1), the salient, albeit contextually incompatible, literal meaning is not dispensed with by contextual information. Rather, because of its salience status and role in comprehension, the literal meaning of irony is accessed and retained by comprehenders. Consequently, it may easily be reused by the discourse participants for special purposes, such as affecting humor. In contrast, its absence or scarcity would be more compatible with the direct access view (according to which no incompatible meanings should be accessed) and the standard pragmatic model (according to which such meanings should undergo suppression).

In Giora and Gur (in press), we tested the predictions of the retention hypothesis by examining the kind of response irony elicits in naturally occurring conversations. Our data come from 1-hour conversations among five Israeli friends. The conversations took place in Tel Aviv in October 1997 and comprise 9380 words. As illustration, consider an English translation of a Hebrew extract (example 15), in which the ironic utterances are underlined, and responses to their literal meaning are in bold. The example comprises about 300 words and (partly) revolves around Benjamin (Bibi) and Sara Netanyahu (the then Israeli Prime Minister and his wife), who, in a newspaper interview, complained about the press harassing them:

(15)   1. A: You don't understand one thing. You think they initiate these things? This
            is maybe the first article they [wrote].

        2. B: [They]
            stay home and after them the paparazzi come . . . and they are simply
            [miserable].

        3. A: [(they) **ruin] their lives**, what do you want?

        4. B: I want to cite the last sentence of the article, yes, out of the heroism's
            mouth [meaning 'out of God's mouth', equivalent to the English idiom
            'out of the horse's mouth'; R.G.] [as they say].

        5. A: [**Out of the baby's mouth.**]

        6. B: **Out of the hero's** mouth. In fact, it's not in this article, it's in the, it's in
            the article that appeared in *Ma'ariv* [an Israeli daily; R.G.], but x Sara
            says that maybe following the tragedy of Princess Diana they will begin
            to understand . . . she and Diana on the same level!

        7. C: So, the last photograph, they chose the picture of Bibi and Sara and their
            two kids on the beach in Caesaria and <xx> ya'eni [a marker for irony;
            R.G.] a *spontaneous* picture, but it's obvious that this picture is carefully
            arranged: the big boy with the father—the small one with the mother, and
            all this.

        8. A: (0.1 second later) It's as if I take a picture of you (C) now, say, you are sit-
            ting next to D (C's wife), because . . . really, come on!

        9. C: One thing is certain, then . . . the paparazzi photographers will not catch
            them at the speed of 160 kph.

        10. Everybody: @ (2 seconds).

        11. D: So she cannot compare herself to Diana.

        12. B: <xx> She is really miserable because they do her injustice.

        13. A: Diana, my ass, this entire story, believe me, I feel like retching.

        14. D: Yes.

        15. A: Big deal! [<xx>]

        16. C: [I don't feel] like retching at all, I feel like sharing the profits.

        17. D: [@@@@]

        18. C: **[I feel like] sharing the profits.** Throw me some bone [equivalent to the
            English idiom 'throw me a scrap'; R.G.].

        19. D: **Open a florist shop.**

LEGEND: [14]

...: half a second break; ..: a shorter break

[ ]: overlap

x: unclear word

<xx>: unclear utterance

@: laughter

(): for words not appearing in the Hebrew text

underlining: ironic utterances

bold: responses to the literal meaning

A sample analysis:

Speaker A (in line 1) sympathizes with the Netanyahus, while speaker B (in line 2) is critical of them and describes them ironically as "miserable." The literal sense of the irony echoes their complaint and indicates that they are far from being miserable and must, in fact, be happy about being so popular in the press. However, A (in line 3) resonates with literal meaning of 'misery' by retorting that their life is "ruined."

In line 4, the reference to Bibi as God ("heroism") is ironic. The next responses referring to him as either "baby" (sort of opposite) or "hero" in line 6 are echoes of the literal meaning of the irony. The irony at the end of line 6, referring to Diana, echoes the literal meaning of a previous irony in line 2, which alludes to the same event through the mention of the "paparazzi." Although the irony in line 6 remains uncommented on at this stage, D is going to refer to it later (in line 11).

The ironic meaning "spontaneous" in line 7 is responded to by A in line 8. A disagrees with C—that is, with the ironic meaning—and attempts to defend the genuine spontaneity of the photograph of the Netanyahus (appearing in the press to affect 'spontaneity' in order to support their claim that they are hounded by the press).

The irony in line 9, which suggests that the couple will never really run away from the paparazzo photographers (see source of the echo in line 2), was responded to by a 2-second laughter.

The irony in line 12 is a repetition of the topic of this conversation. It is a repetition of the literal meaning of the previous ironies, particularly those generated by the self-same speaker.

The irony in line 16 is responded to by laughter in line 17. In line 18, C echoes the literal meaning of his own irony, and in line 19 the literal meaning of his irony is elaborated by D.

Similar analysis of the data as a whole shows that of the 56 identified ironic utterances, 42 (75%) were responded to by reference to their literal meaning. These findings corroborate those of Kotthoff (1998, in press), who shows that in friendly conversations, listeners very often respond to the literal meaning of the ironic utterance while at the same time making it clear that they have also understood the implied meaning. Such findings suggest that the literal meaning of irony is activated and retained by both speakers and addressees. The occurrence of irony in the conversations made its literal meaning available for further discussion and elaboration, as predicted by the graded salience hypothesis, the retention hypothesis, and the indirect negation view. Contra the direct access view, then, irony did not avail only the ironic meaning. Further, contra the traditional (Grice, 1975) and modular views (Fodor, 1983), the literal meaning was not suppressed as irrelevant but was retained for further processes.

Interpretation of unfamiliar, innovative language, then, is a complex process. It involves activating the salient, contextually incompatible meaning initially either before or alongside the contextually compatible nonsalient meaning. In the case of irony, it also involves retention of both meanings for the purpose of a contrastive comparison.

3. What Does Irony Mean?

The various theories in question do not only vary on how they account for comprehension, but also diverge with regard to the interpretation process: what do we mean when we are ironic? According to the classical view (Grice, 1975), we mean the opposite of what we say. But if this is indeed the case, why don't we say what we mean (i.e., the opposite)? Why do we say instead what we don't mean or what we disapprove of? According to the relevance theoretic account (Sperber, 1984; Sperber & Wilson, 1981, 1986/1995; Wilson & Sperber 1992), we resort to irony not when we intend to implicate the opposite (which can be said), but when we wish to dissociate ourselves from someone's utterance, from an opinion of a certain type of person, or from some popular norm or wisdom. Mentioning, alluding to, or representing that opinion enables us to dissociate ourselves from it in a manifestly ridiculing or reproving way. Verbal irony invariably involves an interpretive use of someone's opinion or thought and an attitude of dissociation from the opinion echoed or from what it assumes (Curcó, 1997). Upon this account, the speaker says what she, in fact, disapproves of, in order to distance herself from what she alludes to (or from what is assumed by what she alludes to).

According to the graded salience hypothesis (Giora, 1997b; chapter 2 in this volume) and indirect negation view (Giora, 1995), irony has a different function. The salient literal meaning of irony functions as a reference point relative to which the ironicized situation is to be assessed and criticized. What irony conveys, then, is frustration with or dissociation from what is referred to, rather than from what is said— that is, from the opinion or thought expressed by what is said. Indeed, what is said often alludes to the desired situation/opinion/thought that the criticized state of affairs fails to comply with. The intended meaning is the realization of the extent to which the state of affairs in question has fallen short of expectations usually made explicit by what is said. According to the relevance theoretic account, by saying *What a lovely day for a picnic*, the ironist dissociates herself from the weather forecast and from an opinion or a norm, while ridiculing them; in contrast, according to the indirect negation view, the ironist primarily laments the unfortunate situation (a stormy day) that has fallen short of expectations.

While diverging from the relevance theoretic account, the graded salience hypothesis and indirect negation view of irony are in agreement with proposals by Glucksberg and colleagues (see also Creusere, 1999, 2000). Kreuz and Glucksberg (1989) and Kumon-Nakamura et al. (1995) modified the echoic mention theory. The former proposed that irony is a reminder of an expectation or a norm that has been violated and of the discrepancy between what is said and what should be. According to the latter, irony expresses a speaker's (negative) attitude toward the referent of the ironic utterance (while simultaneously fulfilling other goals, such as being humorous, and making a situation less face threatening by being polite). By assuming pretense while alluding to failed expectations, irony is viewed as allowing the speaker to express a negative attitude about something that went wrong unexpectedly.

Some ironies are prototypically echoic and are better explained by the echoic mention view. In them, the irony targets the opinions echoed. As illustration, consider the following poster, entitled "Guerrilla Girls Explain the Concept of Natural Law" (cited in Crawford, 1995: 162):[15]

(16) • Protecting the rights of the unborn means precisely that. Once you're born, you're on your own.
 • Women who report it are uptight prudes. Women who don't are ambitious whores.
 • Women are paid less in the workplace because they have no business being there.
 • Anyone who is unemployed or homeless deserves it.
 • The people who have the most money are entitled to the best health care.
 • AIDS is a punishment for homosexuality and drug abuse. Only heterosexuals, celebrities, and children deserve a cure.
 • Life is beautiful. Artists, writers, or performers who want to inflict disgusting, homosexual, erotic, satirical, or political images upon the public should have their xxxxxx grants cut off.

"Guerrilla Girls" use sexist norms interpretively while simultaneously projecting an attitude of dissociation, ridicule, and reproof. The opinions and thoughts echoed here are criticized and rejected via irony. (Note that these ironies are also explainable by the pretense view: the ironist assumes the voice of the sexist while allowing the initiated audience to perceive the pretense.)

Most of the ironies in the poster are negative and are used by the authors to dissociate themselves from the opinion echoed and from the persons endorsing them. They are better accounted for by the echoic mention view because they involve allusions to specific attitudes or opinions. To the extent that they do not imply an alternative (as do positive ironies, which make explicit the preferred state of affairs), they may be considered cynic.

However, most negative ironies are not echoic because they do not reflect received opinions or norms, such as when, while walking in a rather posh neighborhood packed with lots of expensive vehicles, I might say, *What a dump!* Such negative irony cannot be easily handled by the relevance theoretic account because it cannot be seen as representing any norm or received opinion (for a similar view, see Attardo, 1998; Clark, 1996; Clark & Gerrig, 1984; Giora, 1995, 1998b). On the face of it, the indirect negation view does not seem to fare better, either. What expectation or desired state of affairs may be expressed by a negative utterance? Contrary to appearances, however, the explicit negative message may convey the ironist's desire that, for example, the posh neighborhood would look like a junkyard. This, for her, may be a better situation than the one she criticizes, because she may be envious of or angry with the rich for having it all (for a similar view, see Cutler, 1974: 118). On the view that irony is critical of a certain situation or opinion, what this negative irony means here is something like 'how far this neighborhood is from being (what I wish it were) a junkyard'. It is not the opinion expressed, then, that is criticized, but the situation it refers to.

To be able to better evaluate the contribution of the echoic mention account and the indirect negation view of irony comprehension, let us consider more complex discourses such as the Walt Disney fictive piece cited at the outset of this chapter. Recall that what this piece confers is the possibility of turning the Old City of Jerusalem (over whose division the Israelis and the Palestinians are unable to agree) into a Disney land. Despite its insincerity, it is not the case that the ironist dissociates herself from what she says with an attitude of ridicule and scorn. On the contrary, the ironist seems to enjoy her fantasy, and even endorse it, suggesting that, though incredible, it is a preferable state of affairs compared to that enforced by the Israeli occupation of Jerusalem. While the indirect negation view is compatible with this interpretation, the echoic mention view seems less so.

Consider, further, the literary piece *Dolly City* by Orly Castel-Bloom (1992) discussed also in Giora (1999, 2002b). *Dolly City* is a fantasy, which, if read only literally, presents Dolly City as a city of outrageous violence, and the protagonist, Dolly, as a ferocious individual. However, if read as an ironic piece, *Dolly City* may be interpreted as a negative irony. Consider the opening scene, which portrays a very cruel ritual, involving a dead goldfish Dolly has hunted in her aquarium:

> I put the fish on the black kitchen marble. I took a dagger, and I started dissecting it. The bastard always kept sliding on the marble, and I had to catch it by the tail and move it back to the scene of the crime. I had worked on this fish for about two hours and a half before I turned its body into small slices some millimeters thick. Then I looked at those pieces. In very ancient times, in the land of Canaan, holy people sacrificed bigger animals than this to God. When they chopped the body of the lamb, big, substantial pieces remained in their hands, bleeding, and their treaty was a treaty. I seasoned the slices of the goldfish, and I put one piece of it on my finger, I lit a match, and I held the fire near the flesh of the fish. Then I leaned my head backward, opened my mouth, and let the first slice of the fish fall directly into my digestive system. (Castel-Bloom, 1992: 9; my translation)

Read along the lines suggested by Sperber and Wilson, the speaker—the implicit author of *Dolly City*—is to be viewed as dissociating herself from what is said: that is, from Dolly's displayed cruelty. However, if read along the lines suggested by the indirect negation view of irony, the actual display of cruelty is to be taken as the preferred state of affairs relative to which the actual state of affairs brought under fire is assessed. On this account, then, what *Dolly City* criticizes is not the protagonist's cruelty but, rather, the brutality of the patriarchs, compared to whose norms Dolly's cruelty is but marginal. If we find Dolly's cruelty revolting, we should be far more critical of the patriarchs' demeanor, which we so inconsistently embrace. *Dolly City*, then, criticizes us by criticizing the patriarchs. This interpretation follows from focusing on the referent of the irony, the object of criticism, rather than on dissociating from what is said. What is said provides a reference point (Dolly's deeds) relative to which what is referred to (the patriarchs' deeds) is appraised and rejected.

Dolly City calls for such comparisons about the major issues of our lives, particularly issues featuring prominently in the Israeli scene. One topic that comes under fire is patriarchal motherhood. Dolly incarnates the "ideal" patriarchal mother who would do practically anything to protect her (not accidentally male) offspring. She is a mother by the book of patriarchy, who, as posited by patriarchy, must be loving by nature and, consequently, must be the primary caretaker, incessantly protecting her child from the world at large—the one who must always worry about her child's health and be wary of the infinite possibilities of evil that might befall him or her. She is, one should keep in mind, a preferred candidate for that role, because she is a physician. As such, she is best equipped to protect her son against all kinds of diseases. Armed with instinctual love, on the one hand, and medical knowledge, on the other, she is, indeed, determined to do away with any possibility that might threaten her son's well-being:

> I made up my mind to get over that terrible fear of losing my child by doing whatever I can to protect him against any kind of disease. I knew I would never be able to keep up with fate, but I was determined, nevertheless, to fight it. I said to myself that the world is full of humps and bottomless holes, pits behind the loquat tree, but, I, as a mother, must fight all these troubles, I have to protect this child against countless ailments and natural disasters. . . .
>
> Between myself and me I have decided that, for a start, I should immunize him against as many diseases as possible. . . . I injected [all the vaccines] at once—even though I knew I must not do it. I couldn't stop myself, couldn't get over the motherly impulse. (p. 18; my translation)

Castel-Bloom examines a mother's relentless, never-to-be-subdued anxiety over the well-being of her child:

> I started checking him up. All was well. The child was O.K., his heart was a sweetheart, I heard no pathological sound. Nevertheless, although the baby was as sound as a bell, I decided to cut him up. I was seized by that chronic doubt I am suffering of. I wanted to inspect my inspection, and then make sure that the inspection was the best possible one, and so on.
>
> I treated him with anesthesia, I put him to sleep, I did it to him. I wrapped my hands in white gloves and started sawing his chest. I could see his inner parts, the heart, the lungs. Having opened him up, I dug in there. And then I picked at his stomach. . . .
>
> Everything was in its place, there was no exception. I verified it again and again, repeated the checkup hundreds of times, opened books, compared findings—all was 100% fine. (p. 25; my translation)

The ideal mother's worries are endless. Soothing one worry just makes place for another: "And so, in spite of the fact that the child did not have cancer, he did not have cancer, in spite of the fact that he did not have cancer, I decided nevertheless to treat him with chemotherapy and large doses of vitamin A. I wanted to be on the safe side" (p. 38; my translation). It turns out, then, that such limitless love, as prescribed by patriarchy, cannot be beneficial. However, if we just interpret the speaker as dissociating herself from what is said, from the cruelty explicitly displayed, we may even end up affirming our values: after all, Dolly is an exaggeration; the values we adhere to and practice seem far less inhumane. But Castel-Bloom would not let us miss the point here:

> Before I go on, I would like to emphasize something: it is important for me that you don't get the impression that I took a child and ruined him. I only wanted to protect him from bad things. I wanted him to live to be a hundred and twenty, and what's wrong with that? I demanded command over all the domains, and what's wrong with that? What is this hypocrisy? In certain communities they are capable of making a man cut off his sister's clitoris with his teeth—am I not allowed then to insist on having monopoly over the protection of my own son? (p. 39; my translation)

If irony implies a speaker's dissociation from what is said, then *Dolly City* is a rejection of a mother who went to the extreme, or rejection of patriarchy taken too literally. However, even if taken more broadly—not simply as a rejection of what is said, but of the attitudes evoked and echoed by what is said (e.g., rejection of the notion of patriarchal instinctual love)—there is an additional layer of meaning missed here, which is allowed by the interpretation proffered by the indirect negation view. According to the indirect negation view, what looks absurd about Dolly's maternal love is a preferred state of affairs—it is a point of reference relative to which what is practiced by "normal" or "sane" patriarchy is condemned as much more absurd or insane. Compared to man-made atrocities that we do not protest, such as the widespread subjugation of women and the "sane" maternal love of "normal" mothers who would agree to their sons' sacrifice in man-made wars, Dolly's insanity is less destructive or immoral. She cannot accept the option of her son's death (resisting the psychiatrist's attempt to "normalize" her; see Giora, 1999a, 2002b):

> You have to remember that it is possible for your child to die in battle. He may die in battle, you have to put this into your head. He may die of drowning, or of a shark, if he falls into the water. You also have to put into your head that he may die of cancer, but it is likely that if he dies soon, he will die in battle. . . . And then if he dies in battle—you will be a bereaved mother, inasmuch as if you die, he will be an orphan. Things have names! Things have identities. For God's sake, Dolly. (p. 98; my translation)

Of such ironic nature is *A Modest Proposal* by Jonathan Swift (1729/1971), which also manifests a negative irony. It details a proposal to serve up Irish babies as food for the rich, so that both the poor and the rich may benefit from it: the former by alleviating their economical distress, the latter by enriching their menu with a new taste of tender flesh. Given the outrageousness and peculiarity of the proposal, it is hard to see how it may be an interpretive use of any received wisdom, opinion, or norm (see also Clark & Gerrig, 1984). Although it is plausible to assume that Swift, being Irish, dissociated himself from what he said, it is still unclear why, in the first place, he would come up with such unprecedented ideas which cannot be attributed to anyone but himself and with which he apparently disagreed. The motivation for using irony provided by the echoic mention view does not seem to apply here.

However, if interpreted along the lines suggested by the indirect negation view, what is said has a specific role: it manifests a reference point relative to which the criticized situation, the real state of affairs, is assessed. The speaker may suggest that, regardless of how horrific what is said is, it is still a preferred situation compared to the way the Irish rich (collaborating with the British) abused the Irish poor. It is, in fact, a *modest* proposal compared to the actual state of affairs. To criticize the rich Irish class of utterly oppressing the poor, Swift envisioned a nightmarish situation that should have aroused disgust in the rich (as well as in others) in order to enlighten them about the atrocities of their own making. (For a similar view concerning the object of criticism, see Booth, 1974.) What Swift dissociated himself from was not so much what was said, but the state of affairs the irony referred to—the actual cruelty and immorality of the rich—which, Swift intended to implicate, were either comparable to or far worse than his "modest" proposal.

In sum, some ironies are expressions of received opinions or thoughts the speaker dissociates herself from. They are better explained by the echoic mention view. Others are better explained by the indirect negation view. On this view, dissociating oneself from what is said provides for a somewhat limited view of the irony. In contrast, perceiving what is said as a reference point of departure from the target of the irony allows for a richer and more accurate interpretation of it. To test these hypothetical interpretations, far more sophisticated tools are needed than are available.

4. Ironic and Literal Interpretations: Different or Equal?

This chapter has been imbued by various voices regarding ironic and literal interpretations. Are they processed differently? Are they similar? Hovering over the chapter, however, is the claim that the relevant comparison is not between literal and nonliteral language but between salient and less or nonsalient meanings. In light of the evidence adduced so far, we may be able to evaluate this claim. Indeed, support for the view that various instances of similar salience should involve equivalent processes comes from findings that familiar ironies and their literal equivalents were processed along the same patterns (Giora & Fein, 1999a).[16] Similarly, instances of unfamiliar metaphor and irony induced similar difficulties (Pexman et al., 2000). In contrast, less salient ironies and their more salient literal interpretations induced different processes, with irony involving a more complex process. The graded salience hypothesis, assuming equivalent processes for similarly salient (e.g., ironic and literal) meanings at the first lexical access phase of comprehension has indeed gained support.

This salience-based "processing-equivalence hypothesis" is not a result of attributing to context a function in modifying processing at the initial lexical phase to the extent that only contextually compatible meanings are activated. On the contrary, since context at this stage is not effective because it does not interact with lexical processes (Giora, Peleg, & Fein, 2001; Peleg et al., 2001, in press), embedding an utterance in different contexts, biasing its interpretation toward different meanings, does not affect initial lexical processes. Even though context may be strong and supportive, and predictive of the compatible meaning, it does not preempt salient though contextually incompatible meanings, such as the salient literal meaning of ironies and the salient figurative meaning of a conventional metaphor used ironically.

In contrast, "the processing-equivalence hypothesis" inspired by the direct access view has not fared well experimentally. Context did not direct comprehension entirely: ironies were not processed only ironically, nor were literals always processed only literally. Specifically, unfamiliar ironies and their literal equivalents were processed differently (in terms of contextual compatibility and processing effort), with irony involving a contextually incompatible (salient) stage initially (Giora & Fein, 1999a; Giora et al., 1998; Pexman et al., 2000). Similarly, at the later retention phase, irony comprehension involved retaining the contextually incompatible salient meaning, whereas its literal counterpart involved only the contextually compatible meaning (Giora & Fein, 1999b). In contrast, utterances sharing similar salience were processed similarly and retained both their contextually compatible but also their contextually incompatible meanings (Giora & Fein, 1999a). The relevant distinction regarding initial processes, then, is not between literal and nonliteral language but between salient and less or nonsalient meanings. Interpreting irony following the initial phase involves some contrastive process (Giora, 1995), which distinguishes irony from literal, as well as from other nonliteral (e.g., metaphoric), interpretations (but see Giora, 2002a).

5. Conclusions

In this chapter I have adduced evidence favoring the graded salience hypothesis and the indirect negation view but questioning the standard pragmatic model and the direct access view. According to the graded salience hypothesis, salient meanings should be accessed initially, regardless of contextual information. Context may affect comprehension immediately and trigger derivation of appropriate meanings, but it is ineffective in sieving out salient but contextually incompatible meanings. Findings from familiar and unfamiliar ironies, obtained by various measures and methodologies, in contrived and spontaneous discourses, show that, contra the direct access view, some meanings are so foremost on our mind, they are always accessed automatically, regardless of contextual information. They further show that, contra the standard pragmatic model, the meanings that are resistant to initial context effects are not (necessarily) literal but salient.

Initial processes, then, involve contextually incompatible meanings. Contra the standard pragmatic model and modular view, they are not discarded automatically. Findings show that rather than suppressing the contextually incompatible salient meaning and replacing it with the intended meaning, irony involves retention of this meaning, as assumed by the indirect negation view, the tinge hypothesis, and the joint pretense view. When a salient though contextually incompatible meaning is conducive to the construction of the utterance interpretation (as it is in irony interpretation), it is retained for further processes. Findings obtained in the lab and from naturally occurring written and conversational discourses support the retention hypothesis, which augments the graded salience hypothesis, and argue against the view that suppression is automatic.

Appendix

The following continues the announcement at the opening of this chapter:

> Officials of the Israeli government were understandably reluctant about confirming the above plans. However one spokesman, Michael Ma'oz of the Foreign Ministry, agreed to discuss some of the issues involved, stressing that none of these statements were, at this moment, more than distant speculations.
>
> When asked about likely opposition from Israel's powerful Orthodox parties, Ma'oz replied that this appears to be less of a problem than previously feared. Disney has agreed to make generous contributions to a number of yeshivahs and other religious institutions. "Many ultra-Orthodox seem quite pleased by the prospect that they can get paid in dollars just for walking around in their traditional clothing. In fact," said Ma'oz, "the rabbis were generally less concerned with the content of the park, which their own people would be unlikely to visit, than with receiving assurances that the Disney folks will not allow the inclusion of any "Reform Street" or "Conservative Square." (A Disney representative did however suggest that non-Orthodox neighbourhoods might be included in prospective satellite parks outside of Israel.)
>
> Asked whether this would contradict Prime Minister Netanyahu's pre-election commitment to an eternally united Israeli Jerusalem, Mr. Ma'oz muttered an obscure comment about Pinocchio's nose, and proceeded to point out how "Egged"'s proposed new combined monorail and roller-coaster would provide welcome relief from the capital's traffic congestion.
>
> A representative of the Jerusalem Waqf, 'Adan al-Duq, was visibly upset when approached with questions about the alleged plan. However, he too acknowledged that the anticipated antagonism from fundamentalist circles would probably not materialize. "The Disney people appear to have learned their lesson from the Aladdin fiasco. They were very reasonable about withdrawing their original suggestion about attaching mouse-ears to the Dome of the Rock, and will definitely not be opening any new tunnels. Also, a private agreement may have been reached with President Arafat." Mr. al-Duq was reluctant to go into detail, but ru-

mors circulating in the Jericho marketplace speak of a Disney commitment to allow Mr. Arafat to fulfill a childhood dream involving wearing a costume (possibly of a character from "Snow White") at the California Disneyland.

Sources in the Holy See hinted at a package deal that would allow for the eventual establishment of a "Vatican Land" in Rome.

The issue that troubles most people about the plan, of course, is the security question: Can the Disney crew maintain law and order in the volatile environment of Jerusalem's Old City? "No problem!" a spokesperson assured us. Remember that the Disney family has official links with at least one world-famous law-enforcement agency. "I can't reveal anything official at this stage, but we expect the area to be policed by an agency that we refer to as the 'Temple Mounties'."

Standing at the foot of the Temple Mount, the Disney representative assured us that every effort would be made not to alter or interfere with the city's traditional religious life-styles and traditions. His assurance was symbolically underscored as the ancient chant of the muezzin filled the air with the proclamation "Allah hu 'Achbar."

5

Metaphors and Idioms

1. The Time Course of Comprehension

When, during the first Intifada, Yitzhak Rabin (then the Israeli defense minister) stated publicly that "we should break their [the Palestinians'] arms and legs," quite a few Israeli soldiers took him literally (as testified by Sela & Mazali, 1993). Apparently, it was the Israeli violent political and military context engendered by Rabin[1] that highlighted the literal meaning of the statement, which could as easily be taken metaphorically, being a conventional metaphor. How metaphors are understood within their context is the focus of this chapter.

As in the previous chapters, here I examine the role context and privileged meanings play in shaping our linguistic behavior. I look into the processes involved in comprehension and production of metaphors and idioms and the temporal stage at which these processes are affected by contextual information.[2] I show that privileged meanings, meanings foremost on our mind, affect comprehension and production primarily, regardless of context or literality. Specifically, I show that access of salient meanings is hard to prevent, even when context is highly supportive of the less or nonsalient meaning, irrespective of whether they are literal or nonliteral. While the literality/nonliterality variable does not play a primary role at the initial stage of language comprehension, it may be a relevant factor in the processes following that stage (see also Gibbs, 1994; but see Giora, 2001, 2002a). Taken together, the findings presented here argue for the claim that rather than assuming different (initial) processes for metaphors, ironies, or literals, it is more plausible to assume different (initial) processes for salient and less or nonsalient language.

This chapter sets out from a variety of perspectives:

- Psychology—the time course of context effects: early (vis-á-vis modularity) and later (vis-á-vis suppression/retention)
- Linguistics—literal versus nonliteral language
- Neuropsychology—hemispheric specialization for metaphor
- Discourse—planned and spontaneous text production

The various perspectives allow us an insight into how processing affects our linguistic behavior in naturally occurring settings.

As in the previous chapters, here, too, the various approaches to metaphor are considered and tested with respect to initial and later processes. The converging data lend support to the graded salience hypothesis.[3]

1.1 Initial Activation Phase

As noted earlier in this volume (chapters 2 and 4), the view proposed here assumes that the initial activation phase involves meanings made available either via a direct look up in the mental lexicon (lexical access) or via integrative mechanisms such as inferencing or guessing that were induced by prior predictive context. In addition, the initial phase may include more than one stage, depending on contextual fit. Thus, if initial access incidentally results in contextual fit, further lexical processes may be invisible; if it does not, however, further processes will ensue as a result of time lapse, either boosting the next available meaning or triggering inferencing (for a similar view, see Hubbell & O'Boyle, 1995; Keysar, 1998). The assumption is that comprehension at the initial phase involves simultaneously activating any information available, whether bottom up (e.g., lexical accessing) or top down (contextual information), with bottom-up processes being automatic and, in many cases, speedier.[4] If top-down, higher level, contextual information and bottom-up lexical information accidentally fit, making up a sensible discourse, no further processing is required. If such initial processes result in a mismatch, further search will be attempted. For instance, if, while we are watching TV expecting the weather forecast, I say, *Here is the weatherman*, letting you know the person forecasting the weather on TV is on, you will instantly access the literal meaning of *weatherman* (on account of its saliency). Because this meaning matches the contextual information, its integration with the context will follow seamlessly. However, if, while we are watching TV, Daniel, my friend, shows up at the door, and I say *Here is the weatherman* (meaning here is the person who knows everything about the weather), the literal meaning you will instantly access (on account of its saliency) will not match the contextual information, and you will probably be searching for an alternative, contextually compatible interpretation. However, if you know that I usually refer to Daniel as the weatherman, this nonliteral meaning will be accessed automatically, too.

1.1.1 Predictions

The various approaches differ with regard to initial processes. Assuming that contextual information interacts with lexical processes, the interactionist, direct access view (see chapters 3–4 in this volume), predicts that, given a constraining context, literal and nonliteral language would be processed initially along the same patterns: each process, whether literal or figurative, would involve only contextually appropriate meanings. In a rich and supportive context, literal utterances would be processed initially only literally, whereas figurative utterances would be processed initially only figuratively. The claim is sweeping, and does not include specific assumptions regarding the degree of salience of the instances in question.

In contrast, the standard pragmatic model (Grice, 1975; Searle, 1979; see also chapter 4 in this volume), which assumes the temporal priority of literal meanings, predicts that, given a supportive context, the initial processing of literal and nonliteral language will differ with regard to contextual compatibility. Since literal and nonliteral language should both be interpreted literally first, regardless of either salience or context, nonliteral (but not literal) interpretation would involve a contextually incompatible phase. Consequently, at a later stage of the lexical access phase, nonliteral language will undergo revisitation and will be processed nonliterally. According to the standard pragmatic model, then, literal and nonliteral utterances involve different processes initially, although both will be processed literally first, regardless of context and salience.

Assuming the superiority of salient over less salient meanings, the graded salience hypothesis (Giora, 1997b; chapters 2–4 in this volume) predicts that, given a similarly supportive context, literal and figurative interpretations will involve similar processes in case they are similarly salient (i.e., coded in the mental lexicon and enjoying similar familiarity, frequency, conventionality, or prototypicality). This "equivalent processes" hypothesis, however, is based on salience rather than on context. While the interactionist, direct access view predicts no differences in processing literal and nonliteral language initially, provided that the context is rich and supportive, the graded salience hypothesis predicts no initial processing difference between literal and nonliteral language, provided salience balance is involved. Thus, when salient language is at stake, the graded salience hypothesis pairs with the direct access view: in both views, the intended salient meaning would be tapped directly, with the exception that, according to the graded salience hypothesis, other salient, though contextually incompatible meanings, would be accessed as well. When nonsalient interpretation is at stake, the predictions of the graded salience hypothesis are somewhat akin to those of the standard pragmatic model: in both views, comprehension would involve a contextually inappropriate meaning initially.

1.2 Later Integration Phase

The various approaches differ also in how they view the second, integration phase. Recall that the second, contextual integration phase either retains the initially activated meanings for further processes, suppresses them as intrusive to the utterance interpretation, or lets them fade (see chapters 2 and 4 in this volume).[5]

1.2.1 Predictions

According to the direct access view, since the first phase involves only contextually compatible meanings, these meanings may seamlessly integrate with contextual information. In contrast, since, according to the standard pragmatic model, comprehending nonliteral language obligatorily involves a contextually incompatible stage, context should suppress the sentence's literal meaning as irrelevant while incorporating the appropriate meaning only (for a similar view, see Gernsbacher, Keysar, Robertson, & Werner, 2001; Keysar, 1989, 1994a). Since the graded salience hypothesis may inform us only about the first phase of comprehension, and since it assumes that the initial access stage may involve contextually inappropriate meanings, it needs to be supplemented by an additional hypothesis. The assumption augmenting the salience hypothesis—the retention hypothesis—assumes that meanings instrumental in the construction of the intended interpretation need not be discarded. For instance, the literal meaning of metaphors need not be suppressed, since, it is assumed, it is supportive of the intended metaphorical meaning. For example, *heartache* (referring conventionally to 'agony' or 'anguish') may benefit both metaphorically and metonymically from the literal/physical meaning of *heartache*. Given that some people really experience some pain in the chest when in agony, this sensation is associated with the emotion causing it and, by extension, stands for it. It also enriches the emotion metaphorically, suggesting that this emotion is so fierce as to be as life threatening as a heartache, thereby amplifying its effect. Similarly, the figurative ('anger') meaning of *boil* benefits from the literal meaning of boiling, suggesting that anger is destructive and uncontrollable, like boiling fluid in a container about to erupt. In contrast, in a literally biasing context, the literal interpretation of figurative language (*get cold feet*) requires the suppression of the salient figurative meaning (*get dismayed*), since it is not conducive to the literal interpretation of the figure ('having cold feet') and may disrupt comprehension (see chapter 2).

In this chapter, I report on the findings of the various approaches regarding the assumed processes involved in the initial and subsequent phases of understanding metaphor vis-à-vis the measures used to test them. Given that the long-standing debates have centered on the literal/figurative distinction, the next sections inevitably address this topic. However, more attention will be paid to the assumption of the graded salience hypothesis that the variable of familiarity, which has been largely overlooked, is essential to the discussion. I will start by looking into the processes involved in the initial phase of comprehending familiar and less or unfamiliar figures, and then examine whether the output of the initial processes is either suppressed or retained for further processes.

2. Familiar and Less Familiar Metaphors

2.1 Initial Processes: Measures and Findings

To test the hypotheses regarding initial processes, measures tapping the very early moments of comprehension should be employed.

2.1.1 Reading Times

Reading times of whole utterances may not reveal the underlying processes involved in comprehension when no differences are found (see Janus & Bever, 1985). However, different reading times may inform us about processing difficulties at the early access phase (see Hubbell & O'Boyle, 1995). Note also that reading times of complete utterances is a measure adept at tapping processes that occur at the message or compositional level without conflating it with word level meanings (see preceding discussion here and in chapter 2). Since the various approaches have different hypotheses about the initial stage, they also vary in how initial processes affect reading times.

According to the direct access view, reading times of the same utterance embedded in equally supportive contexts, whether literal or figurative, should not differ (regardless of salience). Thus, an utterance such as *Jump on it!* will take equally long to read in a metaphorically biasing context (e.g., speaking of an opportunity) and in a literally biasing context (e.g., speaking of a physical object).

Assuming the priority of literal meanings, the standard pragmatic model predicts that an utterance such as *Jump on it!* will take longer to read in a metaphorically biasing context (e.g., the opportunity) than in a literally biasing context (e.g., the object), since in the metaphor-inducing context, the utterance will be processed literally first and metaphorically second, regardless of salience (familiarity).

Assuming the automaticity of salient meanings, the graded salience hypothesis predicts that familiar metaphors (*Jump on it*), whose figurative and literal meanings are similarly salient, will take equally long to read in literally and metaphorically biasing contexts (of similar strength). In both contexts, their salient (contextually compatible and incompatible) meanings will be activated via a direct look up in the mental lexicon (plus an occasional compositional stage in the case of the literal interpretation). In contrast, given similarly supportive contexts, less or unfamiliar metaphors will take longer to read than their literal equivalents, because, unlike the literal interpretation, the metaphoric interpretation does not hinge on the salient interpretation of its components and will require extra processing time for its derivation (but see Peleg et al., 2001, in press).

In Giora, Fein, and Schwartz (1997) and Giora & Fein (1999c), we tested these hypotheses. On the basis of familiarity ratings, 72 Hebrew texts, a couple

of sentences long, were prepared. Of these, 36 contained a metaphorically biasing context (1a; 2a), and 36 contained a literally biasing context (1b; 2b):

(1) *Familiar metaphor*
   a. In order to solve the math problem, the student broke her head [equivalent to the
      English racked her brains].
   b. Because she was so careless when she jumped into the pool, the student broke
      her head.

(2) *Unfamiliar metaphor*
   a. A: My husband is terribly annoyed by his new boss. Every day he comes home
         after work even more depressed than he was the day before. Somehow, he
         cannot adjust himself to the new situation.
      B: *Their bone density is not like ours.*

   b. Our granny had a fracture from just falling off a chair and was rushed to the hos-
      pital. I told my sister I never had a fracture from falling off a chair. She explained
      to me about the elderly. She said: *Their bone density is not like ours.*

As illustrated by figure 5.1, findings indeed show that familiar metaphors
and their literal interpretations took similarly long to read. In contrast, utterances
rated as less and unfamiliar metaphors took longer to read in the metaphorically
than in the literally biasing contexts (for similar findings regarding proverb comprehension, see Katz & Ferretti, 2000, 2001; Turner & Katz, 1997). Taken together, these findings are accountable by the graded salience hypothesis but are
inconsistent with the direct access and standard pragmatic models.

2.1.2 Response Times

Unlike reading times, response times to concepts related to the various meanings of an utterance may reveal which meanings are activated during language
comprehension. For instance (assuming similar salience or frequency of test
words), the time taken to make a decision as to whether a letter string makes
up a word or a nonword may suggest whether the concept associated with the
test word has been activated in the course of comprehension. Short response
times to a test word indicate the accessibility of its meaning; longer response
times suggest that it is less accessible. If the probe is presented immediately
after or while displaying the key (figurative) word(s), response times can be
revealing as to which concepts or meanings are involved in the initial phase of
processing that word or expression. When presented after a delay, response
times can tell us which meanings require extra processing time for their retrieval or derivation.

   According to the direct access view, given a supportive context, readers
would always respond faster to the contextually appropriate test word, since targets activate only the contextually appropriate meaning. Thus, in a literally bi-

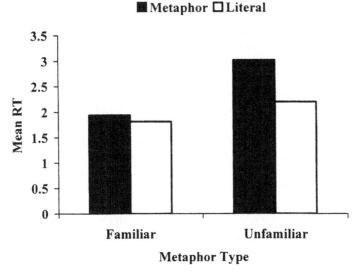

Figure 5.1 Reading times of **familiar and unfamiliar** metaphors in metaphorically and literally biasing contexts.

asing context, the contextually compatible, literally related test word ('hop') of the metaphor (*Jump on it!*) would be responded to faster than would the metaphorically related test word ('utilize'). Similarly, in a metaphorically biasing context (e.g., of chance), the contextually compatible, metaphorically related test word ('utilize') would be responded to faster than would the literally related test word ('hop').

The standard pragmatic model predicts that when response time is measured immediately after offset of the metaphoric target, readers would respond faster to the literally related test word, regardless of context or salience, because metaphors always activate their literal meaning first. Response to the metaphoric meaning ('utilize') would lag behind and would benefit from extra processing time.

According to the graded salience hypothesis, given a supportive (but not a predictive) context, readers would always respond faster to test words related to salient meanings. Given that familiar metaphors have both their literal and figurative meanings coded in the mental lexicon enjoying similar accessibility, response times to test words related to these meanings should not differ. Nor would they benefit from extra processing time. In contrast, less and unfamiliar metaphors should be processed literally initially (since this is their salient meaning) and should benefit from extra processing time.

In Blasko and Connine's (1993) study, participants were presented auditorily familiar and less familiar metaphorical sentences. The task was to make a lexical decision as to whether a visual letter string was a word or a nonword. For instance, after they had heard the last word of the metaphor (*ladder*) in *The belief that* **hard work is a ladder** *is common to this generation*, participants had to decide whether a letter string—either a literally related target ('rungs'), a metaphorically related target ('advance'), or a control ('pastry')—was a word or a nonword. Results showed that, as predicted by the graded salience hypothesis, familiar metaphors facilitated literally as well as metaphorically related test words immediately and also 300 milliseconds after offset of the metaphor. In contrast, less familiar metaphors were processed initially (and also 300 milliseconds after offset of the metaphor) only literally. These findings cannot be accounted for by the standard pragmatic model. They cannot, however, be assessed by the direct access view, since the contexts are rather poor.

It should be noted, further, that, before administering the experiment, Blasko and Connine tested the metaphorically related test words ('advance') in isolation to determine how closely related they were to the most common or central meaning of the metaphors' vehicles (i.e., to the metaphoric constituent *ladder* of the metaphoric utterances *The belief that* **hard work is a ladder** *is common to this generation*). They did not, however, test their affinity to the topic (or target) constituent of the metaphoric expressions (e.g., *hard work*). A close inspection of their materials suggests that more than half of the so-called metaphorically related test words (associated with familiar metaphors) could be easily primed by the topic rather than by the metaphoric constituent of the utterances (the italicized words in the following list) because they were highly related to their meaning as well. Such affinity renders suspect their finding that the metaphors were accessed metaphorically initially:

HIGH FAMILIAR METAPHOR	METAPHORIC TEST WORD
Freedom is truth	liberty
The family is a rock	secure
Adventure is a roller-coaster	daring
The *rocket* was a bullet	speed
Hard work is a ladder	advance
Alcoholism is a parasite	disease
Books are treasure chests	knowledge
Loneliness is a desert	isolate
The old man was a history book	wise
A liar's tongue is a spear	vicious
Rumors were plagues	spreading
Happiness is gold	precious

Another study may partly make up for this drawback as far as familiar (i.e., conventional) metaphors are concerned. In Anaki, Faust, and Kravetz (1998), participants were centrally presented Hebrew word primes (*stinging*) with familiar metaphoric ('stinging remark') and literal ('stinging mosquito') meanings; they then made lexical decisions as to whether letter strings presented to the right (left hemisphere) and left (right hemisphere) visual fields were words or nonwords. The test words were related either to the metaphoric meaning of the priming word (*stinging-insult; rolling-laugh; feeble-explanation*) or to its literal meaning (*stinging-mosquito; rolling-ball; feeble-cripple*). Results showed that familiar metaphors were processed initially both literally and metaphorically (in the left hemisphere, but only metaphorically in the right hemisphere). These findings are consistent with the salience hypothesis, showing that familiar metaphors are accessed initially both literally and metaphorically. They are inconsistent with the standard pragmatic model, which posits the priority of literal meanings, and they cannot be assessed by the direct access view because the stimuli have no context.

A study that may better reflect comprehension of familiar metaphors in context is Williams (1992).[6] Using lexical decision tasks under different delay conditions (at 250, 750, and 1100 milliseconds stimulus onset asynchrony), Williams was able to show that salient meanings of conventional metaphors were activated instantly, regardless of contextual information. Meaning salience was established out of context by obtaining priming effects for the various meanings ('solid'; 'strict') of the metaphorically based polysemous words (*firm*) (relative to unrelated words) in the context of those words only. Priming under this out-of-context condition was then compared with priming from the same words in sentence contexts. Using a video display unit, subjects were first presented with all but the last four words of the sentence in lowercase letters. Upon pressing a button, the remaining four words were added to the sentence, one at a time, at the rate of 250 milliseconds per word. The final word was visible for 250 milliseconds before the whole sentence disappeared from view. The test word was displayed at three different intervals and appeared in capital letters in the same position as the sentence final word. The test word was displayed until the subject made a lexical decision response.

Results showed that metaphorically based polysemies facilitated their salient meanings instantly, regardless of context. For instance, the salient, contextually incompatible (i.e., literal) meaning ('solid') of *firm* was available instantly in the metaphorically biased context (*The schoolteacher was criticized for not being firm*). Similarly, the salient, contextually incompatible (i.e., metaphoric) meaning ('strict') of *firm* was available instantly in the literally biased context (*The couple wanted a bed that was firm*).[7] These findings are consistent with the graded salience hypothesis but incompatible with the direct access and standard pragmatic models (although both views may be said to have predictions only regarding the sentence rather than word meaning).

Hasson (2000) further shows that explicit negation does not inhibit salient metaphorical meanings. Both affirmative (*That train is a rocket*) and negative (*That train is not a rocket*) metaphorical statements facilitated the salient, affirmative related ('fast') probe after a short (150 and even 500 milliseconds) interstimulus interval (ISI). Negative context then did not inhibit salient meanings of familiar metaphors.[8]

As reported in Peleg et al. (2001), we also tested context versus salience effects on metaphor comprehension. We attempted to test the graded salience hypothesis, which assumes that language comprehension involves two distinct mechanisms that do not interact initially but run in parallel: a linguistic mechanism (lexical access) that is modular and stimulus-driven and operates locally, and an expectation-driven, contextual mechanism that operates globally, accumulating information that has already been processed and interfaced with other cognitive processes. We showed, indeed, that a strong context may incur contextual facilitation very early on, even *before* lexical accessing takes place, fostering an impression of a selective/interactive process. We further showed, however, that even when context is strongly predictive of the nonsalient interpretation, the salient but incompatible meaning is activated nonetheless (see also Peleg et al., 2001, in press; Giora, Peleg, & Fein, 2001).

In our study, we engaged novel Hebrew metaphors preceded by a short passage that strongly biased the target last sentence toward the nonsalient (metaphorical) meaning (see example 3). In all the cases, the target metaphorical word was the topic of the context sentence (as well as the topic of the target sentence), creating strong expectations with regard to the target sentence (Ariel, 1990; Giora, 1985a,b; Reinhart, 1980). Our studies show that even in sentence final position (example 3b), where contextual effects must be most pronounced, the salient contextually incompatible meaning of the novel metaphor was accessed, albeit somewhat after the nonsalient contextually compatible meaning was derived.

As illustrated by figure 5.2, when targets were placed in sentence initial position (following a highly predictive discourse context, as in example 3a), responses to the salient contextually incompatible probes (*criminals*) and to the nonsalient contextually compatible probes (*kids*) did not differ, suggesting that they were both facilitated although by different mechanisms. When the targets were placed in sentence final position (following a highly predictive discourse context, as in example 3b), responses to salient incompatible probes were slower than to the contextually compatible probes but faster than to the unrelated probes, suggesting that salient meanings were not preempted, not even at the end of sentences where contextual information must be most effective:

(3) a. Sarit's sons and mine went on fighting continuously. Sarit said to me: These *delinquents** won't let us have a moment of peace.
     (Probes displayed at *: Salient: criminals; Contextually compatible: kids; Unrelated: painters; Nonword: nimvhar)

   b. Sarit's sons and mine went on fighting continuously. Sarit said to me: A moment of peace won't let us have these *delinquents*.*
     (Probes displayed at *: Salient: criminals; Contextually compatible: kids; Unrelated: painters; Nonword: nimvhar)

In all, studies from lexical decision tasks show that salient meanings cannot be filtered out, not even when context is strongly biased in favor of the nonsalient meaning and where its influence must be highly effective.

2.1.3 Moving Windows

Moving windows is a methodology that is adept at detecting locations of ease and difficulty while processing the message as a whole. Recall that self-paced moving windows is a tool in which participants advance a text word by word

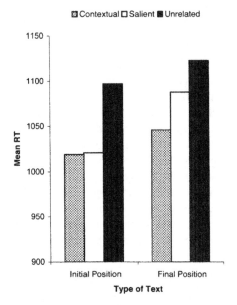

Figure 5.2 Response times to **nonsalient** contextually compatible and **salient** contextually incompatible probes related to targets placed in sentence initial versus sentence final position.

across the screen by pressing a key. Such a procedure reflects the online processes that occur naturally, since it mimics spontaneous reading. Controlling the word-by-word reading process, such procedure allows for the computation of reading latency for each item in the target sentence, for the space following that sentence, and for the first word of the sentence that follows. Reading times following the figurative statement attest to the presence or absence of difficulties that may "spill over" downstream and thus increase the reading times of the subsequent items (see chapter 2 in this volume). In all, short reading times suggest that a meaning is accessed (more or less) directly; longer reading times at the various locations may imply more complex processes that might slow down reading even beyond the key/figurative word, such as at the space following that word and at the first word(s) of the next sentence.

According to the direct access view, in strong contexts, this procedure will detect no differences in reading times of the key (i.e., figurative) words, in the space following the key words, and of the first words of the following sentence embedded in either literally or metaphorically biasing context. Relative to a neutral or poor context, however, reading times of metaphors in a metaphor-inducing context should decrease. This should hold for both familiar and unfamiliar metaphors.

According to the standard pragmatic model, moving windows will detect longer reading times for key (i.e., nonliteral) words in metaphorical utterances than for literally intended words. This should not be sensitive to degree of salience.

According to the graded salience hypothesis, reading times of familiar metaphors and their literal counterparts should not differ. However, given that context may have predictive effects, reading times of targets in a supportive context (whether metaphorically or literally biased) may decrease relative to a neutral, poor context. In contrast, less or nonsalient metaphors should take longer to read than salient targets.

Using this procedure, Pexman, Ferretti, and Katz (2000) presented participants with passages that contained a nonliteral target sentence (which did not appear in text final position and which did not have a plausible literal sense). These sentences were either familiar or less familiar instantiations of conceptual metaphors presented in the metaphoric form 'An X is a Y'. The contexts further varied in strength of weight: they included a speaker of either a high-irony, high-metaphor, neutral, or no occupation statement, and whether they invited an ironic, metaphoric, or neutral interpretation. The following examples illustrate a neutral context (4a; 5a), a high-metaphor occupation speaker (4b; 5b), and a metaphor-inducing context (4c; 5c) of a familiar (example 4) (*Children are precious gems*) and an unfamiliar (example 5) (*Her wedding ring is a "Sorry, we're closed" sign*) metaphor (see Katz & Pexman, 1997):

(4) a. A man was talking to Jodie about his niece and nephew who had visited him recently. During the conversation the man said, "Children are precious gems." This made Jodie think about her cousins.

   b. A scientist was talking to Jodie about his niece and nephew who had visited him recently. During the conversation the man said, "Children are precious gems." This made Jodie think about her cousins.

   c. A scientist was talking to Jodie about his niece and nephew who had visited him recently. The scientist had really enjoyed having the children around. During the conversation the man said, "Children are precious gems." This made Jodie think about her cousins.

(5) a. Sam and his friend were having a conversation about an attractive acquaintance who had recently separated from her husband. Sam's friend said, "Her wedding ring is a 'sorry we're closed' sign." Sam remembered that it would soon be the woman's birthday.

   b. Sam and his friend, a scientist, were having a conversation about an attractive acquaintance who had recently separated from her husband. Sam's friend said, "Her wedding ring is a 'sorry we're closed' sign." Sam remembered that it would soon be the woman's birthday.

   c. Sam and his friend, a scientist, were having a conversation about an attractive acquaintance who had recently separated from her husband and who had not been asked out on any dates. Sam's friend said, "Her wedding ring is a 'sorry we're closed' sign." Sam remembered that it would soon be the woman's birthday.

Results show that reading times for the last, figurative word of the metaphoric items and the space following the statement were shorter for familiar (*gems*) than for less familiar (*sign*) metaphors (relative to a baseline). They also show that metaphors exhibited increased reading time in all three conditions (a–c) at the last, nonliteral word (*gems; sign*) relative to the baseline mean reading time for the first literal words in that statement, regardless of familiarity. As for context effects, reading times of familiar metaphors were not affected when a high-metaphor speaker was mentioned (4b) compared to trials when no occupation was mentioned (4a). However, reading time was shorter for the key, nonliteral word (*gems*) when the context invited a metaphoric reading (4c) than when it did not (4b). The effect disappeared by the pause that follows and, if anything, was slightly longer in the metaphor-inviting case, relative to the neutral control. In both conditions, reading times were back to the baseline by the first word of the next sentence.

Unlike familiar metaphors, however, unfamiliar metaphors in metaphor-inducing contexts (5c) were affected by information about speaker occupation associated with nonliteral language (high-metaphor and high-irony occupations). They exhibited *increased* reading time on the last word (5b) relative to the neutral, no occupation context (5a). In addition, reading time for the last word in the target statement was faster in the metaphor-inviting condition (5c) than in the neutral control (5b). Moreover, reading time was much reduced in the pause after the sentence, especially when the target was in the metaphor-inviting condition. However, in neither case was reading time back to the baseline found at the first part of the sentence or at the first word of the next sentence. So the effects of the unfamiliar items also spilled over and lasted for a longer time than has been found for familiar items.

Familiar and unfamiliar metaphors are processed differently, then. Unfamiliar metaphors take longer to process and are more susceptible to contextual effects than are familiar metaphors. Indeed, since nonsalient meanings rely more heavily on context for their decoding than do salient meanings, they must be more sensitive to contextual information: readers may look for a motivation to use novel language. In the case of the occupation mention, they may have looked for the relevance of this information to the novel utterance (and failed to find it instantly). Similarly, it could easily be the case that what the authors consider a metaphor-inviting context is not so much "metaphor-inviting" as it is more coherent, motivating the next (metaphoric) statement, which, in the preceding examples (ex. 4c and 5c), makes the novel utterance more relevant to the context. It is possible, then, that the contextual effects observed in this study are more directly related to coherence factors than to contextual information that affects metaphor comprehension per se. In any event, it suggests that novelty is more sensitive than salient language to the contextual information on which it depends for its disentanglement.

Note that, despite contextual effects, findings in Pexman et al. (2000) show that less familiar metaphors were read more slowly than were familiar metaphors. Also McGlone, Glucksberg, and Cacciari (1994) found that, although a specific or rich context sped up reading times of both familiar and less familiar idioms relative to a general context, familiar idioms were always read faster. (For similar results concerning familiar and less familiar proverbs, see Turner & Katz, 1997, and Katz & Ferretti, 2000, 2001.)

Even though these findings might be partly in line with the direct access view, attesting to facilitating context effects, they are more fully consistent with the graded salience hypothesis. They show that, as predicted, more familiar language takes less time to understand than does less familiar language, regardless of contextual information. These findings are also partly consistent with the standard pragmatic model because they demonstrate that the metaphorical words took longer to read than the literal (baseline) words, regardless of familiarity. This finding, however, may be a function of wrap up effects (effects caused by tying up loose ends at the end of sentences, inducing an increase in reading times of both literal and nonliteral language).[9] In the absence of literally biasing contexts, it is difficult to determine the cause of the difficulty.

In the final analysis, the balance of evidence adduced from research into initial processes involved in comprehension of familiar and unfamiliar metaphors does not favor the standard pragmatic model. Both familiar and unfamiliar metaphors were shown to follow the salient-first rather than the literal-first processing order. These findings do not favor the direct access view, either. Although some of the evidence supports the direct access view, testifying to contextual effects, in all, the equivalent initial processes attested to (Giora & Fein, 1999c; Williams, 1992) were not a result of contextual information. Rather, they were affected by salience balance. Complementarily, different processes were induced by utterances differing in salience. It should be noted, though, that context strength was manipulated only by two studies (Peleg et al., 2001; Pexman et al., 2000), both of which also attested to facilitative contextual effects (allowed by the graded salience hypothesis as a noninteractive, discrete mechanism; see chapter 2 in this volume). More research is needed to weigh context strength against meaning salience when processing figurative language.

2.1.4 Brain Waves

Additional support for the initial activation of salient (literal and nonliteral) meanings involved in processing familiar metaphors comes from research measuring brain waves—event-related brain potentials recorded from the scalp. N400 brain wave amplitude is largest for contextually incompatible or surprising items (such as semantic anomalies) and smallest for items that can easily integrate with contextual information. Using such measures, Pynte, Besson, Robichon, and Poli (1996) found that, out of context, the last word of familiar metaphors (*Those fighters are lions*) elicited larger N400 components than did the last word of literal sentences (*Those animals are lions*). Such a finding suggests that the incompatible literal meaning of the metaphors was accessed at some point during comprehension. Although Pynte et al. do not consider it, it is quite plausible to assume that the metaphoric meaning ('brave') of the familiar metaphor (*lions*) was also accessed during comprehension of the literal statement, as would be predicted by the graded salience hypothesis, only it did not elevate N400 brain waves since it cohered with the sentential context.

Pynte et al. (1996) erroneously assume, however, that they studied familiar and unfamiliar metaphors. In fact, their targets featured only familiar vehicles (*lions*). Consequently, their 'familiar' (*Those fighters are lions*) and 'unfamiliar' (*Those apprentices are lions*) metaphoric targets differ only in aptness that is, in how similar or relevant their vehicle is to their topic. Unsurprisingly, then, out of context, "familiar" versus "unfamiliar" metaphors did not elicit different responses (experiment 2). Whenever the targets (*lions*) were incompatible with prior context ("They are not idiotic: Those fighters are lions"), they elicited larger N400 amplitude than when cohering with context ("They are not cowardly: Those apprentices are lions") (experiments 3–4). At best, these findings can be taken to suggest that (relatively) familiar metaphors involve their salient metaphoric meaning when they are encountered, regardless of either context or aptness.

2.1.5 Eye Tracking

Like moving windows, eye tracking may be highly precise at detecting locations of ease and difficulty of processing, even though it is similarly blind as to which meanings or senses are activated (chapter 2 in this volume). Using eye-tracking measures, Pickering and Frisson (2001b) and Frisson and Pickering (2001) found that metaphor-based polysemous verbs (*disarmed*) showed sensitivity to context effects only during the later, integration phase. Frequency (or salience) effects were also late, but they were speedier for the frequent sense (literal; see 6a) than for the less frequent sense (metaphoric; see 6b):

(6) a. After the capture of the village, we *disarmed* almost every rebel and sent them to prison for a very long time. (Supportive context biased in favor of the salient meaning.)

   b. With his wit and humor, the speaker *disarmed* almost every critic who was opposed to spending more money on art. (Supportive context biased in favor of the less salient, metaphoric meaning.)

Pickering and Frisson explained these results in terms of the underspecification model for polysemous words introduced by Frazier and Rayner (1990); Frazier, Pacht, and Rayner (1999); and Frisson and Pickering (2001). On this account, the processor activates a single underspecified meaning and then uses evidence from context to home in on the appropriate sense. Context is not used for selecting between meanings, but a rich context is advantageous to the processor and may help specify a precise interpretation for the word. The effect of salience may be due to the fact that it is easier to construct a sentence interpretation when it employs more than a less salient sense.

Further support for the underspecification model comes from the finding that salience and context effects appeared later following polysemous and monosemous verbs than following ambiguous verbs. According to Pickering and Frisson, this supports the view that words with related meanings are accessed like monosemies. They activate a single underspecified meaning, which makes up the core meaning of the various senses (see also Glucksberg, Gildea, & Bookin, 1982) and use contextual information to resolve the ambiguity later on.

Such findings are not inconsistent with a salience-based view, however. They do not preclude the possibility that in both contexts (whether biased in favor of the less or more salient sense), it was the salient sense that was activated initially (see also findings in Garrod & Terras, 2000). Because verbs depend largely on the meanings of their oncoming arguments for their disambiguation, participants may have used the time elapsing from the first encounter of the polysemous verb (*disarmed*) until the encounter of the disambiguating argument (*critic; rebel*) to activate both the salient and the less salient senses. The late salience effects were speedier for the salient than for the less salient senses, probably because the salient sense was more highly activated on account of its salience.

This cannot be attested to, however, because participants had enough time to allow for the less salient sense to be activated alongside the salient sense before the disambiguating context was encountered. Such findings do not preclude the possibility that both senses were activated initially, either (after all, these are conventional metaphors). The late effects may be explained by the retention hypothesis (see chapters 2 and 4 and section 2.2 in this chapter), according to which the literal meaning of a metaphor need not be suppressed as irrelevant but may be retained because it supports the metaphoric sense.

2.1.6 Counterexamples?

Though salience may play a primary role in language comprehension, it is by no means the only factor that affects processing. Two other factors (apart from the contextual mechanism discussed earlier) come to mind: metaphor aptness and processing complexity.

2.1.6.1 ARE APT METAPHORS AN EXCEPTION?   On the face of it, the hypothesis that unfamiliar metaphors (whose metaphoric meaning is not coded in the mental lexicon) should take longer to process than familiar metaphors seemed not to have gained support when apt metaphors were involved. Apt metaphors are those rated high in 'goodness' that is, in getting across the figurative meaning. For some researchers, metaphor aptness (e.g., *That sauna is an oven; That casino is a drug*) is associated with high similarity/shared features (heat; addiction) obtaining between the source/vehicle (*oven; drug*) and the target/topic (*sauna; casino*) domains of the metaphoric expression. Indeed, metaphors judged high in similarity were also judged high in goodness (Chiappe & Kennedy, 1999, 2001; Gentner & Wolff, 1997; Johnson & Malgady, 1979; Katz, 1986; Malgady & Johnson, 1976; Marschark, Katz, & Paivio, 1983; Tourangeau & Rips, 1991; Tourangeau & Sternberg, 1981, 1982) and were also easier or faster to interpret

(Gentner & Wolff, 1997; Johnson & Malgady, 1979; Malgady & Johnson, 1976; Marschark et al., 1983). Indeed, the findings that initial processes are similar for familiar and less familiar metaphors, provided they are apt (Wolff & Gentner, 2000) and that speakers' preference of metaphor over simile when the topic and vehicle exhibit high similarity (Chiappe & Kennedy, 2001) suggest that aptness overrides salience. Other findings hedge this conclusion, however.

For instance, in Blasko and Connine (1993), metaphors rated low in familiarity and high in aptness (i.e., high in their ability to communicate the nonliteral meaning) were processed faster than were low-familiar/low-apt metaphors. Particularly, while both types of metaphor availed their literal meaning instantly, low-familiar/high-apt metaphors also availed their metaphoric meaning instantly. These findings, too, suggest that aptness overrides salience. However, as noted before, a close look at the test words used in Blasko and Connine (1993) suggests that this might be an unwarranted conclusion. Again, as is the case with the familiar metaphors used in their study (see section 2.1.2 in this chapter), more than half of the so-called metaphorically related test words they used could easily be primed by the topic rather than by the metaphoric constituent of the utterances. As stated earlier, here, too, the test words are highly associated with the meaning of both the topic and metaphoric constituents.[10] No wonder they were primed instantly. This is not true of the set of low-familiar/low-apt metaphors, however, in which a smaller number of test words are also highly related to the topic constituents.[11]

Indeed, apt metaphors are difficult to test in this way because of the similarity obtaining between their target (the topic) and source (the vehicle) concepts (see also Chiappe, Kennedy, & Chiappe, 1999).[12]

Still, aptness has been shown to facilitate processing of less familiar metaphors when other measures were used. For instance, in Gentner and Wolff (1997), participants were asked to type interpretations of metaphors displayed on a monitor as soon as they had them well formulated. The time between the appearance of the metaphor and the first keystroke was the dependent measure. One of four alternatives—the topic, the vehicle, both, or neither—was primed by a mention of each of them before the metaphor was displayed. For instance, before displaying *A job is a jail*, one of these alternatives was displayed:

- 'A job is a —', which primed only the topic
- 'A — is a jail', which primed only the vehicle
- 'A job is a jail', which primed both the topic (*job*) and the vehicle (*jail*)
- 'A — is a —', which primed neither

Across the board, apt metaphors were processed faster than were less apt ones. More relevant to our discussion is the finding that among less familiar metaphors, those considered apt were processed faster than those considered less apt, suggesting that aptness compensates for low salience. However, this compensation does not allow apt but less familiar metaphors to be processed as fast as or faster than (both apt and less apt) familiar metaphors, suggesting that, although aptness is a factor in metaphor comprehension, it need not override salience.[13]

2.1.6.2 DOES MAPPING COMPLEXITY OVERRIDE SALIENCE? In a recent study, Coulson and Van Petten (in press) proposed that mapping complexity plays a primary role in language comprehension. Accordingly, the literality /metaphoricity dichotomy should give way to a complexity continuum. To test their view, they used N400 amplitude measures. Recall that N400 is a brain wave whose amplitude is largest for contextually incompatible or surprising items. As such, it is large at the beginning of a sentence, particularly for low-frequency words, but declines with increasing semantic constraints as the sentence proceeds (Van Petten, 1995). Among other things, N400 amplitude measures are sensitive to ease or difficulty of meaning construction. Using such measures, Coulson and Van Petten show that not all literal meanings are alike. Some are more 'literal' than others, the former involving more complex processes (termed literal mappings) typically attributable to metaphors. In their study, sentence-final words (*gem*) were matched across conditions for cloze probability, word length, and word frequency, diverging, however, along a complexity continuum. The literal sense of the target word (*That stone we saw in the natural history museum is a **gem***) involved simple processes and conveyed its conventional, literal meaning. The metaphoric sense (*After giving it some thought, I realized the new idea is a **gem***) involved the most complex processes in which the speaker's idea was linked ana-logically to a gemstone to evoke its brightness and clarity. The intermediate case (*The ring was made of tin, with a pebble instead of a **gem***) involved literal mappings: it prompted readers to map conceptual structure from a different domain. Coulson and Van Petten (in press) claim that, while conveying its conventional meaning, processing *gem* under this condition exploited a correspondence between a worthless toy ring and the more prototypical expensive ring: both are construed as rings; both are worn on the finger; and both have a small, roundish, hard object in the center. Results indeed attest to the hypothesized continuum. They show that while metaphors elicited larger N400s than the literal sentences did, literal mappings fell between metaphors and literals.

These findings can indeed support a continuum hypothesis, which suggests that processing complexity is a crucial factor in comprehension. However, a close look at the items used may allow for an alternative, not mutually exclu-sive, explanation. A review of the items reveals that quite a few of those embed-ded in the "literal mapping" sentences were used in their less-salient/less-proto-typical (although coded) meaning. For instance, in the intermediate condition exemplified in the sentence *The ring was made of tin, with a pebble instead of a **gem***, it is the less salient ('small, roundish form') sense of *gem* that is intended rather than the salient 'brightness', 'valuable', or 'decorative' meaning invited by the literal sentence-context (see also Ortony, Vondruska, Foss, & Jones, 1985). In addition, many of the metaphoric items are not salient, either, which explains the difficulty in processing them. It is thus possible that on top of map-ping complexity, the items also diverge on salience.

In all, findings from metaphor research support the graded salience hypothesis. They demonstrate that salient meanings are always activated initially, regardless of contextual information. Contextual information has not been shown to sieve out contextually incompatible but salient meanings. Rather, salient meanings always popped up. Would contextual information suppress them after a while? Would it sustain them?

2.2 Integration Phase: The Retention/Suppression Hypothesis

The questions addressed in this section relate to the processes involved in comprehending figurative language following the initial activation phase. Which of the meanings made available through the initial process would be retained for further processes, such as alignment or comparison (Gentner & Wolff, 1997; Wolff & Gentner, 2000) or class inclusion (Glucksberg & Keysar, 1990), and which would be discarded as irrelevant (Gernsbacher et al., 2001; Glucksberg, Newsome, & Goldvarg, 2001)? According to the direct access view, only contextually appropriate meanings of sentences (and on the more radical view, also of words) should be available for the later, integration process because they were the only ones activated. Similarly, on the assumption that the contextually incompatible literal meaning of metaphor should be suppressed and replaced by the metaphoric meaning, the standard pragmatic model also predicts that only contextually compatible meanings would be retained for further processes (for a similar view, see Gernsbacher et al., 2001). However, according to the retention hypothesis supplementing the graded salience hypothesis (Giora & Fein, 1999c), meanings conducive to the interpretation of the intended meaning, whether contextually compatible (the figurative meaning of metaphor) or incompatible (the literal meaning of metaphor), would be retained for further processes. In contrast, meanings interfering with the utterance's intended interpretation should be suppressed. For example, the contextually incompatible literal meaning of 'jumping on a solid object' of the familiar metaphor *Jump on it!* should be retained in the metaphor-inducing context (discussing opportunity), since it contributes to its metaphoric interpretation ('grab instantly'). However, when embedded in a literally biasing context, the metaphoric meaning should be suppressed, since, in this context, it has no role in constructing the intended meaning.

In what follows, I examine these predictions regarding comprehension of familiar and less and unfamiliar instances of figurative language. I provide evidence accumulated in my lab and in others', as well as in naturally occurring conversations and written discourse. I start by reviewing results adduced in nonnaturalistic environments where several measures can be employed to test the predictions discussed in this chapter.

2.2.1 *Response Times*

Measuring response times to related, contextually compatible, and contextually incompatible test words in the various contexts after a long delay may be revealing as to which meanings are retained beyond the initial access phase. Indeed, findings in Williams (1992) can be taken to support the retention hypothesis. They show that while salient, contextually compatible, and contextually incompatible meanings of familiar metaphors were facilitated initially in both types of context, it was only the contextually incompatible literal meaning ('solid') in the metaphor-inducing context (*firm teacher*) that remained active after a long delay (of 1100 milliseconds). In contrast, under this condition, the metaphoric meaning ('strict') in the literal-inducing context (*firm bed*) was not available. These findings are consistent with the retention hypothesis but inconsistent with the direct access and standard pragmatic models.

In Hasson (2000), salient but disruptive meanings activated initially ('fast' in *The train to Boston was no rocket*), were deactivated after a long delay (of 1000 milliseconds). Only after such a delay was the appropriate meaning ('slow') of the negative metaphorical statements facilitated.

Unfortunately, such data tapping the retention and suppression processes that might be involved in metaphor comprehension after a long delay are not available for less familiar metaphors. Blasko and Connine (1993) showed that the salient, literal meaning of less familiar metaphors was available both instantly and 300 milliseconds after offset of the metaphoric target sentence, but they did not test the availability of the literal meaning later on, when the figurative meaning becomes available.

2.2.2 Reading Times

Some findings from reading times of whole sentences seem to argue against the retention hypothesis. They show that as predicted by the modular (e.g., Swinney, 1979) and standard pragmatic models (Grice, 1975), contextually inappropriate meanings are suppressed shortly after they have been activated. Specifically, Gernsbacher et al. (2001) aimed to show that the level of activation of information irrelevant to the metaphoric meaning of the metaphor is suppressed. Following Glucksberg and Keysar (1990) and Keysar and Glucksberg (1992), Gernsbacher et al. tested the class inclusion view of metaphor according to which metaphors of the form 'X is a Y' (*That defense lawyer is a shark*) are true category statements. Such statements refer simultaneously to the basic level instance (*shark*) and to the superordinate ad hoc category (of tenacious and vicious things) in which that instance ('shark') is a prototypical member and which it represents. This dual reference is momentary, however. Once the superordinate category has been constructed on the basis of the basic level meanings of the instance, this basic level information is discarded, enabling a straightforward, seamless comprehension of the metaphor. Suppression of basic level information, then, allows for the vehicle to uniquely refer to the superordinate category.

In their study, Gernsbacher et al. (2001) presented participants with metaphoric (*That defense lawyer is a shark*) and literal (*That large hammerhead is a shark*) class inclusion statements as primes, followed by basic level statements. Their findings show first that metaphor comprehension involves enhancement of meanings relevant to the superordinate interpretation of the metaphor: metaphoric but not literal class inclusion statements facilitated reading times of statements (*Sharks are tenacious*) related to the superordinate category meaning of the metaphor (tenacity).

However, the difference between the amount of enhancement induced by metaphoric versus literal primes can be attributed to the fact that about half of the metaphoric primes contained apt metaphors—metaphors whose topic and vehicle share salient features. For instance, it is possible that *My uncle's surgeon is a butcher* primed *Butchers use knives* to a greater degree than did the literal prime *My father's brother is a butcher* because both *surgeon* and *butcher* in the metaphoric prime could prime *use knives*, while in the literal prime only one constituent (*butcher*) could prime the target *use knives*. About half of the metaphoric primes were less apt, however, and would support the class inclusion theory more strongly if they were shown to be as effective primes as were apt metaphors (on how topic specificity affects metaphor processing, see Glucksberg, McGlone, & Manferdi, 1997).

Second and more important, Gernsbacher et al.'s findings show that metaphor comprehension involves suppression: reading times of basic level instantiations (*Sharks are good swimmers*) were slower following a metaphoric class inclusion statement (*That defense lawyer is a shark*) than following a literal class inclusion (baseline) prime (*That large hammerhead is a shark*). Gernsbacher et al. concluded that *basic-level* meanings, irrelevant to the superordinate metaphoric interpretation on account of their basic-level abstraction, are suppressed. Basic-level properties such as 'good swimmers' are dampened, they contend, because, having been activated and used for the construction of the metaphorical meaning, they may then get in the way and interfere with comprehension. Their suppression should allow for a fast and frictionless interpretation of the metaphor, which explains people's reported insensitivity to any "anomaly" involved in metaphor comprehension.

To show that once the superordinate meaning is constructed, the basic-level concept that has contributed to its construction is suppressed, it is not enough to show that basic-level meanings that could not apparently contribute to the construction of the ad hoc superordinate category are suppressed. These might be suppressed because they were never relevant to the superordinate category to begin with: 'good swimmers' has nothing to do with being tenacious or vicious, and this irrelevance has nothing to do with basic-level abstraction. However, *Butchers use knives* does contain basic-level concepts that are conducive to the superordinate meanings of *butcher* in *My uncle's surgeon is a butcher*, and so does *Airplanes have wings*, whose basic-level concepts are relevant to the superordinate category entitled *airplanes* in *My mother says that birds are airplanes*. Similarly, *Sieves have holes* contains basic-level information that is relevant to the superordinate meaning of *sieve* in *In old age, her memory was a sieve*. To convince us that basic-level concepts are dampened on account of their basic-level abstraction (which might confuse comprehenders and foster an impression of "anomaly" or category mistake), Gernsbacher et al. should attest to the suppression of basic-level but *relevant* concepts, such as those that might have some constructive role in metaphor interpretation but get discarded after being used, as they claim, on the basis of their basic-level abstraction.

It is also possible that some of these basic-level properties have not been activated at all on account of their low salience. For instance, 'swimming' is a lower salience property of *sharks* than is either 'ferocity' or 'jaws' (which might be more relevant, though, in the case of the literal prime condition).

The assumption that it is low salience (rather than low relevance) that accounts for the low levels of activation of the literal meanings tested in Gernsbacher et al. gains support from reanalysis of findings in Glucksberg et al. (2001), who attempted to replicate Gernsbacher et al. by testing the availability of relevant versus irrelevant properties. Indeed, in their study, a metaphorically irrelevant literal sentence probe such as *Geese can swim* was read more slowly than was a metaphorically relevant literal sentence probe *Geese are vicious* (which contains a metaphor-relevant property 'vicious'), following a metaphor prime *My lawyer was a shark*. A closer look, however, reveals that the probe sentences containing metaphorically relevant property ('viciousness') were always read faster than the probe sentence substantiating metaphorically irrelevant property ('swimming'), irrespective of prime context (about sharks), suggesting that relevance and salience might be conflated. Thus, *Geese are vicious* took almost equally long to read (1578 milliseconds versus 1568 milliseconds) whether the prime was metaphoric ('My lawyer is a shark') or literal ('This hammerhead is a shark'), but faster than *Geese can swim*, whether preceded by a literal (1701 milliseconds) or a metaphoric (1926 milliseconds) prime. Such findings suggest that there was no inhibition of irrelevant properties: apparently, *Geese can swim* is relevant in the context of the literal prime ('This hammerhead is a shark') in which 'swimming' is relevant, but was nevertheless read more slowly than the "relevant" *Geese are vicious*. Instead, the metaphorically irrelevant properties were also low salience properties. The salience-based explanation, therefore, seems to account for all these findings: low salience probes took longer to read than high salience probes in all (relevant and irrelevant) conditions.[14]

Recall, further, that the suppression hypothesis has not gained support from findings by Giora and Fein (1999c) and Williams (1992). Alternatively, it has been proposed here that suppression is more likely to take place where meanings, activated on account of their salience, are detrimental to the interpretation process.

In sum, the findings reviewed here are consistent with the retention hypothesis. They show that contextually inappropriate meanings are not suppressed en bloc. Only meanings that interfere with the utterance interpretation are discarded (see also chapter 6 in this volume). In contrast, meanings contributing to utterance interpretation are retained even if they do not make up the intended meaning.

2.2.3 Word Fragment Completion

In word fragment completion tests, participants are asked to complete a fragmented word (t-b-e) with the first word that comes to mind (for a review, see chapters 2 and 4 in this volume). Because it is an offline measure, word fragment completion testing may suggest which meanings are retained after the initial access phase. According to the direct access view, word fragment completion tests would favor the contextually appropriate meaning in either context, regardless of familiarity. The standard pragmatic model has the same prediction. According to the retention hypothesis (supplementing the graded salience hypothesis), word fragment completion tests will favor both meanings in the metaphor-inducing context (in which both meanings are conducive to the construction of the metaphoric meaning), but only the literal meaning in the literally biasing context (in which the metaphoric meaning usually plays no role in constructing the literal meaning). This prediction is particularly pertinent to unfamiliar metaphors (example 2 in this chapter), because unfamiliar metaphors usually have only one salient meaning: the literal meaning. In the literal context, then, it should be the only one accessed. In contrast, familiar metaphors (example 1 here) usually have at least two salient meanings: the literal and the metaphoric meanings. Therefore, they should be accessed in both the literal- and metaphor-inducing contexts, and they should undergo suppression when they are irrelevant.

In Giora and Fein (1999c) we tested these predictions. Materials (in Hebrew) were those used and rated for familiarity in Giora et al. (1997). A pretest established that in the absence of context, there was no difference between literally and metaphorically related test words in terms of salience. In the experiment, participants read familiar, less familiar, and unfamiliar metaphors that were embedded in either a metaphor- or a literal-inducing context, and they were asked to complete two fragmented words with the first word that came to mind.

As illustrated by figure 5.3, results demonstrate that familiar metaphors (*In order to solve the math problem, the student broke her head*) retained both the metaphoric ('effort') and the literal ('wound') meanings in the metaphorically biasing context. However, in the literally biasing context (*Because she was so careless when she jumped into the pool, the student broke her head*), the metaphoric meaning was significantly less available than the literal meaning. Similarly, results demonstrated that less and unfamiliar metaphors facilitated their literal meaning in both types of context, while their metaphoric meaning was more available in the metaphorically biasing context.

To control for the possibility that it was context rather than salience that affected the results, the experiment was repeated with the contexts only. In the absence of target sentences, no differences were found between literally and metaphorically related test words.

The finding that the metaphoric meaning of familiar metaphors was less available than the literal meaning in the *literally* biasing context is susceptible to two interpretations. Either the metaphorical meaning of the salient metaphors was inhibited by literally biasing contextual information (as would be predicted by the direct access view), or, having been activated, it was undergoing suppression (as would be predicted by the retention hypothesis). In light of previous findings, we favored the suppression hypothesis. Recall that in Williams (1992),

Familiar Metaphors

■ Compatible responses ☐ Incompatible responses

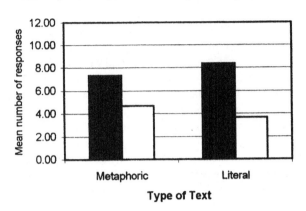

Less-Familiar Metaphors

■ Compatible responses ☐ Incompatible responses

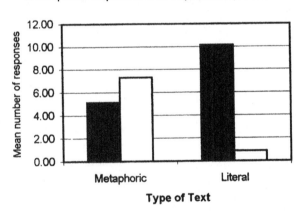

Figure 5.3 Mean number of compatible and incompatible responses in metaphorically and literally biasing texts, for **familiar** (*top panel*), **less familiar** (*bottom panel*), and **unfamiliar** (*next panel*) metaphors.

familiar metaphors were shown to activate their salient, contextually incompatible, metaphoric meaning initially, in the context biasing their interpretation toward the literal meaning. However, after a delay, this meaning was less available. In addition, our findings regarding less familiar metaphors show that metaphorically related test words were hardly facilitated when less familiar metaphors were embedded in literally biasing contexts, suggesting that this

Unfamiliar Metaphors

■ Compatible responses □ Incompatible responses

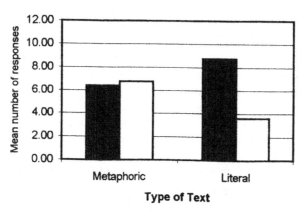

Figure 5.3 (continued)

meaning was not activated there (figure 5.3). This difference in the amount of facilitation of metaphorically related test words in the literally biasing context between familiar and less familiar metaphors further supports the hypothesis that while the metaphorical meaning of familiar metaphors was activated and suppressed, it was not activated upon processing less familiar metaphors. Less familiar metaphors do not have a salient metaphoric meaning at their disposal (but see note 12).

These findings are consistent with the view that salient, contextually incompatible meanings are retained insofar as they are functional. They are discarded, if they are not. Since the salient, contextually incompatible, literal meaning of metaphor plays a role in metaphor interpretation, it was retained in the metaphor-inducing context. Complementarily, since the metaphoric meaning of the same utterance embedded in a literally biasing context does not partake in constructing the literal interpretation, it was deactivated. These results cannot be accommodated by the direct access view. While according to the direct access view only the contextually appropriate, literally related words should be facilitated by the literal targets, and only the contextually appropriate, metaphorically related words should be facilitated by the metaphorical targets, this was not the case. Neither can these findings be accommodated by the standard pragmatic model, according to which the contextually incompatible literal meaning of metaphor should be rejected and replaced.

2.2.4 Spontaneous Response

Spontaneous responses to metaphoric utterances in naturally occurring conversations and written texts may also indicate which meanings have been kept in the mind of the producer and the interlocutor. Addressing a certain meaning and elaborating on it testifies to its availability due to activation and retention. Of particular interest are meanings deemed irrelevant in a certain context (e.g., the literal meaning of utterances intended nonliterally). In the final analysis, what we are interested in is what happens outside the lab—that is, in the processes involved in spontaneous (both spoken and written) speech.

2.2.4.1 CONVERSATION   The graded salience hypothesis is consistent with the view that naturally occurring conversations would abound in "dialogic" turns in which participants resonate with meanings brought up by the interlocutors' speech, including their own (Du Bois, 1998, 2000a). Unlike producing a written discourse, engaging in naturally occurring conversation (in which long pauses or silent turns are unacceptable) implies being involved in a time-constrained activity. Time constraints make resonating with already retrieved salient meanings a more economical and plausible strategy than innovating. While innovating is effortful, resonating with salient meanings requires less effort and should therefore facilitate the discourse flow.

According to the graded salience hypothesis, resonating with salient meanings need not always imply resonating with the intended meaning. In the case of metaphor, it may also involve contextually inappropriate meanings that have been retained on account of the role they play in the utterance interpretation. For example, the literal meaning of metaphor need not be suppressed, even though it is contextually incompatible, since it benefits the utterance interpretation (via comparison processes à la Gentner & Wolff, 1997, or class inclusion, à la Glucksberg & Keysar, 1990). Thus, a conversational response to the salient, albeit contextually incompatible, literal meaning of *both* familiar and less familiar metaphors is consistent with the view that salient meanings should not be bypassed.

To illustrate what is meant by resonating with the various meanings evoked and retained by metaphor, consider an extract from a recorded conversation (on a book on death), which took place between Pamela and Darryl in their bedroom (Du Bois, 2000b). (The metaphors are bolded. Utterances that are being responded to, whether in the immediate context or later on, are underlined. For the full text, see the appendix in this chapter.)

(7)   1. PAMELA: Well you're right,
    2. I think they're probably **flip** sides.
    3. DARRYL: (TSK) I mean who [are you].
    4. PAMELA: [But I'm] —
    5. DARRYL: **Pollyanna?**
    6. PAMELA: ... (SWALLOW) (TSK) ha=rdly=.
    7. DARRYL: @@@
    8. PAMELA: Hardly=,
    9. Look **where I've come from**.
    10. ... (H) I mean,
    11. ... % (Hx) ... (H) % This chapter on *heaven an hell*,
    12. it's really interesting.
    13. DARRYL: ... Why,
    14. PAMELA: I used to have this,

15. .. sort of,

16. .. % standard li=ne,

17. that,

18. ... % there were **two things I got out of= .. my marriage**.

19. One was= a name that was easy to spell,

20. and one was a %,

21. .. (H) a child.

22. (Hx) .. % ... that=,

23. ... really got me **grounded**.

24. But,

25. (H) the fact of the matter is,

26. ... (H) that the marriage itself=,

27. I mean as **h=ellish** as it was,

28. ... % .. It's like **it pulled me under,**

29. **like a giant octopus,**

30. **or a giant,**

31. % ... **giant shark.**

32. (H) **And it pulled me all the way under**.

33. **and then,**

34. **(H) ... and there I was,**

35. **it was like the silent scream,**

36. **and then,**

37. .. then I found that .. **I% was on my own two feet** again.

38. **and it r=eally was —**

39. (H) .. (Hx) ... % .. % (Hx) (H) (TSK)

40. S- what was **hell** in that .. that marriage became,

41. ... became **a way out for me**.

42. ... it was the **flip** side.

43. (H) .. It's like sometimes **you go through things,**

44. ... and **you come out the other side of them,**

45. <WH you WH> .. **come out so much better.**

46. ... (H) and if I hadn't had that,

47. if I hadn't had —

48. [(H)]

49. DARRYL: [**It's not the way**] with food.

50. PAMELA: ... What do you mean.

51. DARRYL: ...(H) **What goes in [one way,**

52. **PAMELA:**   [@ @ @ @ @

53. **DARRYL:** <@ **doesn't come out** XXX @> @ @ @ @ @ @ @ @ @ @].

54. PAMELA: (H) <@ kay @>,

55. (H)]

56. **comes out very hellish.**

57. DARRYL: (H) Yeah=.

58. PAMELA: **Very hellish.**

59. DARRYL: .. So what <X did that [have to d]o X> —

60. PAMELA: [But it's so] good /god/ —

61. k=- <u>**so good going down**</u>.
62. th-,
63. [I mean],
64. DARRYL: [what did] —
65. PAMELA: there's there's the opposites again.
66. DARRYL: it's it's [ma-] —
67. PAMELA: **[the] food is like,**
68. all [2unique2],
69. DARRYL: [2hey2].
70. PAMELA: and [3wonderful,
71. DARRYL: [3i- **it's <u>major-league</u>3**] **Yin and Yang.**
72. PAMELA: and **<u>heavenly</u>3**]
73. . ... (TSK) <u>**major league**</u>.
74. DARRYL: .. What does that have to do with heaven and hell in the book.

LEGEND:[15]
...: half a second break; . .: a shorter break
[ ]: overlap
x: unclear word
<xx>: unclear utterance
@: laughter
<u>underlined</u>: Utterances resonated with
bold: Metaphors

As predicted by the graded salience and retention hypotheses, *both* less familiar, but even more so, familiar metaphors evoked and retained their salient, contextually incompatible, literal meaning, so that this meaning became available for interlocutors to respond to. Of the 23 metaphors, only 4 (lines 5, 18, 35, 71) remained unaddressed, of which only one is unfamiliar (*silent scream*, line 35). Of the remaining 18, whose literal meaning was either repeated or elaborated on, only one is new (lines 28–32). Indeed this one has gained a major elaboration by the speaker herself:

(7.1)   It's like it pulled me under,
        like a giant octopus,
        or a giant,
        ... giant shark.
        And it pulled me all the way under.

This excerpt is highly repetitive: *pulled me under* is mentioned twice, *giant* is mentioned three times, and *octopus* is emphasized by the addition of *shark*—a member of the same category. Thus the literal meaning of the metaphor *pulled me under, like a giant octopus* is immediately responded to by the very same speaker, who harps on it, attesting to its availability. This novel metaphor may be viewed as a new instantiation of the root metaphor (Lakoff &

Johnson, 1980) DOWN IS SUBDUED, with the addition of the overwhelming power of wild ocean animals.[16]

Following this segment, there is an intervening metaphor (*silent scream,* line 35) that does not cohere with the preceding metaphor in that its source domain (literal meaning) is not associated with the source domain of the previous metaphor. However, immediately following (in line 37) is a familiar coherent figure (*was on my own two feet*), which echoes the literal meaning of a somewhat remote metaphor (*grounded*) and the previous one through a reversal: having been pulled *down*, the speaker is now *on* her two feet—that is, erect and steady—drawing on the root metaphor UP IS RESISTANT. The coherent figure attests to the availability of the salient meaning (of being pulled *down*) which has been activated and retained: the speaker is using the vertical domain of "up and down" to describe her emotional transitions in the course of her marriage.

Other related metaphors she is using draw on the "in and out" (rather than "down and up") aspects of space (lines 41–45):

(7.2)   that marriage became,
    ... became a way *out* for me.
    ... it was the flip side.
    .. It's like sometimes you go *through* things,
    ... and you come *out* the other side of them,
    you .. come *out* so much better.

With the exception of the familiar metaphor *flip side*, the literal meaning of 'being in and out of some space' is elaborated on and responded to by the same speaker. Both *going through things* and *coming out of them* are familiar metaphors, drawing on similar spatial dimensions to describe emotional states. These spatial dimensions, which make up the salient literal meaning, are retained by the same speaker. Having been activated, these salient meanings are made available for her for further elaboration.

Indeed, the addressee attends to these salient meanings and, having processed them, he picks them up for "irrelevant" humorous purposes:

(7.3)   DARRYL: It's not the way with food.
    PAMELA: ... What do you mean.
    DARRYL: ... What *goes in* one way,
    PAMELA: @@@@@
    DARRYL: doesn't *come out* @@@@@@@@@@@].
    PAMELA: @ kay @,
        comes out very hellish.
    DARRYL: Yeah.
    PAMELA: Very hellish.
    DARRYL: .. So what did that have to do
    PAMELA: But it's so good /god/ —
        so good going down

The addressee attends to the literal meaning (*going through* and *coming out of*) and draws a negative analogy. (Note that even if this elaboration is not metaphorical and the analogy is literal, this does not hamper the analysis attesting that salient meanings are not suppressed when functional and can, therefore, be resonated with.) The contextually irrelevant meaning does not escape him; he does not suppress it. Rather, he picks it up for further elaboration and comic relief. This small excerpt ends in resonating with the literal meaning of the previous metaphor 'so good *going down*' (line 61), attesting to its salience and retention.

Now salient (literal) correspondences are established. Previously the metaphor *hell* was employed to characterize the marriage she was *going through* (line 40). Now *hellish* is used to describe the outcome (what *comes out*) of a similar though different process. *Hellish* is repeated twice here, by the same speaker who also introduced it (in its metaphoric sense) for the first time.

Hell and *heaven* are very accessible here, both literally and metaphorically. Being first introduced through their literal meaning only—through the chapter's title (line 11)—they made available their salient metaphoric meaning as well. *Hell* is later used three times metaphorically (lines 40, 56, and 58) and one more time literally (line 74); *Heaven* is later used once metaphorically (line 72) and once literally (line 74).

Other salient meanings keep recurring. The familiar metaphor *flip side* occurs twice (lines 2 and 42); *Where I have come from* (line 9) is not repeated or elaborated on in this quoted segment, but it recurs later on in the conversation, probably also on account of it being one of the discourse topics (see also Giora, 1985a, b). It refers metaphorically to life before birth. And *major league,* intended metaphorically, occurs twice.

The conversation on the whole is very repetitive, echoing salient meanings that have been activated and reused for all kinds of purposes. The salient literal meanings of metaphors, not least familiar metaphors, are recycled, as predicted by the graded salience and retention hypotheses. Similarly, familiar metaphoric meanings are also resonated with, as predicted.

Particularly interesting are elaborations on the unintended meaning, which are extended either metaphorically or literally, such as line 641 (see appendix), in which Darryl elaborates on the literal meaning of Pamela's metaphor to the extent that it becomes funny:

(8)   PAMELA: (...) what if you **took the same ... spacesuit**?
       ... and you *put another spirit into it.*
       ... It would be a different person,
       DARRYL: **It'd say,**
       let me out .

As he does in lines 778 and 788 in which, again, the literal meaning is responded to, evoking an irrelevant association for humorous purposes:

(9) PAMELA: Maybe he's a **very old soul**.
     DARRYL: .. (Hx)
     PAMELA: ... please.
     DARRYL: like Old King Cole
     PAMELA: [2@@@2]
     $ DARRYL LAUGHS NINE SECONDS, AND PAMELA JOINS FOR
        TWO MORE
     Hm=.
        ...   Well,
     (Hx)
     DARRYL: If **he's a very old soul,**
                 he should keep it to himself.

Or in line 816, where the literal meaning (*gone*) of the dying metaphor is
extended literally:

(10) PAMELA: ... (H) I just think it's so wei=rd,
                    that **they're go=ne**.
                    ... and **where did they go to**.

Of particular interest are some of the errors and puns, which can be explained by resonating with salient, though contextually inappropriate, meanings. In the following, Darryl mistakes Pamela's metaphoric meaning (bolded
and underlined) for the salient literal meaning (underlined):

(11) PAMELA: well,
                  n- n- —
                  Maybe I —
                  maybe I'm just eager to **get back to where I was**.
                  may-] —
       DARRYL: Back into the womb?
       PAMELA: no no no,

Note further the error and echoing of sounds (underlined), made available
through prior activation, which introduced irrelevant but salient meanings to
the discourse that caused laughter (marked by @):

(12) PAMELA: ... Being here is,
                   .. is so illusive sometimes.
                   ... I mean .. illusionary.
       DARRYL: ... Those are two different words,
                    and they mean two different things.
       PAMELA: Well it's illusionary.
                   ... I take back what I said about @illusive,
       DARRYL: @@

PAMELA: @@ @@@@@@
DARRYL: Y- .. you may be <u>elusive,</u>

Of the 120 metaphoric utterances (in bold) found in the half-hour conversation (see appendix), about 20 are less or unfamiliar metaphors.[17] Of the 20 less or unfamiliar metaphoric utterances, 7 (35%) are not resonated with: that is, there is no response to either their literal or metaphoric meaning (note, however, that some novel metaphors are extensions of metaphors previously activated in the discourse). The remaining 13 (65%) have their salient, literal meaning extended by either their producer or the addressee. Of the remaining 100 familiar metaphors, 20 (20%) go unresponded to. All the remaining 80 (80%) metaphoric utterances have literal extensions or repetitions—elaborations of both the speaker's and the addressee's, suggesting that the salient but contextually inappropriate meaning is activated and retained in the minds of both the producer and the comprehender. Examination of this naturally occurring conversation suggests that, as predicted by the graded salience and retention hypotheses, metaphors, not least familiar metaphors, are processed both literally and metaphorically. Moreover, their salient, literal meaning is retained and may be resonated with for further processes.

2.2.4.2 WRITTEN DISCOURSE   In what follows, I focus on the processes involved in written text production. Would they mirror those involved in text comprehension? On the face of it, it seems plausible to assume that at least in one respect they should not: since authors know what's on their mind—they know what they mean before the articulation of this meaning—they would access only that intended meaning. Text production, it might be assumed, would not involve accessing and retaining unintended meanings of a word selected for expressing a certain meaning or concept. Rather, it's the word's intended meaning—the one compatible with the context—that must be involved exclusively. In the case of metaphors, for example, this means that only the metaphorical meaning of the metaphor is tapped, thus inhibiting the unintended literal meaning.

As a working hypothesis, let us assume that the processes involved in text production indeed mirror those involved in text comprehension. On this assumption, the various views would differ only insofar as contextually incompatible meanings are concerned. In the case of metaphor, this would usually involve the literal meaning. Whereas the direct access view would predict the exclusive activation and retention of the compatible metaphoric meaning, particularly of familiar metaphors, with no traces of the literal meaning (Gibbs, 1980; Keysar, Shen, Glucksberg, & Horton, 2000), the standard pragmatic model would predict the initial activation and subsequent suppression of that incompatible literal meaning of both familiar and unfamiliar metaphors. Assuming the activation of the literal meaning of both familiar and unfamiliar metaphors on account of its salience, the retention hypothesis would predict retention of the literal meaning, on account of its nonintrusive but rather instrumental role in metaphor interpretation.

One way to test these predictions is to study the ecology of metaphors in naturally occurring discourses. Mention of any of the meanings of a metaphor after that metaphor has been mentioned, either in the metaphor's immediate neighborhood or in the next two or three clauses, reflects the availability of that meaning in the mind of the producer. Thus, if familiar and unfamiliar metaphors both prime their unintended literal meaning indistinguishably, this would support the graded salience hypothesis. However, if none prime their unintended literal meanings, this would be partly more consistent with the direct access and standard pragmatic views. If only unfamiliar metaphors prime their unintended literal meaning, this would also be consistent with the version of the direct access view proposed by Keysar et al. (2000). Whereas discourses not involving incompatible meanings need not argue against the graded salience hypothesis, discourses involving incompatible meanings that are non-salient would (this has not been tested here, however; but see Ariel, 2002b).[18]

In Giora and Balaban (2001), we tested these hypotheses. Our materials were Hebrew metaphors used in newspaper articles. We collected 60 metaphors from the columns' section of *Ha'aretz*, an Israeli daily. These were equally split: 30 involved some mention or echo of their (unintended) literal meaning—that is, a word semantically related to their literal meaning, in the same or next clause(s) (13a–c)—and 30 did not (14a–c).

(13) a. The strikes in the education system took place when the union was putting up a **fight** against the government. In this fight, threats, sanctions, and even a general strike were the **weapons**. (*Ha'aretz*, 4 September 1997: B1)

   b. In this situation, the Treasury [department] looks like **an island** of sanity in a **sea** of unconstrained demands. (*Ha'aretz*, 12 September 1997: B1)

   c. Politically, the present Croatian leaders' wishing to **blur** the **impression** of the "Ustasha" rehabilitation is understandable. But they will find it difficult to **erase the** moral **stain** of their attempt to rehabilitate the murderers and their accomplices. (*Ha'aretz*, 3 September 1997: B1)[19]

(14) a. He **lost** his health, and his spirit **broke**. (*Ha'aretz*, 1 September 1997: B1)

   b. Every honest and benevolent person should **have given a shoulder** to the minister of the Treasury so that he can **succeed** in implementing his plan. (*Ha'aretz*, 4 September 1997: B1)

   c. In her position as the mother of the future king, [Diana] was **stuck as a bone in the throat** of the British monarchy. And from this position and being so bright, she **opened a window** into the inhumanity of the royal family. (*Ha'aretz*, 2 September 1997: B1)

A total of 40 native speakers of Hebrew rated the metaphors on a 1–7 familiarity scale. Findings showed that, as predicted by the graded salience hypothesis, metaphors followed by a mention of their literal meaning did not differ in familiarity from those that were not followed by the literal meaning. Thus, the metaphors whose literal meaning was echoed and elaborated on in the immediate or next clause(s) were not evaluated as more or less familiar than those that received no literal extension. Moreover, a check of the number of metaphors that received the highest familiarity rates (6–7) reveals that 15 of them belonged in the group of 30 metaphors that had literal extensions (13a–c) and 17 belonged in the other group of 30 metaphors whose literal meaning was not elaborated on (14b–c).

Our findings are consistent with the hypothesis that lexical access in text production is governed by salience. Context did not block activation of salient though incompatible meanings. Even highly familiar metaphors, whose metaphoric meaning may be processed directly and at times before the literal meaning, activated their salient, literal meaning upon their production, even though this meaning was incompatible with contextual information. These findings further suggest that meanings made available to the processor are not discarded automatically but may be retained for further processes, regardless of their contextual fit. The processes involved in text production, then, are at least partially similar to those involved in text comprehension. To a certain extent, both comprehension and production are affected by salience. (See, however, Shen & Balaban, 1999, on lack of metaphorical coherence.)

3. Familiar and Less Familiar Idioms

3.1 Initial Activation Phase: Measures and Findings

It is interesting to look into how idioms are processed initially, since they mostly constitute a highly entrenched instance of figurative language. Apparently, they are more familiar than their literal interpretation (for a corpus-based assessment, see Moon, 1998; for intuited assessments see Popiel & McRae, 1988). Would familiar idioms induce response patterns similar to familiar metaphors? Would familiar and less familiar idioms be processed differently? There are very few studies looking into familiar versus less familiar idioms. The few that did consider salience as a variable reported differences on account of the degree of salience.

3.1.1 Reading Times

According to the graded salience hypothesis, familiar idiomatic utterances should be processed faster than less familiar idiomatic utterances. Indeed, reading times for familiar idioms were faster than for less familiar idioms (Cronk, Lima, & Schweigert, 1993; Cronk & Schweigert, 1992; Gibbs, 1994: 96; Schraw, Trathen, Reynolds, & Lapan, 1988; Schweigert, 1986, 1991). Moreover, embedded in the same context, less familiar (variant) idioms (*didn't spill a single bean*) took longer to read than their familiar canonical origins (*spill the beans*). These findings suggest that, inconsistently with the direct access view, salience overrides context effects (at the initial access phase). While a supportive (specific) context plays a role in comprehension, speeding up reading times of both familiar and less familiar idioms relative to a general context, familiar idioms were always read faster (McGlone et al., 1994).

According to the graded salience hypothesis but in disagreement with the standard pragmatic model and the interactionist direct access view, processing familiar idioms in appropriate (idiomatic) contexts should be faster than processing their literal equivalents in appropriate (literal) contexts, and faster than processing similar literal sentences. Indeed, as reported in Gibbs (1980), idioms such as *spill the beans* were read faster in an idiomatically than in a literally biasing context. Similarly, as reported in Gibbs and Gonzales (1985), Gibbs, Nayak, & Cutting (1989), and McGlone et al. (1994), idioms were read faster than their literal controls or paraphrases. In Connine, Blasko, Brandt, and Kaplan Layer (1992), response times to the last word of idiomatic phrases such as *get off my back* were faster than to similar nonidiomatic phrases such as *get off my pack*. In addition, frozenness affected idiom identification to a greater extent than familiarity (but see Gibbs et al., 1989, for conflicting results showing that flexible idioms such as *lay down the law* were verified more speedily than were unanalyzable/frozen idioms such as *kick the bucket*).

3.1.2 Response Times

Similarly, findings in Van de Voort and Vonk (1995) show that familiar idioms (whose more salient meaning is idiomatic) are automatically processed idiomatically. Variant idioms took longer to process than nonmodified idioms did, while the opposite was true for their literal controls. Specifically, subjects took longer to make a lexical decision to target words (*bag*) in internally modified idioms (*She let the fat cat out of the **bag***) than in nonmodified versions (*She let the cat out of the **bag***), thus suggesting that the internal modification inhibited the idiomatic meaning, which then had to be revisited. The response times for target words in the literal controls showed a reverse pattern. Lexical decisions to target words (*closet*) in internally modified sentences (*She let the fat cat out of the **closet***) were faster than in the nonmodified sentences (*She let the cat out of the **closet***), thus suggesting that the nonmodified sentences were processed idiomatically initially and had to be revisited.

3.2 Later Integration Phase: Measures and Findings

On the assumption that the idiomatic meaning of familiar idioms is more salient than their literal interpretation, the graded salience hypothesis predicts that processing familiar idioms (*kick the bucket*) should evoke their idiomatic meaning ('die') in the context that biases their meaning toward either the idiomatic or the literal interpretation. According to the retention hypothesis, the salient idiomatic meaning should be suppressed in the literally biasing context since it is not instrumental in that context. However, since the idiomatic meaning is highly salient, it might be difficult to suppress even when it is inappropriate (recall the *cold feet* example in chapter 2). Specifically, the idiomatic meaning in the context biased toward the literal interpretation might show higher levels of retention than the literal meaning of the target sentence in the context biased toward the idiomatic meaning, thus disproving the suppression/retention hypothesis.

In contrast, processing less familiar idioms should activate their salient, literal meaning regardless of context. Because it is less salient, the idiomatic interpretation relies on the more salient literal meaning, which would, therefore, be retained in the idiom-inducing context. In the literally biasing context, the literal meaning would be retained to a greater extent than the idiomatic meaning since it is the intended meaning in this context. Less salient idioms, then, would exhibit retention of their salient literal meaning in both types of context since in both types of context they are functional.

The direct access and standard pragmatic models have different predictions. On both views, only contextually compatible meanings should be retained.

3.2.1 Word Fragment Completion

In Giora and Fein (1999c), we tested these hypotheses. We asked participants who have read familiar and less familiar idioms embedded in idiomatically and literally biasing contexts to complete one of two fragmented words. The participants were primary school students, aged 12–13. They familiarized themselves with the idioms through their studies at school. For a year they were taught idioms systematically, in an alphabetical order. At the end of the year, their knowledge of the idioms was tested. On the basis of the results of the test, the idioms in the experiment were divided into familiar and less familiar idioms.

The fragmented test words they were asked to complete were tested for their salience out of context and were not found to be different. The context texts were one-sentence long, biased either toward the idiomatic meaning of the target (15a, where *on one leg* means 'briefly') or toward its literal interpretation (15b):

(15)   a. He told me the whole story *on one leg.*
       b. In the zoo, I saw a stork standing *on one leg.*

As illustrated in figure 5.4, the salient idiomatic meanings of the familiar targets (e.g., 'briefly') were retained regardless of context. Further, their contextually incompatible idiomatic meanings were retained to a greater extent in the literal context (15b) than was the contextually incompatible literal meaning (e.g., 'toe') in the idiomatic context (15a).

In contrast, less familiar targets induced a different response pattern. As illustrated by figure 5.4, the salient literal meanings of the less familiar targets were highly retained in both types of context, irrespective of contextual bias. As found for less familiar metaphors, the difference between the retention of the idiomatic and literal meanings in the idiomatically biased context was smaller than, and in the opposite direction to, the difference between that of the literal and idiomatic meanings in the literally biased context. While these findings are partially accountable by the retention/suppression hypothesis, they are inconsistent with both the standard pragmatic and the direct access views.

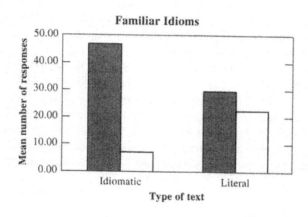

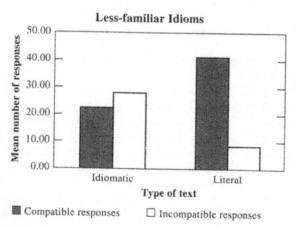

Figure 5.4 Mean number of compatible and incompatible responses in idiomatically and literally biasing texts, for **familiar** (*top panel*) and **less-familiar** idioms (*bottom panel*).

In sum, measures tapping later, integrative processes show that, as predicted by the graded salience and retention hypotheses, salient idioms are processed idiomatically, regardless of context. However, since their idiomatic meaning is so salient, it is hard to suppress in spite of contextual information to the contrary. Less familiar idioms resemble less familiar metaphors. They are processed literally in both types of context and retain the contextually incompatible literal meaning even after a while.

4. Metaphor, Irony, and Literal Language: Different or Equal?

At this stage it is possible to shed some new light on some of the unresolved enigmas occupying the minds of linguists and psycholinguists for over two decades. The question regarding the processes involved in literal versus nonliteral language or the question regarding the processes involved in metaphor versus irony may be reexamined in light of the data presented in the previous chapters and in the literature in general.

Indeed, review of the findings presented so far suggests that the relevant factor determining differences or similarity in early processes is not the literality or nonliterality of the utterances in question but, rather, their degree of familiarity. Instances of language use sharing similar salience were shown to be processed initially along the same patterns, regardless of the kind of trope. Utterances distinguishable in terms of familiarity involved different processes. Insights gained in neurological experiments may also serve to support these claims.

4.1 Irony versus Metaphor

4.1.1 Early Activation Processes

According to the graded salience hypothesis, comprehension of metaphor and irony should not differ at the initial access phase, provided they share similar salience. Thus, familiar instances of metaphor and irony should be processed initially both literally and figuratively because both their figurative and literal interpretations are similarly accessible (either coded in the mental lexicon or hinging on the salient literal meanings of their components). Indeed, the evidence presented in chapters 4–5 in this volume show that familiar instances of metaphor and irony activated their salient (figurative and literal) meanings initially, regardless of contextual information (Giora & Fein, 1999a; Williams, 1992).

Complementarily, less familiar instances of irony and metaphor should also be processed similarly, though differing from familiar instances. They should activate their salient meaning automatically, in parallel to and at times before deriving their nonsalient, contextually compatible interpretation. Indeed, findings by Giora, Fein, and Schwartz (1998), Giora and Fein (1999a), Pexman et al. (2000), and Schwoebel, Dews, Winner, and Srinivas (2000) lend support to this view. They show that nonconventional ironies activate their salient (literal) meaning initially, before activating their nonsalient (ironic) interpretation (Giora & Fein, 1999a; Giora et al., 1998). They also show that nonconventional ironies and metaphors take longer to read than their more accessible literal counterparts (Dews & Winner, 1997; Giora et al., 1997, 1998). Fine-tuned online measures also show that nonconventional ironies take longer to read than their more salient literal (Schwoebel et al., 2000) and metaphoric equivalents (Pexman et al., 2000).

Recall that Pexman et al. (2000) embedded familiar and less familiar metaphors (16a) in irony inducing contexts (16b):

(16)　a. Jan and her cousin, a factory worker, were waiting in line at the supermarket checkout. The cashier was working very efficiently. About the cashier, the factory worker said:
　　　"Her mind is an active volcano." (An extra sentence follows here).

　　　b. Jan and her cousin, a factory worker, were waiting in line at the supermarket checkout. The cashier was having difficulty counting change for the customer ahead of them in line. About the cashier, the factory worker said:
　　　"Her mind is an active volcano." (An extra sentence follows here).

They found that, in these contexts, reading times of less familiar (metaphoric and ironic) items, measured at various locations—that is, at the figurative key word (*volcano*) of the statement, at the space following that word, and at the first word of the next sentence—increased relative to familiar items (embedded in metaphor-inviting contexts). Such findings contrast familiar and unfamiliar metaphors but equate unfamiliar instances of irony and metaphor.

Findings by Colston and Gibbs (2002) and Gibbs (1998a), allegedly attesting to different processes involved in comprehending irony and metaphor, can also be interpreted along the same lines. For example, Colston and Gibbs showed that utterances (*This one's really sharp*) embedded in irony-inducing contexts (17b) take longer to read than when embedded in metaphor-inducing contexts (17a):

(17)　a. You are a teacher at an elementary school. You are discussing a new student with your assistant teacher. The student did extremely well on her entrance examinations. You say to your assistant,
　　　"This one's really sharp."

　　　b. You are a teacher at an elementary school. You are gathering teaching supplies with your assistant teacher. Some of the scissors you have are in really bad shape. You find one pair that won't cut anything. You say to your assistant,
　　　"This one's really sharp."

However, an inspection of the stimuli reveals that while many of the metaphoric items might be conventional and thus have salient meanings, their ironic uses are less salient and are more dependent on contextual information for their interpretation. This, however, has not been established (out of or in a neutral context).

4.1.2 Later Integration Processes

Although irony and metaphor may be processed similarly initially, provided they share similar salience, they may nevertheless differ at the integration phase following the initial lexical access phase. According to the indirect negation view (Giora, 1995) and the retention hypothesis supplementing the graded salience hypothesis (Giora & Fein, 1999c), the salient, contextually incompatible (literal) meaning of both irony and metaphor should be retained for further processes. Indeed, findings show that, in the figuratively biasing context, instances of familiar and unfamiliar ironies and metaphors retain their salient, contextually incompatible literal meaning (Giora et al, 1998; Giora & Fein, 1999a,b,c; Williams, 1992). They show that when so-called irrelevant meanings partake in constructing the compatible meaning, they are not suppressed.

It should be noted, however, that irony and metaphor may have additional processes apart from those examined here, along which they may nevertheless differ (even when they converge in salience). For instance, while irony uses salient incompatible meanings for the purposes of contrastive comparison (Colston & O'Brien, 2000; Dews & Winner, 1995, 1997, 1999; Giora, 1995; Winner, 1988), in metaphor, the literal and the figurative meanings invite a search for similarities (Dews & Winner, 1997; Gentner & Wolff, 1997; Shen, 1989; Winner, 1988; Wolff & Gentner, 2000). Specifically, according to the class inclusion view (Glucksberg & Keysar, 1990; Shen, 1991, 1992, 1995; see also Glucksberg, 1989, 1991, 1998, 2001), the salient literal meaning of the metaphor vehicle (*gems* in *Children are precious gems*) represents the (abstract) ad hoc category of 'precious things'—the figurative meaning of the metaphor. In this category, 'children' and real-life/literal 'gems' are included as marginal and prototypical members, respectively. Indeed, class membership assumes some similarity (among other things) between category members. Although the class inclusion view rejects the retention hypothesis, positing suppression of the literal meaning following the construction of the category (see Gernsbacher et al., 2001; Glucksberg et al., 2001), this hypothesis has not gained enough support.

According to the alignment theory (Gentner & Wolff, 1997), processing novel metaphors involves an alignment process first, comparing the literal (topic) and figurative (vehicle) constituents of the metaphor before mapping relational properties from the source (vehicle) to the topic domain. Metaphors containing conventional vehicles, however, are processed only via class inclusion—that is, via mapping of properties from the vehicle to the topic domain (Bowdle & Gentner, 1995, 1999, 2001; Gentner & Bowdle, 2001).[20]

These differences in irony and metaphor interpretation (following the initial access phase) cannot be attested to by the findings reported here. The literal meaning, shown to be retained by both irony and metaphor, is instrumental in both kinds of comparison (whether via alignment or contrast). Different measures should be used to highlight the differences in irony and metaphor interpretations following the initial access phase.

4.1.3 Hemispheric Perspective

The question concerning the processes induced by metaphor and irony may benefit from research taking a hemispheric perspective. Research into hemisphere involvement in language comprehension reveals that the left hemisphere is sensitive to salient meanings (Burgess & Simpson, 1988a), whereas the right hemisphere specializes in linguistic reinterpretation (Bihrle, Brownell, Powelson, & Gardner, 1986; Brownell, Michel, Powelson & Gardner, 1983; Brownell & Potter, Bihrle, & Gardner, 1986; Zaidel, 1979). The graded salience hypothesis thus predicts a selective right-hemisphere involvement in comprehension of nonsalient language (e.g., irony) and a left-hemisphere involvement in processing salient language (e.g., conventional metaphors). If familiar metaphors are shown to behave like other instances of salient language, involving the left hemisphere, while unfamiliar ironies are shown to behave like other instances of nonsalient language, involving the right hemisphere, this will be consistent with the view that the factor determining the type of processing is neither literality (or nonliterality) nor type of trope, but degree of salience.

In the studies reported in Giora, Zaidel, Soroker, Batori, and Kasher (2000), we tested these hypotheses using the Hebrew adaptation of the Sarcasm Comprehension and Metaphor Comprehension subtests of Gardner and Brownell's (1986) Right Hemisphere Communication Battery (H[ebrew] RHCB). These subtests were administered to 27 right-brain damaged, 31 left-brain damaged, and 21 age-matched normal controls. To control for a confounding language deficit, the patients were also tested on a Hebrew adaptation of the Western Aphasia Battery.

The Sarcasm subtest of Gardner and Brownell (1986) comprises six vignettes (e.g., example 18), each followed by a factual question (18.2) and a metalinguistic question (18.1):

(18)   Anne and Roger were lawyers in the same law firm. Anne hated Roger because he often teased her for defending clients who couldn't afford to pay her fee. One day Anne was at the courthouse while Roger was defending a very wealthy man. He did a terrible job, completely mishandling what should have been a simple case. Anne said to another attorney, "Roger handled that case well."

Questions
1. When Anne said that Roger handled the case well, Anne was:
    a. making a mistake
    b. telling the truth
    c. telling a lie
    d. being sarcastic

2. Based on what you heard in the story, which of the following is true?
    a. Roger handled the case poorly
    b. Roger did a good job on the case.
    c. Roger was a tax lawyer.

The participants were tested individually. They listened to a recorded version of the vignettes, one at a time. When the recording of each vignette was over, they were asked to answer the comprehension question, then they were asked to select the most suitable choice in the metalinguistic question.

Analysis of the responses to the metalinguistic questions shows that, when the presence of aphasia is neutralized (using the aphasia quotient obtained from pretesting on the Hebrew adaptation of the Western Aphasia Battery as a covariate), left-brain-damaged individuals outperformed right-brain-damaged individuals. Such results imply right-hemisphere involvement in comprehension of nonsalient utterances (irony).

To test for familiar metaphor comprehension, 17 normal, 31 left-brain-damaged, and 27 right-brain-damaged individuals were administered the Verbal Metaphor subtest of the HRHCB (Gardner and Brownell, 1986). The test contains four highly conventional metaphors: *broken heart, warm heart, lend a hand, a hard man.* The participants had to provide oral verbal explications of the four metaphoric phrases.

Results show that performance by right-brain-damaged and normal controls (who understood all the metaphors perfectly) did not vary significantly. In contrast, left-brain-damaged individuals performed significantly worse than right-brain-damaged participants. The analysis of the results was not affected when aphasia was used as a covariate.[21]

These results are consistent with findings by Zaidel and Kasher (1989) and by Spence, Zaidel, and Kasher (1990) as they all suggest left-hemisphere involvement in comprehension of salient meanings. Spence et al. showed that commissurotomy individuals (whose free-field performance is presumably controlled by their disconnected left hemisphere) performed significantly worse than normal controls on all the tests except for conventional verbal metaphor. Complementarily, they are also consistent with findings by Bottini et al. (1994) which indicate right-hemisphere contribution to comprehension of unfamiliar metaphors.

However, they stand in contrast to findings by Gardner and Brownell and their colleagues (Brownell, 1988; Brownell, Potter, Michelow, & Gardner, 1984; Gardner & Brownell, 1986; Winner & Gardner, 1977; see also Van Lancker & Kempler, 1987, 1993). In these studies, right-brain-damaged participants tended to be biased toward the literal interpretation of verbal metaphors, while left-brain-damaged participants had a preserved sensitivity to the metaphoric interpretation. However, these studies tended to include pictorial multiple choices and thus involved pictorial interpretation. Indeed, in our studies, we found a poor correlation between performance on the Pictorial Metaphor subtest and the Verbal Metaphor subtest of the RHCB among right-brain-damaged individuals (Zaidel, Kasher, Batori, Soroker, & Graves, 2002).

Our findings seem to also somewhat disagree with findings by Anaki et al. (1998). Recall that in Anaki et al., conventional metaphors were processed initially both literally and metaphorically in the left hemisphere, but only metaphorically in the right hemisphere. Moreover, after a delay, the metaphoric meaning was retained only in the right hemisphere, while in the left hemisphere it was suppressed, retaining only the literal meaning. Such findings are consistent with the consensual division of labor between the hemispheres, associating the left hemisphere with sensitivity to literal meanings and the right hemisphere with sensitivity to nonliteral meanings. However, while in Anaki et al., the metaphors (*stinging*) had both literal and nonliteral meanings, our items had only one such metaphor (*lend a hand*). Indeed, with regard to this metaphor there was no difference in the bias toward the literal interpretation assigned by left-brain- and right-brain-damaged individuals (19% vs. 17%, respectively). In contrast, those with left brain damage had substantially more errors (21%) than those with right brain damage (7%) on the three metaphors that had no plausible literal interpretation. These findings, however, tie up with findings, suggesting that, unlike the left hemisphere, the right hemisphere is associated with peripheral meanings (Titone, 1998).

Taken together, these findings argue for the claim that, rather than assuming different processes for metaphor and irony comprehension, it is more plausible to assume different processes for utterances differing in salience and similar processes for utterance sharing similar salience (assuming, of course, that late processes show residue of early processes).

5. Literal versus Nonliteral Language

5.1 Early Activation Processes

According to the direct access view which assumes that rich and supportive context significantly governs comprehension, literal and nonliteral language should not be processed differently initially. Given equally strong contexts, both literal and nonliteral interpretations should be processed along the same patterns: they should be tapped directly, without any contextual incompatible interpretive phase at all (Sperber & Wilson, 1985/1996; for a review, see Gibbs, 1994). According to the graded salience hypothesis, the relevant distinction is not between literal and nonliteral language but between salient and nonsalient language. Salient language is assumed to be accessed via a direct look up in the mental lexicon. In contrast, nonsalient interpretations require inferential processes. Thus, ironies and literals would involve similar access processes if they are similarly salient. They would not involve similar access processes if they are different in salience.

In review of the findings presented in this book, it seems safe to conclude that initial differences between literal and nonliteral language are primarily a matter of salience imbalance rather than a matter of literality or nonliterality. Findings show that understanding salient language (metaphor and idiom) differs from understanding less or nonsalient language (metaphor and idiom). The various measures used to examine the underlying processes involved suggest that this difference goes beyond the extra length of time taken to process novel language and has to do with the requirement to revisit salient meanings when these meanings are used unconventionally. For instance, unfamiliar metaphors took longer to read than familiar metaphors relative to their literal controls (see Giora & Fein 1999c) or relative to a neutral control (see Pexman et al., 2000), and less familiar (variant) idioms took longer to read than their conventional forms (McGlone et al. 1994; Van de Voort & Vonk, 1995). In addition, familiar metaphors were processed figuratively initially (Anaki et al., 1998; Blasko & Connine, 1993; Williams, 1992), since their figurative meaning is salient. In contrast, less familiar metaphors were processed (only) literally initially, since only their literal meaning is salient.[22] Their figurative meaning lagged behind (with the exception of apt metaphors; Blasko & Connine, 1993; Gentner & Wolff, 1997; see the preceding discussion here), because it is nonsalient and has to be inferred.

Similarly, when salience was balanced, literal and figurative uses of language were processed along similar patterns. For instance, enjoying similar salience, familiar metaphors and their literal interpretations took equally long to read (Giora & Fein, 1999c) and activated their salient metaphorically and literally related concepts initially (Williams, 1992), regardless of contextual information. In contrast, unfamiliar metaphors took longer to read than their more accessible literal interpretations (Brisard, Frisson, and Sandra, 2001; Giora & Fein, 1999c).

Contrary to appearances, however, and although they suggest equivalent processes, these findings cannot be interpreted along the lines proposed by the direct access view. On the direct access view, processes should be affected by contextual information: embedded in a metaphorically biasing context, metaphors should be interpreted metaphorically exclusively. Similarly, embedded in literally biasing contexts, their counterparts should be interpreted literally exclusively. This, however, was not attested to. Alongside salient and contextually compatible meanings, salient but contextually incompatible meanings were available as well. In the metaphorically biasing context, it was the salient, contextually incompatible literal meaning that was always facilitated. In the literally biasing context, it was the salient, contextually incompatible metaphoric meaning that was accessed. Even though familiar metaphor and literal language involve similar lexical processes, these processes are not those predicted by the direct access view. Rather, they are motivated by salience and are impervious to inhibitory contextual effects.

5.2. Later Integration Processes

Unlike initial processes, later processes may distinguish literal from nonliteral language (see also Reinhart, 1976; for a different view, see chapter 7 in this volume; Giora, 2002a). Thus, familiar metaphors that avail their salient but contextually incompatible meanings in both the literally and the metaphori-

cally biasing contexts retain their literal meaning in the metaphorically biasing context but suppress their metaphoric meaning in the literally biasing context (Giora & Fein, 1999c; Williams, 1992). It seems that while the literal
meaning of metaphors is conducive to the interpretation of both salient and
nonsalient metaphor, the reverse is incorrect: metaphorical meanings do not
partake in constructing the literal interpretation of utterances (Giora & Fein,
1999c).[23]

6. Summary and Conclusions

The evidence presented so far supports the hypothesis that salience plays a primary role in determining the initial processes involved in language comprehension and production. Salient (conventional, familiar, frequent, prototypical)
meanings were shown to be accessed automatically, regardless of context, and,
when inappropriate, to be redressed and adjusted to contextual information and
authorial intent. Heavily weighted contextual information sped up activation
of contextually appropriate meanings. However, it was less successful at pre-
empting contextually inappropriate but (highly) salient meanings. Mostly, context became effective postlexically, either retaining contextually appropriate
and inappropriate meanings, allowing retrieval of less salient meanings, or
suppressing inappropriate meanings.

Thus, in an appropriate context, familiar idioms (*spill the beans*), whose
nonliteral meaning is salient, were shown to be processed nonliterally (e.g.,
'secret') initially and faster than were less familiar idioms (*didn't spill a single
bean*). Familiar metaphors (e.g., *stinging*), whose literal and nonliteral meanings are salient, were initially processed both literally ('mosquito') and figuratively ('remark'). In addition, such phrases took less time to comprehend than
did unfamiliar metaphors. Furthermore, unfamiliar metaphors (*Their bone
density is not like ours*) took longer to comprehend than their more accessible,
literal interpretations.

Whereas activation of salient meanings was immediate, irrespective of
contextual compatibility, suppression of contextually incompatible meanings
(e.g., the literal meaning of metaphors) was not automatic. The graded salience
and retention hypotheses, then, are only partly consistent with the modular assumptions that "the lexicon proposes and context disposes" (Bates, 1999). The
lexicon indeed "proposes"; however, access is salience-ordered rather than
only exhaustive. Besides, context does not always "dispose"; indeed, it tends
to discard contextually incompatible meanings when they are detrimental to
the intended meaning (e.g., the nonliteral meanings of salient metaphors embedded in literally biasing contexts). However, when contextually incompatible meanings are conducive to the intended meaning (e.g., the literal meaning
of metaphors), they are retained rather than suppressed and are used for various purposes, such as allowing for comparison and mapping processes. Moreover, suppression is not always effective even when it is required. Evidence
suggests that some highly salient meanings resist suppression even when they

are contextually irrelevant (the idiomatic meanings of familiar idioms embedded in a literally biased context).

These experimental findings have important implications for an understanding of the human mind. At first, they appear to paint a picture of the mind as unparsimonious: the mind activates every possible meaning, without tailoring initial access to contextual information. Consequently, on various occasions, contextually incompatible information is tapped either solely or in addition to contextually compatible information, and wastefully, so it seems. Yet, the experimental results presented here show that such salient, though unintended meanings are used thoughtfully, after all. For instance, resonating with the salient literally related meaning of metaphors allowed for the elaboration of the next text segment and served the purposes of introducing humorous turns (lines 49–53 and 640–641 in the appendix), innovating (lines 28–33, 328, 637–638, and 816–817 in the appendix), and agreeing (lines 453–458 and 699 in the appendix) and disagreeing with an idea (lines 663–665 and 788–789 in the appendix). Both speakers and writers go on harping on the same strings for the purpose of being coherent, cohesive, and pleasing. Although the mind may not be always economical, it is not wasteful, either.

Appendix

Transcription title: A Book about Death
Recording date: June 1989
Recording time: late evening
Recording location: Santa Barbara
Language: English
Setting: bedroom of private home
Participant names changed in speaker labels and utterances

1. PAMELA: Well you're right,
2. I think they're probably **flip** sides.
3. DARRYL: (TSK) I mean who [are you].
4. PAMELA: [But I'm] --
5. DARRYL: **Pollyanna**?
6. PAMELA: ... (SWALLOW) (TSK) ha=rdly=.
7. DARRYL: @@@
8. PAMELA: Hardly=,
9. Look **where I've come from**.
10. ... (H) I mean,
11. .. % (Hx) ... (H) % This chapter on heaven an hell,
12. it's really interesting.
13. DARRYL: ... Why,
14. PAMELA: I used to have this,
15. .. sort of,
16. .. % standard li=ne,

17.   that,
18.   ... % there were **two things I got out of=** .. **my marriage**.
19.   One was= a name that was easy to spell,
20.   and one was a %,
21.   .. (H) a child.
22.   (Hx) .. % ... that=,
23.   ... really got me **grounded**.
24.   But,
25.   (H) the fact of the matter is,
26.   ... (H) that the marriage itself=,
27.   I mean as **h=ellish** as it was,
28.   ... % .. It's like **it pulled me under,**
29.   **like a giant octopus,**
30.   **or a giant,**
31.   % ... **giant shark.**
32.   (H) **And it pulled me all the way under.**
33.   **and then,**
34.   (H) ... **and there I was,**
35.   **it was like the silent scream,**
36.   **and then,**
37.   .. **then I found that** .. **I% was on my own two feet** again.
38.   **and it r=eally was --**
39.   (H) .. (Hx) ... % .. % (Hx) (H) (TSK)
40.   **S- what was hell** in that .. that marriage became,
41.   ... **became a way out for me.**
42.   ... it was the **flip** side.
43.   (H) .. It's like sometimes **you go through things,**
44.   ... **and you come out the other side of them,**
45.   <WH you WH> .. **come out so much better.**
46.   ... (H) and if I hadn't had that,
47.   if I hadn't had --
48.   [(H)]
49.   DARRYL: **[It's not the way]** with food.
50.   PAMELA: ... What do you mean.
51.   DARRYL: ... (H) **What goes in [one way,**
52.   **PAMELA:**   [@ @ @ @ @
53.   **DARRYL:** <@ **doesn't come out** XXX @> @ @ @ @ @ @ @ @ @ @].
54.   PAMELA: (H) <@ kay @>,
55.   (H)]
56.   **comes out very hellish.**
57.   DARRYL: (H) Yeah=.
58.   PAMELA: **Very hellish.**
59.   DARRYL: .. So what <X did that [have to d]o X> --
60.   PAMELA: [But it's so] good /god/ --
61.   k=- **so good going down.**
62.   th-,

63. [I mean],
64. DARRYL: [what did] --
65. PAMELA: there's there's the opposites again.
66. DARRYL: it's it's [ma-] --
67. PAMELA: **[the] food is like,**
68. all [2unique2],
69. DARRYL: [2hey2].
70. PAMELA: and [3wonderful,
71. DARRYL: [3i- **it's major-league**3] **Yin and Yang**.
72. PAMELA: and **heavenly**3]
73. ... (TSK) **major league**.
74. DARRYL: .. What does that have to do with <u>heaven and hell</u> in the book.
75. PAMELA: ... Well,
76. ... % I'm just sort of= reiterating.
77. ... I could read you some.
78. DARRYL: [No].
79. PAMELA: [I] mean is that allowed?
80. DARRYL: ... No I I don't want to hear anything out of a book with,
81. .. chapter called heaven and hell.
82. PAMELA: You don't.
83. DARRYL: .. No.
84. PAMELA: Nkay.
85. Well then let's talk about [our vacation].
86. DARRYL: [I'm gonna be] **closed-minded** about it.
87. PAMELA: (TSK) ... Oh dear.
88. (Hx)
89. DARRYL: (H) [but,
90. PAMELA: [that's **hell**].
91. DARRYL: .. I] didn't like the book,
92. the way I --
93. the minute I looked at it.
94. PAMELA: ... You didn't.
95. DARRYL: No.
96. PAMELA: That's cause you,
97. DARRYL: ... That's because I have my own ideas about it,
98. I guess.
99. That I'm .. pretty comfortable with.
100. PAMELA: ... Ah.
101. DARRYL: ... I don't like re- --
102. I don't like reading books about what other people think about dying.
103. ... And I,
104. .. consider myself a real free [thinker when it comes to that] stuff.
105. PAMELA: [(TSK) (H) Well].
106. DARRYL: [2and that's2] --
107. PAMELA: [2<% remember2],
108. remember it in the movie %>,

109.   in Beetle Juice?

110.   the h=andbook for the recently deceased?

111.   DARRYL: Yeah?

112.   PAMELA: <X I mean X> books,

113.   wor=ds.

114.   I mean,

115.   ... n- they just become handbooks.

116.   You **distill** them.

117.   and use them in your own way.

118.   DARRYL: ... <P No P>,

119.   ... no,

120.   .. no I don't.

121.   .. I don't.

122.   ... (H) I,

123.   ... I come up with my own ideas about that stuff.

124.   PAMELA: ... And **where do you get the ideas**.

125.   DARRYL: ... Thought.

126.   PAMELA: ... And **where do you get those thoughts**?

127.   DARRYL: Processing what goes on around me.

128.   PAMELA: ... Well?

129.   ... Isn't= a book part of what goes on [around you]?

130.   DARRYL: [(H) Well %],

131.   ... % more from an oblique sou=rce.

132.   You know,

133.   <X when X> you're reading fiction,

134.   or,

135.   .. (H) or articles,

136.   or history or something like that,

137.   (H) but .. but,

138.   t- for me it's very difficult,

139.   to pick up a b=ook about d=eath.

140.   .. (H) that someone's written about death,

141.   Because it's [**bullshit**.

142.   PAMELA: [(H) @% well --

143.   DARRYL: Who knows what death] is.

144.   PAMELA: what --

145.   d- %>] --

146.   %What what this man has put in the boo- --

147.   You haven't read the book,

148.   one.

149.   You haven't read the book,

150.   so you don't know.

151.   ... [I haven't read the book so I don't know,

152.   DARRYL: [Yeah but I do know,

153.   it it's an awfully,

154.   it's it's] an awfully presumptuous thing,

155. PAMELA: but (H)],
156. DARRYL: to sit down and write a book about [death,
157. PAMELA: [d- --
158. DARRYL: when you haven't died].
159. PAMELA: It has,
160.   it] has,
161.   it has stories in there from,
162.   (H) from the Zen= an=d,
163.   .. f- it just **pools** on other different --
164. DARRYL: Wel[l the Zen can be **bullshit** too].
165. PAMELA: [% .. different sources].
166. DARRYL: I mean,
167.   [whoever wrote the book of Zen wasn't dead either.
168. PAMELA: [Well <F it .. might all= be **bullshit** F>,
169. DARRYL: @(Hx)]
170. PAMELA: But,
171.   you g- you g- you've gotta] **pull these ideas from your environment,**
172.   and what's gone on before=.
173.   ... (H) th- Th- %**the things I know most,**
174.   **about life and death** come from .. from= .. my g=randmother.
175.   ... (H) And having **gone through** all that %.
176.   ... with her.
177.   (H) And then it was interesting,
178.   cause reading I did after that,
179.   **substantiated** that experience.
180.   (H) For two months=,
181.   prior to her death,
182.   did I tell you this?
183.   that she dreamt?
184.   (H) about .. um,
185.   ... (H) she had this dream of falling off a building.
186.   .. (H) down o- --
187.   (H) just like that,
188.   .. that cartoon we saw.
189. DARRYL: ... Falling?
190.   .. Yeah,
191. PAMELA: The animation [cartoon].
192. DARRYL: [Yeah] .. yeah .. yeah.
193. PAMELA: (H) And it was like that.
194.   And that's what she was dreaming about.
195.   ... And then she said that she dreamt about,
196.   (H) u=m,
197.   .. all of her relatives,
198.   ... that had died.
199.   ... She wasn't dreaming about anybody who was living,
200.   but who had die=d.

201. DARRYL: (H)
202. PAMELA: ... And I read that l=ater.
203.   You know it was much later I read that in a book where,
204.   (H) ... u=m,
205.   ... (H) people who .. %had .. % technically died,
206.   and then have been revived.
207.   ... (H) saw .. relatives coming for them.
208. DARRYL: I've read that.
209. PAMELA: (H) Course that may be what happens=,
210.   .. prior to the big,
211.   ... the **big nothing**.
212. DARRYL: ... (H) So why are you reading a book about dying,
213. PAMELA: ... <P I don't know P>.
214. DARRYL: .. You don't know?
215. PAMELA: .. I have an interest in it.
216. DARRYL: Why.
217.   ... You're alive.
218.   Why are you r=eading a book about dying.
219. PAMELA: ... I've always been interested in it.
220. DARRYL: % <W Why W>.
221.   ... I mean,
222.   you know,
223.   y=ou ask someone why they're interested in electronics,
224.   and they can probably tell you.
225.   (H)
226. PAMELA: ... @@@@@
227.   (H) Well,
228.   I don't know,
229.   I guess it must,
230.   fo- some reason,
231.   %I was fascinated with that movie last night.
232.   .. with,
233.   ... (H) with uh,
234.   Lilian Gish and [B-],
235. DARRYL: [@]@@@
236. PAMELA: <@ and Bette Davis.
237.   (H) I couldn't believe.
238.   (H)@>
239.   These two old,
240.   ... I don't know,
241.   ... (Hx) I wanna say **windba=gs**.
242.   ... ha- but what h=appens to them,
243.   I,
244.   (H) Here's Betty Davis.
245.   I mean,
246. DARRYL: <VOX Sa=rah= VOX>?

247.   PAMELA: <X<@ z- yeah @>X: --
248.   (H) This incredible ... film **legend**.
249.   ... And we think of her in Jezebe=l,
250.   we think of her,
251.   (H) you know,
252.   smoking (H) .. cigarette smoke into the faces of .. William Holden and,
253.   (H) and the like.
254.   DARRYL: I don't,
255.   I've never seen those movies.
256.   PAMELA: ... (TSK) You've never seen Betty Davis movie?
257.   You've heard Kim- --
258.   % the song Betty Davis Eye=s?
259.   DARRYL: Sure.
260.   PAMELA: (H) ... And she's got,
261.   She got,
262.   The woman's got a re=p.
263.   DARRYL: (YAWN)
264.   PAMELA: And so she .. she lives,
265.   and,
266.   DARRYL: <YWN yeah YWN>.
267.   PAMELA: I guess it's j- looking at my mother,
268.   too,
269.   I n- --
270.   % (Hx)
271.   DARRYL: ... What does that have to do with why you're reading a book on death?
272.   [(H)]
273.   PAMELA: [(H)] .. I've always been interested in death.
274.   DARRYL: ... <F Why= F>.
275.   (H)
276.   PAMELA: Why,
277.   DARRYL: <WH @@ WH>
278.   PAMELA: ... (H) @@ [yeah I'm laughing].
279.   DARRYL: [What is] --
280.   PAMELA: (H) I'm thinking one thing my mother always used to say=,
281.   when I wouldn't go bicycling with my [father],
282.   DARRYL: [<@ ~Pamela],
283.   you are [2@@@,
284.   PAMELA: [2she would say2],
285.   DARRYL: You are @@@ @:2] --
286.   PAMELA: She would say,
287.   (H) <Q you'll be s=orry when we're dead Q>.
288.   DARRYL: @because you would[n't bicycling]?
289.   PAMELA: [@@ <@mm@>].
290.   because I wouldn't go bicycling with my father.
291.   DARRYL: Oh.

292. So i- w=- it's it's= --
293. (Hx)
294. PAMELA: You know,
295. (H) and I h- --
296. **I bit my tongue the other day**,
297. because remember,
298. .. you said to #Deven,
299. well,
300. I really want to **spend time** with you?
301. DARRYL: Yeah?
302. PAMELA: And then we went to the Chalk .. Fair,
303. and then he **took off** with #Tobias?
304. DARRYL: The Chop Fair?
305. PAMELA: The Chalk.
306. DARRYL: [Oh,
307. PAMELA: [The Chalk Fair].
308. DARRYL: .. unhunh]?
309. PAMELA: (H) and he **took off** with #Tobias?
310. DARRYL: Yeah?
311. PAMELA: ... Is that,
312. that,
313. .. that .. I wanted to say with him well your dad wanted to **spend time** with you today.
314. ... and why did you **run off**.
315. ... (TSK) And I didn't,
316. because I remembered,
317. ... (H) that my mother tried to guilt me the same way.
318. DARRYL: ... <YWN So that's why you're interested in death YWN>?
319. PAMELA: (SIGH)
320. DARRYL: (YAWN) (TSK)
321. PAMELA: ... (TSK) (TSK) <X maybe X> it's because my parents were ol=d?
322. when I was young?
323. very very young?
324. ... I've always=,
325. ... thought it's w=eird,
326. that we've been --
327. ... (H) I look down at my **body?**
328. **... and I f=eel like I'm in a spaceship**.
329. DARRYL: ... Yeah?
330. PAMELA: [@]@@@@
331. DARRYL: [<WH @@ WH>]
332. PAMELA: [2(H) I just,
333. DARRYL: [2That's why you're interested in death?
334. PAMELA: (H) n- and,
335. DARRYL: @@2]
336. PAMELA: I just2] think it's <MRC so damn weird MRC> **we're here**.

337. DARRYL: ... yeah?
338. ... Yeah,
339. well it i=s.
340. PAMELA: and,
341. and I was **constructed**,
342. ... inside of some w=oman's w=omb,
343. ... (H) and I was [... **burped out**],
344. DARRYL: [(H) So (H),
345. so **you're running**,
346. **you're running down the road**,
347. **all the way to the very end**.
348. Hunh?
349. PAMELA: . .. (H)
350. DARRYL: n- you're **you're you're already standing at the end of [the road]**,
351. PAMELA: [(H)]
352. DARRYL: .. [2trying to **figure out what hap2**]pens **there**?
353. PAMELA: [2%== well2],
354. % n- n- --
355. Maybe I --
356. maybe I'm just eager to **get back to where I wa=s**.
357. (H) [may-] --
358. DARRYL: [Back] into the womb?
359. PAMELA: % no no no,
360. I --
361. maybe,
362. .. maybe this whole **lifetime was just a really rude @interruption**.
363. DARRYL: of @what,
364. @ [<@ of what @>],
365. PAMELA: [<@ of what]ever it was @> I was doing,
366. before I was,
367. (H) **before my number came up**.
368. ... (H) and I was told I had to **come ba=ck here**.
369. (H)
370. DARRYL: ... (H) What if.
371. What .. if=.
372. PAMELA: (Hx) Unhu=nh.
373. DARRYL: What if worrying about that,
374. PAMELA: %See,
375. This is what you told #Deven.
376. DARRYL: well,
377. what if worrying about that,
378. has **got in the way=**,
379. ... **gotten in the way**,
380. of you making positive choices for yourself in your life.
381. ... (H) Instead of just worrying about,

382. w- that **you're he=re**,
383. ... and making the best out of it.
384. PAMELA: ... **Being here is=**,
385. .. is so <u>illusive</u> sometimes.
386. ... I mean .. <u>illusionary</u>.
387. DARRYL: ... Those are two different words=,
388. and they mean two different things.
389. PAMELA: Well it's <u>illusionary</u>.
390. ... I take back what I said about @<u>illusive</u>,
391. DARRYL: @@
392. PAMELA: (H) [@@ (H) @@@@]@@@ (H)
393. DARRYL: [Y- .. you may be <u>elusive</u>],
394. (H)
395. ... Well,
396. PAMELA: Mm,
397. DARRYL: Yeah but .. but .. but=,
398. % to me the whole point is is,
399. ... you have no idea,
400. what happens before or after.
401. ... You have no idea.
402. ... You can read books about it,
403. and you can .. (H) talk about it,
404. ... but the most pragmatic thing to do is,
405. to just ... live it.
406. PAMELA: ... Hm.
407. DARRYL: ... **Learn the rules of the game**,
408. **... play the game**,
409. PAMELA: For what.
410. DARRYL: ... For whatever you wa=nt.
411. ... For what%ever you wa=nt.
412. ... Be a= doctor,
413. or a screen writer,
414. or an actress,
415. or a philanthropist,
416. or= an explorer=?
417. PAMELA: ... <VOX An explorer VOX>.
418. DARRYL: ... Do what you want,
419. with the **time you have**.
420. Learn,
421. ... give,
422. ... whatever.
423. PAMELA: ... Love?
424. DARRYL: %Lo=ve?
425. PAMELA: [<VOX Love]?
426. DARRYL: [@@@]
427. PAMELA: (H) Could [2I2] love you?

428. DARRYL: [2X2]
429. @
430. PAMELA: @@@ @@@
431. (H) Could I love you_**while I'm here** VOX>?
432. .. (H) (Hx)
433. DARRYL: (H)
434. PAMELA: ... (H)
435. DARRYL: Don't make light of what I'm saying.
436. PAMELA: ... N=o.
437. ... Think about the kids.
438. What are --
439. Who are,
440. who are these kids.
441. ... <W Who are these **kids** W>.
442. .. @ (H)
443. ... These little **seedpods,**
444. ... (H) that **have been sent** [_our way_].
445. DARRYL: [(H)] (Hx)
446. ... Well,
447. .. sometimes for me,
448. they are a **whip and a hairshirt.**
449. PAMELA: @[@@@@@]
450. DARRYL: [<WH @@@@ WH>]
451. PAMELA: (H) They're little,
452. .. little,
453. ... **little** _lessons_.
454. @@@ (H)
455. DARRYL: ... (TSK) .. Yeah,
456. ah,
457. yeah I mean,
458. sometimes **I have** _to be_ [_real prep_-] --
459. PAMELA: [(GASP)]
460. DARRYL: .. What.
461. PAMELA: XX,
462. #Natalie asked me about Santa Claus today.
463. DARRYL: What did she,
464. [what did she say],
465. PAMELA: [In the laundro]mat.
466. She said,
467. .. mom,
468. Santa Claus isn't,
469. ... I mean,
470. d- is there a for real sa- Santa Claus?
471. .. I said a for real Santa Claus,
472. you mean a man who lives .. at the north pole?
473. .. (H) she said yeah,

474. I said no.
475. ... (H) And she said,
476. well,
477. who are the other ones.
478. I said well,
479. they're the spirit of Santa Claus,
480. and,
481. ... (H) They represent Santa Claus.
482. they --
483. (H) They're a picture [of Santa Claus].
484. DARRYL: [they're Santa Claus's] agents.
485. PAMELA: .. @@@
486. (H) They're pictures of Santa Claus.
487. ... Is my mike on.
488. DARRYL: Unhunh?
489. PAMELA: Oh,
490. [Okay.
491. DARRYL: [(H) It sure is,
492. PAMELA: (H) and],
493. DARRYL: You just] damn near broke the damn needle there?
494. PAMELA: And then she said,
495. ... and then she said well,
496. who fills the stockings.
497. ... and I kind of,
498. I said,
499. ... **love fills the stockings**.
500. DARRYL: Oh Go=d,
501. [~Pamela].
502. PAMELA: [@@@ She] said,
503. (H) she said,
504. oh you mean,
505. ... adults=?
506. DARRYL: (H)
507. PAMELA: ... Adults who wanna show you how much they care,
508. and I said,
509. ... (H) Yeah.
510. Adults=,
511. adults around who love you.
512. ... Fill those stockings.
513. ... (H) And I said,
514. She said but some adults= talk about Santa Claus,
515. I said that's because,
516. .. they wanna believe in Santa Claus.
517. (H) And that's what I told her,
518. I said,
519. I wanna believe in Santa Claus.

520.   .. In fact sometimes I d=o believe in Santa Claus.
521.   ... and that,
522.   ... that really [**satisfied** her].
523.   DARRYL: [(H)]
524.   PAMELA: (H) [<F But I thought] it was very pragmatic of her to ask about that in June F>.
525.   DARRYL: [yeah but what d-],
526.   PAMELA: (H) I thought to myself,
527.   if she asked me that,
528.   like,
529.   [on] [2Christmas2] [3Eve3],
530.   DARRYL: [Well] [2she2]   [3must have gotten some3] sort of a signal somewhere.
531.   >ENV: [2((MICROPHONE))2]
532.   PAMELA: Today in the laundromat?
533.   DARRYL: <X I mean X> what does that have to do with death.
534.   ... <WH @@@ WH>
535.   PAMELA: ... Well,
536.   .. we were talking about
537.   .. death= and illusions,
538.   DARRYL: (H)
539.   PAMELA: The illusions of this life,
540.   .. (H) You know,
541.   I --
542.   (H) .. % I,
543.   % I,
544.   DARRYL: X X [X],
545.   PAMELA: [<VOX My] favorite word when I was twelve VOX>,
546.   ... was paradox.
547.   DARRYL: ... <YWN why YWN>.
548.   PAMELA: (H) Because,
549.   ... I thought,
550.   .. any wor=d,
551.   ... that was defined.
552.   .. I mean I remember the definition.
553.   .. (H) that I learned in seventh grade.
554.   .. (H) That was paradox.
555.   .. (H) Seemingly contrary.
556.   DARRYL: ... (TSK) [Seemingly <P X X X P>].
557.   PAMELA: [seemingly con-],
558.   (H) And I had a hard time with the definition.
559.   .. (H) so I thought .. God.
560.   (H) a wor=d.
561.   (H) .. that I'm supposed to lear=n,
562.   (H) and I get this definition,
563.   and I don't even understand [the defini=tion].

564. DARRYL: [the definition=] of the word paradox,
565. is by design ambiguous.
566. ... **Chew on this one**.
567. An ambiguous paradox.
568. PAMELA: ... Is that redundant?
569. DARRYL: Yes.
570. PAMELA: [@ (GROAN) @] @@ (H)
571. DARRYL: [@ (GROAN) <WH @@ WH>]
572. PAMELA: ... Well,
573. .. that was age twelve.
574. .. so %-,
575. that was very close to #Deven's age,
576. when,
577. ... (H) I sort of=,
578. .. **bit my teeth into that one**.
579. DARRYL: **Bit your teeth**,
580. hunh?
581. PAMELA: (H) And then,
582. yeah.
583. DARRYL: [@@@@]@@
584. PAMELA: [as I went],
585. @@@[2@@@@2]
586. DARRYL: [2@@@@@@@@2]
587. PAMELA: (H) I,
588. DARRYL: (H) @@
589. PAMELA: **Took a bite**?
590. DARRYL: <@ is,
591. **is that like c=utting it [in the] nip**= @>?
592. PAMELA: [@@]
593. DARRYL: @@@@@@@@@
594. PAMELA: (H) ... I,
595. I get a little [ahead <@ of myself @>.
596. DARRYL: [@@@@@ (H)]
597. <@ Yeah I guess you do @>.
598. @@@@@ (H)
599. PAMELA: [(H) Oh God I hope this doesn't] all sound real s=tupid.
600. DARRYL: [(H) X= @]
601. PAMELA: @@@
602. (H) ... Well.
603. .. % From,
604. .. from twelve to seventeen,
605. then,
606. ... that went from paradox,
607. ... to,
608. ... **the invisible**,
609. .. **interfacing with the visible**.

610. DARRYL: ... (TSK) Hunh?
611. PAMELA: @@@
612. **The invisible**.
613. **... inter[facing] with the visible**.
614. DARRYL: [facing X]
615. PAMELA: (H) For everything you see.
616. You can look at me and I'm a body.
617. (H) You see eyes,
618. ... you see .. body,
619. you see hair,
620. you see,
621. @@[@@@]
622. DARRYL: [@@@]@@
623. PAMELA: ((SLAP)) <@ S- get your hands off me @>.
624. [(H)]
625. DARRYL: [(H)]
626. PAMELA: Y=ou <HI see HI> all those things,
627. right?
628. DARRYL: [<VOX yea=h VOX>].
629. PAMELA: [But there's] **there's me**=,
630. **insi=de**.
631. .. that's ... invisible.
632. DARRYL: ... It's not,
633. ... it's it's n-,
634. it's it's,
635. PAMELA: (H) I mean,
636. (H) what if,
637. what if you **took the same ... spacesuit**?
638. **... and you put another spirit into it**.
639. ... It would be [a different person,
640. DARRYL: [<@ **It'd say,**
641. **let me out** @>.
642. $ SIX SECONDS OF MUTUAL LAUGHTER
643. PAMELA: It would be,
644. .. a different person.
645. DARRYL: ... <X You're X> [right].
646. PAMELA: [I] wouldn't [2be2] me.
647. DARRYL: [2right2].
648. That's right.
649. It'd be a different [personality].
650. PAMELA: [(H)] So .. I,
651. .. I,
652. ... I think it's=,
653. [very fascinating],
654. DARRYL: [Of course that's a hypothetical],
655. [2how do you know that2].

656.   PAMELA: [2(H)2] It's very [interesti- --
657.   DARRYL: [maybe,
658.   may-,
659.   PAMELA: (Hx)
660.   DARRYL: Maybe,
661.   PAMELA: @@@]
662.   DARRYL: May=be=],
663.   Maybe the **spacesuit** has something to do=,
664.   with,
665.   .. with **who's inside of it**.
666.   .. (H) I mean you don't know [that].
667.   PAMELA: [(TSK) (H)] Wouldn't that be f- a fascinating
       [2experiment2].
668.   DARRYL: [2<A well no,
669.   be2]cause look A>.
670.   .. **genes**.
671.   .. **genetic makeup**.
672.   .. It's proven.
673.   .. and **that's part of the spacesuit**,
674.   **if you wanna use that**.
675.   ... that that your **genetic makeup**,
676.   .. **largely determines who you are**.
677.   PAMELA: .. You mean .. **the chemical bath I sit in**?
678.   DARRYL: Yeah.
679.   ... As it were.
680.   .. (H) (Hx)
681.   PAMELA: ... Hm=.
682.   .. sort of **dictates how I feel about being in** [.. **this spacesuit**].
683.   DARRYL: [Ye=s.
684.   yes right].
685.   .. r- you know,
686.   and it depends on your **brain dolphin** level,
687.   [and],
688.   PAMELA: [(H)] **My brain dolphin**,
689.   XX [X] X,
690.   that's **sweet**.
691.   DARRYL: [mm],
692.   ... you [2know2]?
693.   PAMELA: [2hunh2].
694.   DARRYL: <X i- depend am- X>,
695.   yeah.
696.   Yeah.
697.   ... A lot of it has to do with the with the,
698.   .. the r=- --
699.   ... (TSK) (H) **five dollars and ninety-eight cents worth of**
700.   **chemicals and compounds that make you**.

701. PAMELA: ... % We could **spend a lot of our life**,
702. trying to,
703. to contradict that.
704. DARRYL: <F Why= F>.
705. PAMELA: (H) Well,
706. [Because],
707. DARRYL: [@@@] @
708. PAMELA: (H) <@ it may be @> **a very bad [chemi]cal bath**.
709. DARRYL: [(H)] @@@
710. PAMELA: (H) We [may],
711. DARRYL: [(SNIFF)]
712. PAMELA: %b- **been put into something that's completely acid**,
713. **to our true essence**.
714. (H)
715. DARRYL: .. Yeah,
716. but we [have no choice in that matter].
717. PAMELA: [and we **spend a lifetime**],
718. ... that's right.
719. ... n- well,
720. no (H) apparent choice.
721. ... No choice=,
722. ... that we know of.
723. DARRYL: ... mn yeah.
724. ... hm .. hm .. y- .. yeah.
725. ... but but rather than than,
726. PAMELA: ... (H) I mean I'm not,
727. .. I'm not,
728. ... **I'm not all bent out of shape about [it]**.
729. DARRYL: [@]@@[2@@@2]
730. PAMELA: [2(H) but I've just2],
731. <X but I was [thi- X>] --
732. DARRYL: [<@ X you're] just [2really interested in dea=th @>.
733. PAMELA: [2my yearning,
734. my yearning2],
735. DARRYL: @@@@@@2]
736. PAMELA: my yearning is n- --
737. .. [2maybe2] **not to run ahead** and,
738. DARRYL: [2(H)2]
739. PAMELA: .. and,
740. ... and,
741. **and get to the exit**.
742. (H) as --
743. ... ()
744. DARRYL: (H) [w-] --
745. PAMELA: [I] mean maybe it's the yearning %,
746. .. for **where I was before I was born**.

747. DARRYL: (H) Well how is <u>write</u> - --748.<u>reading a book written</u> by some **schmuck,**
749. who thinks he's an expert on d=eath,
750. (H)
751. PAMELA: Well he may or may not be a **schmuck,**
752. ~Darryl.
753. DARRYL: ... (H) Anyone who sits down to write a <u>book</u> about d=eath,
754. .. with the hopes of **enlightening,**
755. his fellow human beings,
756. (H) .. is in my **book** a **schmuck.**
757. PAMELA: ... (TSK) (H) Well now,
758. ... <VOX them's **fightin'** [wor=ds,
759. DARRYL: [@@@@@@]
760. PAMELA: boy= VOX>.
761. @ <@ you could @> --
762. (H)
763. DARRYL: Who the hell is someone,
764. .. anyone,
765. who's <@ living,
766. to sit down @> and write a book about dea=th.
767. ... @[@]@@@@@ (H)
768. PAMELA: [@]
769. DARRYL: Now really.
770. PAMELA: (H)
771. DARRYL: You know?
772. %it's like,
773. % it's these --
774. .. %this --
775. %this is the .. person who **falls under that .. that,**
776. **(H) .. category of expert** that I disdain so much.
777. ... I know a [lot about-] --
778. PAMELA: [(H) Maybe] he's a <MRC **very old soul** MRC>.
779. (Hx)
780. DARRYL: .. (Hx)
781. PAMELA: ... plea=[se].
782. DARRYL: [<@ <u>like Old] [2King Cole</u> @>2]
783. PAMELA: [2@@@2]
784. $ DARRYL LAUGHS NINE SECONDS, AND PAMELA JOINS FOR TWO MORE
785. Hm=.
786. ... (TSK) (H) Well,
787. (Hx)
788. DARRYL: (TSK) If **he's a very old soul,**
789. **he should keep it to [himself.**
790. PAMELA: [(H)] You know,
791. % % (Hx)

792.   ... I felt 1- after #Gretchen died,
793.   it was all .. rather unfair.
794.   I mean,
795.   % % **the** <u>tides</u> at work,
796.   **... just <u>swept over</u>** her so quickly.
797.   ...(H) and it [was like],
798.   DARRYL: [But really] not so quickly,
799.   it was,
800.   <X<P yeah P>X>,
801.   I mean,
802.   it was something that had started in her a very long time ago.
803.   PAMELA: ... She was **gone** in less than,
804.   ... five months.
805.   .. six --
806.   eight months.
807.   DARRYL: ... (H) (THROAT)
808.   PAMELA: ... And it just=,
809.   ... amazes me=.
810.   (H) I mean,
811.   you can't **drag** on and on and on about a fellow creature who's **gone**,
812.   (H) ... but I still miss my grandmother.
813.   ... and I,
814.   ... I certainly miss my do=g.
815.   ... (H) I just think it's so wei=rd,
816.   that **they're go=ne**.
817.   **... and <u>where did they go to</u>**.

6

Jokes

Most theories of joke comprehension focus on one type of jokes—semantic jokes that involve double entendre.[1] Looking into this genre, most theorists proposed that jokes involve entertaining two incompatible interpretations. The following joke may serve to illustrate the claim:

(1) Q: Do you believe in clubs for young men?
     A: Only when kindness fails.

According to Attardo (1994, 1996a,b, 2000, 2001) and Attardo, Attardo, Baltes, and Petray (1994), processing a joke begins with processing one sense (the 'social groups' meaning of the ambiguous word *clubs*) which is retained up to the point at which the initial interpretation no longer makes sense (*fails*). At this point, termed the disjunctor, the interpretation process is disrupted. If the disruption is minimal, it affects reinterpretation of the initial sense, resulting in a different/opposed sense (which would now be 'sticks'). If it is not minimal, the comprehender may dismiss the text as ill-formed. Attardo and his colleagues assume Raskin's (1985) view of jokes as centering on opposition relations obtaining between the two senses/scripts ('social groups' vs. 'sticks').[2]

For Coulson and Kutas (1998, 2001; see also Coulson, 2001: 77–82), it is script-shifting (from the 'social groups' to the 'sticks' script) termed "frame shifting" that accounts for joke comprehension. Compared to alternative surprise endings that do not involve script or frame shifting, jokes' endings are costly precisely because of the need to switch from one script or frame to another.

Curcó (1995, 1996a,b, 1998) assumes a different processing model in which an assumption that is weakly manifest (the 'social groups' meaning of *clubs*) becomes strongly manifest upon encounter of the "target assumption" (involving the 'stick' meaning of *clubs*). The contrast between the two assumptions triggers this shift from weak to strong manifestation and makes up joke comprehension. Such a view thus assumes that the initial interpretation (the 'social groups' meaning) of the ambiguity involved (*clubs*) is retained for contrastive purposes.

De Palma and Weiner (1992), Giora (1991), and Weiner (1996) posit that the structure of jokes is categorial (à la Rosch, 1973), starting with the most prototypical (salient) member of the set and ending with a highly marginal (less salient) member.[3] Such a view suggests that a humorous "surprise" does not hinge on a stark difference between two interpretations. Rather, it depends on the likelihood of the less accessible/salient interpretation to be relevant to and included within the category proposed initially. A humorous surprise, then, does not constitute an entirely unthinkable option (Giora, 1991), but only a less salient one—one that should not have but which nevertheless has escaped our attention because of our salience-prone mind (on how salience is defined in terms of familiarity, frequency, conventionality, and prototypicality, see chapter 2 in this volume).[4]

In Giora (1991, 1995), however, I further proposed that unlike other "nonliteral" discourses that retain incompatible interpretations (irony and metaphor; see chapters 4–5 in this volume), joke comprehension involves attenuation of the salient but contextually incompatible meaning (the 'social groups' interpretation of *club*) following the disjunctor point (*fail*). Here I examine this suppression assumption within the framework of the graded salience view of joke comprehension (for a similar view, see Gernsbacher & Robertson, 1995).

1. The Role of Salience and Context in Joke Comprehension

Most jokes make up a discourse that best exposes our tendency to opt for the salient interpretation first. They exploit the fact that we wear mental blinkers, which, in the absence of apparent evidence to the contrary, keep us attending to the most salient interpretation initially. Note how we are caught entirely off guard when we realize that a person who has a *drinking problem* is, in fact, one who spills liquid all over himself while drinking (*Flying High* by Abrahams, Zucker, & Zucker, 1980). Jokes indeed tend to involve some salience imbalance that invites the comprehender to process the more salient but eventually incompatible meaning first ('drinking alcohol excessively') in order to dispense with it and activate a less salient but congruent meaning.

To lead our "one-track mind" down "the garden path," the initial context of a joke is usually unambiguous, compatible with the salient meaning, so that this interpretation is retained up until the punch line, at which point a sudden incongruity forces reinterpretation. The following joke (taken from Coulson & Kutas, 1998) illustrates the role of salience in joke interpretation and the collaborative function of a supportive context (see also chapter 2 in this volume):

(2) By the time Mary had had her fourteenth child,
      she'd finally run out of names
      to call her husband.

The salient meaning of *names* is associated with 'proper names'. In addition, the most plausible interpretation of *name calling* in the context of childbirth is also associated with 'proper names'. Furthermore, the most plausible interpretation of 'running out of *names*' in the context of the birth of a fourteenth child is further supportive of the 'proper names' interpretation. Salience and contextual information harmonize here: contextual information is highly supportive and predictive of the salient meaning of the polysemous word. The punch line, therefore, comes as a sheer surprise.

The strongly felt mismatch of meaning salience and context at the disjunctor point triggers the need for a revisitation. The more salient meaning or script ('proper names') has to be abandoned in favor of a less salient interpretation or script ('derogatory epithets').[5]

Note that even when the initial context is supportive of the less salient meaning, the salient meaning is activated initially, regardless of context. As illustration, consider the following jokes. They all hinge on the ambiguous nature of words that have more than one coded meaning but at least one highly salient meaning, which is activated faster, accidentally resulting in contextual misfit, allowing for the next coded meaning to reach sufficient levels of activation as well. In (3), the salient meaning of the punch line is syntactic information; in (4), it is the idiomatic meaning that is more salient:

(3) What do you call Santa's helpers?
      Subordinate Clauses.

(4) How do you get holy water?
      Boil the hell out of it.

Revisitation of salient meanings rather than mere surprise ending may indeed be a major factor in accounting for the largely acknowledged difficulty of joke interpretation. Indeed, as shown by Coulson and Kutas (1998), other forms of discourse involving less salient, unexpected items, which do not require reinterpretation (or script-shift) of salient meanings, have been found to be less effort consuming. For instance, in their study, nonjoke texts (5a), having an equally unpredictable (low cloze probability) ending as jokes (5b), diverging from jokes in that they do not involve reinterpretation (of salient meanings or scripts), were faster to read than jokes:

(5) By the time Mary had had her fourteenth child, she'd finally run out of names to call her
      (a) offspring [*Nonjoke ending*]
      (b) husband [*Joke ending*]

Crucially, then, for a joke to be understood it should involve revisitation of initially activated concepts. Such revisitation, it is hypothesized here, involves suppression of the initially activated concept(s) so that the compatible meaning may get across.

2. The Suppression Hypothesis

The theory of joke comprehension proposed here assumes that understanding a joke involves a sequential process upon which a salient meaning of a key word or expression is activated initially[6] and suppressed at the punch line, disjunctor position, or even later on. At this point, this meaning has no role in constructing the intended meaning. Rather, it may stand in the way and interfere with comprehension. According to the retention hypothesis (Giora & Fein, 1999c; see also chapters 2, 4–5 in this volume), meanings are retained as long as they are conducive to the interpretation process but discarded if they interfere with comprehension. Indeed, comprehenders who are less able at suppressing salient meanings have been shown to be poor comprehenders (Gernsbacher, 1990, 1993; see also chapter 3 in this volume).[7]

In a pilot study (Colston, Giora, & Katz, 2000), we tested the suppression hypothesis. We aimed to show that the meaning activated initially is suppressed later on, at offset of the punch line. In our study, participants were presented 36 contrived jokes (6 below) and 12 nonjoke fillers. The jokes involved an ambiguous word (*ear*) whose less salient meaning ('corn') is the contextually appropriate meaning following the second line and at the punch line position:

(6)   My friend asked me to look at his ear*
       but it was covered with butter*
       and salt.*

---

probes (displayed at *):
Related salient meaning: hearing
Related less salient meaning: corn
Unrelated: address
Nonword: drammer

Participants self-paced their readings of jokes (and nonjokes), which were displayed line by line on a computer screen. They had to make lexical decisions as to whether a letter string, displayed on the screen immediately after offset of each line (see * in example 6), was a word or a nonword in English.

Results indeed demonstrate that, as anticipated, the original meaning of the key word (*ear*) assumed to be salient ('hearing') was available immediately after offset of the key word (at the end of the first line).[8] Similarly, after offset of the second segment, its levels of activation were still marginally significant.

However, at the final punch line position, the initially activated meaning was no longer available: it was no more activated than the unrelated probe, suggesting that, at this point, it underwent suppression (see figure 6.1; for similar results, see also Vaid, Heredia, Hull, Martinez, & Gerkens, 2001; Vaid, Hull, Gerkens, & Heredia, 2000; and Vaid, Hull, Heredia, Gerkens, & Martinez, in press). As for the less salient appropriate meaning, it never reached sufficient levels of activation, suggesting that immediately after offset of the joke, comprehenders have not yet captured the intended meaning that might have required longer processing time). However, Vaid et al., who provided for a longer delay, found priming effects for the less salient apprpriate meaning.

The suppression hypothesis may indeed account for other findings regarding joke comprehension. Given that suppression comes with a cost (Gernsbacher, 1990), the suppression hypothesis predicts that an interpretation process that does not require suppression would be less costly than one that requires suppression. This prediction is consistent with the findings in Coulson and Kutas (1998) discussed earlier. Consider, again, example (5). While both *husband* and *offspring* were shown to be similarly unpredictable or probable given the preceding context (having cloze probability of 4% and 2%, respectively), only *husband* will induce suppression of the salient meaning of ('proper') 'name' so that a less salient concept ('epithets associated with insult') will be activated. In contrast, although *offspring* is a low probability ending, suppressing the originally highly salient meaning of 'name' is not required. On the contrary, like the probable ending 'child', *offspring* involves retaining the notion of 'proper name' with which it is consistent, since, like 'child', it represents the same probable concept, only by means of an unexpected word. No wonder it took less time to process than *husband*.

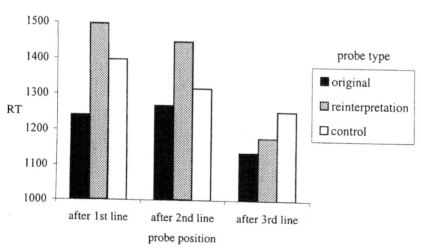

Figure 6.1 Mean response time (RT, in milliseconds) to probes presented immediately (0 ISI) after the first, the second, and the third line of the joke.

Or, consider another example (taken from Coulson & Kutas, 1998b):

(7)   He is so modest he pulls down the shade to change his
         mind [*Joke ending*]
         jacket [*Nonjoke ending*]
         clothes [*Conventional ending*]

According to the suppression hypothesis, for the joke to get through, the salient meaning of *change* ('replace', 'take off clothes'), which is also the one invited by the context (having a cloze probability of 42%), has to be suppressed so that a less salient meaning of *change* ('change of mind'), having a cloze probability of 6%), can be evoked and integrated into the context. Although *changing a jacket* is a less salient, less frequent expression than *changing clothes* (having a cloze probability of 3%), it need not involve suppressing the salient ('replace') meaning of *change*, because it is an extension of that self-same meaning. Indeed, subjects took less time to read the nonjoke (*jacket*) than the joke (*mind*) ending.

Assuming the graded salience hypothesis, the suppression hypothesis further predicts that the more salient the information, the more difficult it is to suppress (Giora, 1997b; see also chapters 2 and 8 in this volume).[9] Findings in Coulson and Kutas (1998, 2001) serve to support this hypothesis as well. They show that when the meaning to be rejected is not (what I term) highly salient (having a low cloze probability), joke comprehension is less costly than when it is.

In Coulson and Kutas, experimental sentences were divided into two classes of sentences, determined by the probability of the most popular response for each sentence on a separately administered cloze task. For what they term "low constraint" sentences, this value was less than 40%; for what they term "high constraint" sentences, this value was greater than 40%. Note that, in this case, high and low constraint sentences correspond to high and low salient meanings (of those key words to be reinterpreted at the punch line), although for probability to be correlated with salience, it should be measured in a neutral rather than in a highly biased sentence context. As illustration, consider the following low constraint (8) and high constraint (9–10) sentence jokes (cloze probability percentages in parentheses):

(8)   Statistics indicate that Americans spend $80 million a year on games of chance, mostly
         weddings (0%) [*Joke ending*]
         dice (4%) [*Nonjoke ending*]
         gambling (16%) [*Conventional ending*]

The most popular ending of (8) constitutes only 16% of the possible endings, suggesting that there are many more possible endings. This indicates that the most popular ('gambling') meaning of *game of chance* (on which one can spend a lot of money) is not what is termed here highly salient: given these results, it is not necessarily the first meaning that comes to mind. In contrast, the most popular endings in (9) and (10) have a lot fewer competitors, suggesting that they are foremost on one's mind:

(9) I decided to start saving for a rainy day, so I went to a savings and loan and deposited my
     umbrella (0%) [*Joke ending*]
     paycheck (4%) [*Nonjoke ending*]
     money (64%) [*Conventional ending*]

(10) When I asked him how long I should cook the noodles he said at least ten
      inches (0%) [*Joke ending*]
      seconds (0%) [*Nonjoke ending*]
      minutes (96.39%) [*Conventional ending*]

The cloze probability (64% and 96.39%) for the endings of (9) and (10), respectively, attest to the high salience of the meanings ('money', 'time') associated with the 'key' words (*savings, how long*) involved in these jokes. According to the graded salience hypothesis, suppressing such highly salient meanings should be more difficult than suppressing less salient meanings. Indeed, using moving windows (see chapter 2 in this volume), Coulson and Kutas (1998) showed that jokes involving highly salient meanings (9–10) took longer to read than nonjokes and jokes involving less salient meanings (8). The latter did not exhibit a significant difference from nonjoke endings.

Moreover, as predicted by the suppression hypothesis, these results were more pronounced for participants who exhibited comprehension of the jokes than for those who did not. Given that suppression is costly (Gernsbacher, 1990) and that good comprehenders outperform poor comprehenders when processing requires suppression (Gernsbacher & Robertson, 1995), such results are consistent with the suppression hypothesis.

Findings from event-related brain potentials lend further support to the hypothesis that joke comprehension involves suppression. In another study, Coulson and Kutas (2001) compared event-related brain potentials recorded from the scalp as participants read joke and nonjoke sentences. As mentioned earlier, the difficulty of integrating a given word into an established context is correlated with N400 brain wave amplitude. N400 brain wave amplitude is largest for items with low cloze probability such as semantic anomalies, and it is smallest for easily integrated items with high cloze probability such as best completions. Accordingly, the suppression hypothesis predicts that joke comprehension would involve N400 amplitude to a greater extent than nonjokes. It also predicts that the effect would be greatest for jokes involving highly salient meanings than for those involving less salient meanings, since salient meanings are harder to suppress. Moreover, it predicts that this effect would be more pronounced among good than among poor comprehenders (cf. Gernsbacher & Robertson, 1995).

Findings in Coulson and Kutas (2001) indeed serve to support the suppression hypothesis. They show that jokes elicited larger N400 components than nonjokes (ending with similarly cloze probability items) and that this effect was greatest when highly salient meanings (in high constraint sentence jokes) were involved (examples 9–10). Furthermore, they showed that this pattern was most pronounced among participants whose performance on the comprehension questions suggested that they understood most of the jokes, thus also suggesting that they suppressed the incompatible, though salient, meaning.

It could be argued that cloze probability reflects probability within a context—the extent to which a context is predictive—not salience. This is certainly true but should be taken with a grain of salt with regard to the studies in question. Consider, for instance, example (7). Given a context in which one is very shy, it is much more plausible that one would pull down the shade to change his or her jacket (the low probability item) than his or her clothes (the high probability item), the latter being the norm, and does not require an extremely shy person. However, the collocation 'change clothes' is more salient (frequent/conventional) than 'change a jacket'; hence the high cloze probability of the former relative to the low cloze probability of the latter. Similarly, 'saving money' and 'saving a paycheck' (example 9) mean more or less the same thing and should be equally predictable in the given context. They differ in terms of salience, however. While the collocation 'saving money' is very salient (familiar/conventional), 'saving a paycheck' is not. No wonder the former obtained a high cloze probability, while the latter did not. Cloze probability indeed measures predictability or probability within a context. This need not obscure salience or familiarity effects altogether, particularly not in a joke context in which context is presumed to be highly supportive of the salient meaning.

For Coulson and Kutas (Coulson, 2001; Coulson & Kutas, 2001), however, these findings support the hypothesis that joke comprehension involves a frame shift. Frame shifting occurs when elements of a given message-level representation are mapped onto a new frame. Jokes, they contend, are deliberately constructed to suggest one frame while evoking elements consistent with another. The notion of frame shifting is not inconsistent with the assumption of the graded salience hypothesis concerning joke comprehension. It is plausible to assume that a word meaning involves activating its unmarked contextual information or frame. Moreover, jokes do not always hinge on explicit word meanings but, rather, on frame anticipation. Although the following joke may involve a less salient reading of *something* as referring to humans, it is possible that contextual information such as 'frame' plays a highly significant role in its initial interpretation (as 'a drink'):

(11)   When I asked the bartender for something cold and full of rum, she recommended her husband.

However, it seems that the graded salience hypothesis augmented with the retention/suppression hypothesis can better account for some of the findings in Coulson and Kutas (1998, 2001). For instance, the finding in Coulson and Kutas (1998) that nonhumorous texts involving frame shifting (12 below) were easier to process than jokes is not explainable by the frame shifting hypothesis. On its own, this hypothesis cannot explain why texts akin in frame shifting would nevertheless differ in processing costs:[10]

(12)   The veterans were suing the government because they had been exposed to dangerous ideas.

In contrast, the suppression hypothesis can account for this finding. While nonjokes may involve a surprise ending, jokes involve, in addition, a process of suppression. Processing less humorous texts such as (12) need not involve suppression of information evoked initially, since its comprehensibility relies on retaining that plausible meaning (e.g., 'radioactivity', 'toxins') with which to compare the surprise ending in order to render it meaningful. In other words, while such texts may be more difficult to read than texts containing more plausible (though not less surprising) endings, their comprehension need not involve discarding salient information. This may explain why they are easier to process than jokes, which involve suppression of such information. Frame shifting may be akin to salience reshuffling. But, as proposed earlier, reinterpretation of salient meanings on its own will not suffice to account for the processing difficulty involved in jokes.[11] Reinterpretation that involves suppression may.

In sum, while jokes and other tropes (irony, metaphor) share similar early processes activating salient meanings initially, they diverge with regard to integration processes. Whereas understanding irony and metaphor involves retention of salient, though contextually incompatible meanings (cf. chapters 4 and 5 in this volume), joke interpretation does not. Unlike irony and metaphor, which often use these salient meanings in the processes of their interpretation, such meanings are not instrumental in the comprehension of many jokes and may even get in the way. They are, therefore, discarded, at least momentarily. More research is required to shed light on the issues discussed here.

One cannot end a chapter on jokes without a punch line, however. My excuse for citing the following joke is its persuasive power as to the role of salience in joke interpretation:

(13)   A bus stops and two Italian men get on. They sit down and engage in an animated conversation. The lady sitting behind them ignores them at first, but her attention is galvanized when she hears one of the men say the following:

"Emma come first. Den I come. Den two asses come together. I come once-amore. Two asses, they come together again. I come again and pee twice. Then I come one lasta time."

"You foul-mouthed swine," retorted the lady indignantly. "In this country we don't talk about our sex lives in public!"

"Hey, coola down lady," said the man. "Who talkin' abouta sexa? I'm a justa tellin' my frienda how to spella 'Mississippi'."

BET YA READ IT TWICE!

7

Innovation

1. On the Role of Salience in Aesthetic Innovation

1.1 The Optimal Innovation Hypothesis

It seems appropriate at this stage to address a question long overdue, related to the "other side" of salience—the issue of novelty and creativity. Indeed, at first blush, novelty appears to be the opposite of salience (familiarity), presumably occupying the extreme end position on the scale. According to the graded salience hypothesis (Giora, 1997b; chapter 2 in this volume), however, novelty stands in some complementary relation to salience. Since salience is a graded notion, it follows that innovativeness is graded, too. It requires just a small step away from salience and can gradually evolve to pure novelty. Indeed, I will argue that it is not extreme novelty but "optimal" innovation—novelty that allows for the recoverability of the familiar—that is most pleasurable. While the common view focuses on the role of sheer novelty in aesthetics (Brinker, 1988), this chapter sheds light on the part salience/familiarity plays in affecting pleasure.[1]

For innovation to be "optimal" it should involve

(1) a. a novel response, but
     b. such that would also allow for the recovery of a salient meaning from which
        that novel meaning stems, in order that the similarity and difference between
        them may be assessable (the optimal innovation hypothesis).

To the extent that pleasure hinges on recognizing the familiar in the novel (Berlyne, 1971; Freud, 1905), it is optimal innovation that should induce the most pleasing effect: while optimal creativity is innovative enough to involve a transformation of a familiar meaning, it also allows for the retrieval of that meaning. The notion of optimal innovation thus excludes innovations such as variants of salient meanings, on the one hand, and pure innovations, on the other. Variations and variants (*a single piece of paper*, which stems from *a piece of paper*) do not meet the first requirement (1a above). Although they involve a slight change, this modification does not result in a novel response (as opposed to, e.g., *a peace of paper*). Neither are pure innovations "optimally innovative" since they do not meet the second requirement (1b above): no familiar meaning is recoverable and instrumental in the construction of the novel meaning (e.g., *grok; spandy-wear*).[2]

As illustration of an optimal innovation, consider the following poem by Efrat Mishori (1999: 237), translated from Hebrew (by Rachel Tzvia Back), which deconstructs the concept of motherhood (Hebrew *imahoot*) and allows for a new insight into it:

(2) *The Wall of Motherhood*

> The two
> sides
> of
> the wall
> of motherhood
> are the same
> as
> the two
> sides
> of
> a piece
> of flat
> paper
> not
> exactly
> because
> the wall
> of motherhoo
> d is like
> this poem
> it i
> s
> rea
> son and also
> res
> ult
> of
> the wall of m
> otherhood
> (1994)

The poem experiments with the "other side" of motherhood and ends up concluding that it amounts to the annihilation of the self. When *imahoot* is broken up into *i-mahoot* (translated into *m-otherhood*), it results in assigning the word an additional, new meaning, that of 'non-essence', or 'being depleted of that which is essential to the self', without discarding its conventional meaning. The pleasure we experience while encountering the new meaning (*i-mahoot; m-otherhood*) derives from the new insight we gain into possible aspects of a salient concept that we haven't processed automatically but that nevertheless makes sense in light of the salient meaning.

Or consider *Nolad met* (*Born Dead*)—the Hebrew title of a photo exhibition by Yehudit Matzkel (1999) who photographed engravings on tombstones in Israeli military cemeteries. In Hebrew, *met* is a homograph ambiguous between 'dead' and 'died'. *Nolad met* (*Born Dead*) is optimally innovative in that it involves a change of a salient convention of engraving on the tombstone, in two separate lines, the deceased's date of birth (*Born*) and his or her date of death (*Met* in the sense of 'died'). This change in segmentation, which allows for the two separate items (*Born. . . Died. . .*) to be viewed as a single unit, results in a new response (*Born Dead*; complying with requirement 1a above) that allows for the salient original

> *Nolad (Born. . .)*
> *Met (Died. . .)*

to be nevertheless recovered and reconsidered (complying with requirement 1b above). Given the Israeli militaristic scene, the exhibition projects Israeli women's anger and anguish that their sons and daughters (who, at birth, are prospective soldiers) are "born dead."

Copywriters are well aware of the appeal of such creativity. Recall the advertisement *Core soft helps you get* **A'Head** (see chapter 1), where the salient *ahead* is broken up to point to an alternative nonsalient interpretation (see also Goldenberg, Mazursky, & Solomon, 1999a,b on pictorial innovations in ads).

Indeed, throughout this book, I have considered such aesthetic innovations. Nonsalient puns (*a peace of paper*), metaphors (*Her wedding ring is a "sorry we're closed" sign*), ironies (*read my lipstick*), and jokes (*How do you get holy water? Boil the hell out of it*) are all instances of novelty that resides in salience. They all harp on old, salient strings, involving a slight twist that results in some change of the original, salient meaning, which is still recoverable and partakes in the construction of the new meaning.

Various findings presented in this book suggest that linguistic innovation is intertwined with salience (see also Clark & Gerrig, 1983). The instances of novel nonsalient language I have looked into indicate that aesthetic creativity is, at least to a certain extent, a matter of graded innovativeness. It is not a total surprise that is pleasing, but a somewhat novel interpretation that could be assigned to a familiar meaning that did not come to mind immediately (see also Giora, 1991). This may explain why the surprise endings (in terms of cloze probability) in Coulson and Kutas (1998; see also Coulson, 2001: 77–82) that did not involve reinterpretation of salient meaning (or script) were not considered humorous or pleasing. Thus, while (3b) is a joke, (3a) is not, although both share similar (cloze) surprise values:

(3)   By the time Mary had had her fourteenth child, she'd finally run out of names to
        call her
        (a) offspring [*Nonjoke ending*]
        (b) husband [*Joke ending*]

No wonder joke endings took longer to read than similarly surprising nonjoke endings. Whereas the latter involve accessing and reinterpreting a salient meaning (or script), the former do not.

Although most of the innovations dealt with in this book are tropes, the notion of optimal innovation is not exclusively related to figurative language. Literal innovations may also be optimally creative in that they involve a novel response that allows for the retrieval of a salient one. For example, the funniness or pleasure derivable from *What's the difference between roast beef and pea soup? Anyone can roast beef* or from *We're not God but we do save soles* (a sign on a shoe repair store in New York City) lies in that the homophones *pea* and *soles* involve accessing their salient literal meanings (*pee* and *souls*). Similarly, the novel, 'otherhood' sense inherent in the salient meaning of *motherhood* is a literal optimal innovation. Some optimal innovations involve not only a change of their own meaning (*herstory*) but also a change of the meaning ('his-story') of the origin (*history*) from which they stem.

Complementarily, salient figurative language may also be subject to optimal innovativeness. Recall the novel sense attributed to salient metaphors such as *Children are precious gems* when used ironically, or the novel meaning invoked by *jump on it* when used literally, (cf. chapter 5), or the less salient ('about') sense of the figurative ('accessible') meaning invited by the title of this book: *On Our Mind*. Optimal innovation, then, is not a matter of figurativeness. Rather, it is a matter of degree of salience: it consists in allowing for some apparently "unthinkable" insights into salient concepts, regardless of whether they are literal or figurative. Needless to say, figurative language may be innovative. It turns out, though, that most novel metaphors are not pure innovations but rooted in salient metaphoric concepts (see Gibbs, 1991, 1994; Lakoff & Johnson, 1980). Findings show that while conventional (instantiations of root) metaphors (*We have come thus far*) do not involve activating their root metaphors (LOVE IS A JOURNEY), metaphors rated as novel do (Keysar, Shen, Glucksberg, & Horton, 2000).

The mind, then, is poetic not only because of the possibility that thought is intrinsically metaphoric (as argued by Gibbs, 1994, and Lakoff & Johnson, 1980)—that is, not only because "the systematic, conceptual underpinnings of the vast number of linguistic expressions . . . are metaphorical and creative" (Gibbs, 1991: 88)—but also because it is constantly in search of novelty, regardless of whether it is figurative or literal. Indeed, more often than not, novelty is induced by de-automatizing salient meanings than by inventing entirely new ones. To date, this mechanism has been considered the defining feature of poetic language. A whole school of thought (the Russian formalism, e.g., Shklovsky, 1917/1965, and the Linguistic Circle of Prague, e.g., Mukařovský, 1932/1964, 1978; for a review, see Miall & Kuiken, 1994, and Renan, 1984; for a similar view, see Berlyne, 1960; Schopenhauer, 1969; Townsend, 1997) has been devoted to research into literary ways of 'making strange' (*ostranenie* in Russian) or 'foregrounding' salient, entrenched meanings that are retrieved automatically. De-familiarizing salient meanings and conventions is considered an attention-getting device resulting in novel insights (Jakobson, 1960; see also Lakoff & Turner, 1989: 215). Recently, Lakoff and Johnson (1980) and Gibbs (1994) have enlightened us with respect to the ubiquity of poetics and the extent to which creativity pervades literature and everyday language as well.

Novelty and salience, then, are intertwined and feed on each other. On the one hand, the constant pursuit of novel experiences is driven by the waning and aging of meanings. It is a reaction against the process of bleaching, of becoming salient, yielded by repetitive exposure. On the other hand, since salient meanings are most available, they are the best candidates amenable to refurbishment and sensitization. It is not just that salient meanings are highly accessible—foremost on our mind. They are also prevalent. According to Erman and Warren (2001), about half of our written (52.3%) and spoken (58.6%) language is made up of routines—fixed expressions whose meanings and forms have been conventionalized and lexicalized.[3] They are thus a ready prey for our novelty-craving mind.

1.2 Tests of the Optimal Innovation Hypothesis

In our lab, we examined some aspects of the optimal innovation hypothesis. For instance, in Giora (2002c); Giora, Fein, Kronrod, Elnatan, and Zur (2002); Giora, Kronrod, Elnatan, and Fein (2001); Kronrod (2001); and Kronrod, Giora, and Fein (2000), we aimed to show that an optimal innovation is most pleasurable. To do that we produced (Hebrew) quartets containing items (equivalent to examples 5–7) that differed from each other in terms of how removed they were from the source, fixed expression (equivalent to example 4). The first variation was a variant of the fixed expression, made up by inserting only a slight modification to the fixed expression, such that did not affect a novel response (example 5). The optimally innovative variation involved some minimal change that resulted in meaning transformation but such that allowed for the recovery of the salient interpretation from which it derives (example 6). The pure innovation was made up by inserting two modifications into the salient expression so that its meaning becomes less accessible (example 7). A similarity rating test confirmed degrees of deviation from the original fixed expression. As illustration, consider the English (contrived) examples (4–7):

(4)   Body and soul (salient, fixed expression)
(5)   Bodies and souls (variant version)
(6)   Body and sole (optimal innovation)
(7)   Bobby and Saul (pure innovation)

To show that familiarity plays a crucial role in affecting pleasure, we first established the relative degree of salience of each item. Our findings show that the four variations were significantly distinct in terms of familiarity/salience (measured on a 1–7 familiarity scale), with the fixed expression being most familiar (mean = 6.79), the variant version being slightly less familiar (mean = 5.52), the optimal innovation occupying a mid position on the familiarity scale (mean = 4.04), and the pure innovation being most novel (mean = 2.02).

To show that an optimal innovation (6) is more pleasurable than either the salient, fixed expression from which it derives (4), or a variant version of that expression (5), or a pure innovation (7), we asked subjects to rate the various targets on a (1–7) liking scale. Our findings show that, as predicted, the various versions were distinctly different on the aesthetics scale. The optimal innovation achieved the highest score (mean = 5.31). Least pleasurable was the pure innovation (mean = 2.56). The fixed expression and its variant version occupied mid position on the pleasure scale (3.79 and 3.42, respectively), with the fixed expression being significantly more pleasurable. Such findings attest to the major role salience plays in affecting pleasure ratings, particularly in novelty.

In Elnatan (2002); Giora, Fein, et al. (2002); and Giora, Kronrod et al. (2001), we tested identical items. We aimed to show that familiar items would be rated as less pleasurable than their optimally innovative interpretations induced by a late context. In these studies, readers were presented familiar Hebrew idioms (8) followed by a one-sentence context biasing them either toward their salient, idiomatic (8a) meaning ('feeling confused') or toward their less salient ('political') interpretation (8b):

(8)   You don't know your right from left?
      a. *The Comprehensive Lexicon* will teach you whatever you don't know.
      b. Buy *The Comprehensive Guide for the Political Factions in Israel.*

Results show that the optimally innovative interpretation (suggested by, e.g., 8b) was rated as significantly more pleasurable than the salient, conventional one (suggested by, e.g., 8a).

If, indeed, optimal innovations involve recovering the salient meaning from which they stem, salient meanings would take a shorter time to read following optimal innovations than following pure innovations, which do not allow access of salient meanings. Complementarily, an utterance would take shorter to read following a context that is compatible with its salient interpretation than following a context that invites an optimally innovative interpretation. To test these hypotheses, we used reading times. As predicted, reading time of the salient, fixed expression (example 4) was shorter following the optimal innovation (example 6) than following the pure innovation (example 7), suggesting that the optimal innovation involved processing the salient expression from which it derives (Kronrod et al., 2000). Complementarily, in Elnatan (2002), Giora, Fein, et al. (2002), and Giora, Kronrod et al. (2001), an optimally innovative interpretation (9d) took longer to read following the idiomatic expression

(9a) than following a context that does not require such interpretation (9b), but somewhat shorter than following an unrelated control context (9c). Compared to deriving the salient interpretation only, the optimally innovative interpretation is more effortful, because it involves deriving the salient meaning and more. It is, however, less effortful than trying to make sense of an interpretation that is incoherent and does not involve any familiar meaning:

(9)   a. You don't know your right from left?
       b. If you want to familiarize yourself with the political situation in Israel,
       c. If you are the type that sings in the shower,
       d. Buy *The Comprehensive Guide for the Political Factions in Israel.*

Such findings are consistent with our assumption that, on top of deriving a novel interpretation, optimal innovations involve processing a salient meaning as well. They further attest to the role of salience in aesthetics: they show that it is the salience factor in innovativeness rather than pure novelty that accounts for the pleasure it induces.

Pleasure, then, is a function of both salience and innovativeness. It is the surprise experienced in suddenly discovering some novelty where it is least expected, or the gratification in discovering the familiar in the novel, which attenuates the novelty and makes it easier to accommodate. Indeed, familiarity (though less so excessive familiarity) is known to be a factor in pleasure or liking (on the various aesthetic effects of mere exposure, see Bornstein & D'Agostino, 1992; Harrison, 1977; Kunst-Wilson & Zajonc, 1980; Zajonc, 1968, 2000), as also attested to by our findings (Kronrod et al., 2000). It is not the most familiar, then, that is least enjoyable but, rather, the most novel that is least pleasing. Pleasure, however, resides half way between high salience and high novelty.

The insistence throughout this book on the salience factor involved in literal and nonliteral language comprehension is, in effect, an attempt to also pursue that which is aesthetic about language and thought. The assumption of the direct access view (cf. chapters 1–2) that rich and supportive contexts may enable comprehenders to bypass salient meanings ignores a whole range of possible aesthetic effects.

2. A Change of Mind: On Awareness and Innovation

> This invasion of one's mind by ready-made phrases ... can only be prevented if one is constantly on guard against them, and every such phrase anesthetizes a portion of one's brain.
> —George Orwell, *Politics and the English Language*

Optimal innovation—the estrangement of the conventional—may be gratifying partly because it is, in fact, a mode of subversiveness. Even while aiming at pleasing, it pulls the rug from under salient/consensual routines, turning them into an object of scrutiny. Novelty, then, may be subversive both in aesthetics and in thought. Though aesthetics may draw attention to form, it also de-automatizes meaning. It stems from a rebellious mind that intends to affect a change of mind.

When Marilyn French (1977) entitled her book *The Women's Room,* replacing (the crossed-over) *Ladies'* by *Women's,* she was innovative while being defiant—drawing our attention to the euphemistic use of *Ladies* as a conventional referring expression to women. When Mary Daly (1978) entitled her book *Gyn/ ecology,* she protested oppressing ideologies while proposing an alternative that allows women to have control over their own environment. When Jennifer Coates (1986) entitled her book *Women, Men and Language,* she subverted the canonical order by giving priority to women over men. When, in 1998, a new group of Israeli feminists, aiming at de-militarizing the Israeli society while legitimizing conscientious objection to conscription, called themselves *New Profile,* they protested *profile 21*—the derogatory and punitive military classification used to designate those who refuse to join the compulsory military service. These are just a few examples. They suggest that de-automatizing salient language may be motivated not only by the search for aesthetic novelty but also by dissidence—by a change of mind seeking to affect social and political change. Such change may be assessed relative to the (normative) salient meaning from which it both stems and deviates and which it revokes. No wonder such innovations echo the salient norms and meanings that they question. This is true of both revolutions and counterrevolutions alike. Orwell's (*Nineteen Eighty-Four*) Newspeak instances are a fictional example; *feminazi* is a real one.

Indeed, in Giora (2002d) and in Ariel and Giora (1998), we looked into narrative, power of speech, and stylistic norms of female and male journalists, authors, and scriptwriters writing in Hebrew between the 1930s and the 1990s. We showed that only feminist writers introduced linguistic innovations, diverging from norms that reflect men's perspectives and interests. By contrast, the stylistic conventions used by nonfeminist writers (both women and men) projected the dominant, male-oriented worldview. Thus, while nonfeminist writers tended to present more women than men by using their first name and family status rather than via functional/professional descriptions (10), feminist writers reversed the pattern (11–12). They also reversed the tendency to anchor women to men (p. 73):

(10)   His [anchoring] sister [family+anchored] Bilha [first name], who works with him, an architect [functional] too, a woman [sex-based] divorced three times [family] (Hareven 1982: 14).

(11)   Anita Hill [full name], a law professor in Oklahoma University [functional], who blamed the judge [functional] Thomas Clarence [full name] . . . (Krasin, 1992a, 23: 8)

(12)   I was not impressed by the baby face [external description] of William Kennedy-Smith [full name]. . . . In contrast, the prosecutor [functional], Patricia Bowman [full name], impressed me deeply (Krasin, 1992b, 23: 9).

That language change is motivated by social awareness is also made manifest in Peleg (1992), who showed that dissident Jews of oriental (Mizrachi) origin, protesting their marginalization in the Israeli society, adopt a divergence strategy (Giles, 1984). They revive the original stylistic and lexical features of their variety of Hebrew while rejecting the dominant groups' variety.

Subversive innovation may take various forms, but the most popular is probably verbal hygiene (Cameron, 1995)—the attempt to "cleanse" the language and divest it of its salient, offensive connotations. At times, verbal hygiene involves replacing offensive language with "politically correct" or euphemistic language (for example, the replacement of *disabled* with *physically challenged* or *woman* with *lady*). At times, however, it is obtained by challenging salient meanings via a defiant use: by deliberately insisting on, rather than avoiding, their usage. Such practice endows them with new meanings as when the "derogatory" *woman, feminist,* and *Jew* assume positive connotations in positive contexts (cf. *The Women's Room*, or the title of a Singaporean newspaper article *I Am Woman, Hear Me Roar* echoing cat woman in *Batman Returns*). Exemplary in this respect is working-class speakers' resistance to Standard English which gives allegiance to the vernacular, thereby endowing it with covert prestige (Coates, 1996). Verbal hygiene may, indeed, be effective as long as it is novel. Once its novelty wanes, it becomes euphemistic—a target for subversion and counterrevolution (cf. Bergvall, Bing, & Freed, 1996).

The morale of this chapter is highly predictable: highly novel language and thought will be less attractive and catchy, and easier to shirk off. (No wonder some important scientific and artistic discoveries are rejected with vehemence when they first appear on the scene.) Effective novelty (attractive, affecting change), by contrast, induces change but is rooted in salience to the extent that it allows for the recoverability of the familiar.

8

Evidence from Other Research

Having discussed evidence adduced primarily in my lab, it is timely at this stage to review contemporary literature to see whether its array of findings can be accounted for by the graded salience hypothesis (Giora, 1997b, 1999b; chapter 2 in this volume).

1. The Temporal Aspects of Context Effects: Processing Models

Recall that according to the interactionist, direct access view (cf. chapter 3 in this volume), processing language involves a single mechanism that is sensitive to both linguistic and nonlinguistic information and allows for contextual information to interact with lexical processes very early on. Such processes result in tapping the appropriate interpretation directly, with no recourse to contextually incompatible information. Thus, when context is specific and supportive, literal and nonliteral language involve equivalent processes.

Proponents of this view argue against the context-resistant approach, dubbed "the standard pragmatic model," according to which interpreting an utterance figuratively is a post-access procedure, upon which the literal interpretation is activated initially, regardless of context; moreover, because it is inappropriate, the interpretation is adjusted to contextual information. On this view, only literal language is understood directly.

Alternatively, the graded salience hypothesis assumes that comprehension involves two distinct mechanisms that do not interact at the initial comprehension stage: a contextual, central system mechanism, which may have rapid predictive effects, and a lexical accessing mechanism (among others), which is modular—automatic and impervious to context effects. Lexical access is salience sensitive: salient (familiar, frequent) meanings are accessed automatically upon encounter of the linguistic stimulus, regardless of context; less salient meanings lag behind. Although context may avail the appropriate meaning immediately via the predictive and inferential mechanism, it does not block salient meanings even when they are inappropriate. Understanding unfamiliar uses of familiar instances may be rapid due to a strongly predictive context, but it would not be selective: salient, though contextually incompatible meanings would emerge nonetheless on account of their salience (see chapters 2–3 in this volume).

Like the direct access view, the graded salience hypothesis dispenses with the literal/figurative divide regarding initial processes. It assumes, instead, the salient-nonsalient continuum. It thus predicts that alternative interpretations of similar salience would be activated in parallel (for instance, the literal and figurative meanings of familiar metaphors), regardless of context. Utterances diverging in salience (such as the ironic versus literal interpretations of unfamiliar ironies and the literal and idiomatic interpretations of familiar idioms) would involve different processes. Initially, nonsalient, novel uses of familiar language would involve salient, albeit contextually incompatible meaning. Contextual information will be operative, too, either preceding, coinciding, or following the output of lexical processing. But it will affect the latter only post-lexically. When these parallel operations (of the contextual and the lexical mechanisms) result in conflicting outputs (that are anticipated upon encounter of novel uses of language), consequent revisitation processes will follow.

2. On the Superiority of Salient Meanings: The Case of Figurative Language

2.1 The Standard Pragmatic Model: Counterevidence

The following facts cannot be accounted for by the traditional view: they show that context facilitates initial comprehension of figurative language. For instance, some studies attest that a rich context neutralizes the difference between comprehension of literal and nonliteral language. Contexts longer than three sentences induced similar reading times for (nonsalient) metaphoric and (relatively more salient/accessible) literal interpretations (Inhoff, Lima, & Carroll, 1984; Ortony, Schallert, Reynolds, & Antos, 1978; Shinjo & Myers, 1978). Similarly, Gerrig and Healy (1983), who manipulated metaphor and context ordering, showed that metaphors followed by a context phrase took longer to read than when preceded by a context. (The ordering manipulation, however, did not affect comprehension of literal sentences). Kemper (1981), who investigated comprehension of proverbs, also found that the length of the paragraph affected proverb interpretation: the longer the paragraph, the faster it took to interpret it figuratively. Turner and Katz (1997), Katz and Ferretti (2000, 2001), and Katz, Ferretti, and Taylor (1999) showed that familiar proverbs did not take longer to read in figuratively than in literally biasing contexts (but see Katz and Ferretti's, 2000 experiment 2 for counterexamples). Similarly, Pickering and Frisson (2001a) found no difficulty with unfamiliar metonymies (*read Needham*) compared to familiar ones (*read Dickens*) when preceded by a predictive context.

Apparently, these findings can be accounted for by the interactionist/direct access approach. According to the direct access view, elaborated and supportive contextual information interacts with lexical processes very early on and preselects the contextually appropriate meaning. Hence, the facilitation effects and equal reading times.

These findings can also be accounted for by the graded salience hypothesis. For instance, equal reading times for similarly familiar utterances is anticipated (Turner & Katz, 1997; Giora & Fein, 1999c). But even equal reading times for more and less familiar utterances need not necessarily disconfirm the graded salience hypothesis because the graded salience hypothesis allows for facilitative contextual effects. To disprove the graded salience hypothesis, salient (but contextually incompatible meanings) should be shown to be blocked upon encounter. Given that salient meanings should be activated irrespective of contextual information, the graded salience hypothesis thus anticipates processing difficulties upon encountering a less salient meaning that should involve accessing its salient, albeit inappropriate, meaning as well. For example, it predicts processing difficulties upon encountering *troops* while reading *Regardless of the danger, the troops marched on* in the metaphor-inducing context (speaking of ruthless kids, see Ortony et al., 1978). Encountering *troops* should involve processing difficulties such as found for unbalanced ambiguous words embedded in contexts biasing their interpretation toward their less salient (subordinate) meaning (Rayner, Pacht, & Duffy, 1994; cf. chapter 3 in this volume). Indeed, findings by Janus and Bever (1985), who measured reading times at the locus of the figurative information (*troops*) rather than at the end of the sentence, exhibited longer reading times for the nonsalient (figurative) than for the salient (literal) word.

Janus and Bever (1985) tested the hypothesis that the equal reading times found for literal and metaphoric utterances in Ortony et al.'s (1978) study were not affected by the prior rich context, but by the extra processing at the end of sentences (attested to by Abrams & Bever, 1969, and Just & Carpenter, 1980). This extra processing masked the difference in processing times for comprehension of literal versus metaphorical sentences and fostered an illusion of equivalence. Criticizing Ortony et al.'s methodology, but using their materials, Janus and Bever measured reading times at the end of target (vehicle) phrases rather than at the end of target sentences. Their findings show that even when the context is rich, novel metaphors present some difficulty to comprehenders (see also Brisard, Frisson, & Sandra, 2001; and see Gibbs & Gerrig, 1989, on the possibility that equal reading times of whole sentences may mask underlying processes). That rich and supportive context does not block salient though incompatible meanings has also been shown by Peleg, Giora, and Fein (2001, in press; cf. chapter 3 in this volume).

Findings regarding comprehension of idiomatic language do not corroborate the traditional view, either. They show that nonliteral meanings are activated first. For instance, in a conversational context, idioms took longer to be understood literally than figuratively (Gibbs, 1980). In Hillert and Swinney (2001), idioms were not processed literally first. In Van de Voort and Vonk (1995), familiar idioms, whose more salient meaning is idiomatic, were automatically processed idiomatically. Variant idioms, however, took longer to process than nonmodified idioms, while the opposite was true for their literal controls. A similar tendency was found in Ortony et al. (1978). Needham (1992), too, disconfirmed the hypothesis that literal meaning is activated during comprehension of idiomatic utterances. He presented participants with three target sentences preceded by a context that had a title. The targets were an idiom, a literal (anaphor) target, or a control phrase. The test word for all the three cases was identical and appeared previously in the text, but it was related only to the literal interpretation of the idiom and to the literal (anaphor) target. Participants were told to decide as quickly as possible whether the test word had occurred in the passage:

(1)   *Title*: Carol lets out a secret

Carol was cooking dinner for Bob. After dinner, there was going to be a surprise birthday party for him. She was putting some vegetables in a pan. She had poured some drinks for the two of them. She got nervous talking to Bob.

She spilled the beans when* [*Idiom*]

She spilled the carrots when* [*Anaphor*]

She spilled the beer when* [*Control*]

The test word for all three cases was *pan*, presented at *

Although participants' response time in the three conditions did not differ significantly across subjects, and only marginally across items, there was a significant effect of condition on error rates across subjects and materials. The error rate for the literal (anaphor) condition was significantly lower than for either the idiom or the control condition, suggesting that the literal meaning was computed only for the literal target.

Most of these findings are accountable by the direct access hypothesis (Gibbs, 1984), which does not require that the literal interpretation of the figurative utterance be computed. They can also be accounted for by the graded salience hypothesis, which predicts that salient meanings, such as the conventional (figurative) meaning of idioms would be processed initially, regardless of context.

2.2 The Direct Access View: Counterevidence

Let us consider other findings, which are problematic for the interactionist, direct access view. They suggest that the contextually incompatible literal meaning of figurative language is activated and at times even triggers a sequential process. Such findings can be accounted for by the graded salience hypothesis, however, as well as by the traditional view. For instance, in Turner and Katz (1997) and Katz and Ferretti (2000, 2001), unfamiliar proverbs took longer to read in figuratively than in literally biasing contexts. In Honeck, Welge, and Temple (1998), participants took longer to judge whether a less familiar proverb was an appropriate restatement of the paragraph topic than its literal counterpart. Looking into familiar and unfamiliar producer-for-product metonymies with literal expressions, Pickering and Frisson (2001a) found that, whereas familiar metonymies (*read Dickens*) incurred no difficulty, expressions that can be interpreted as unfamiliar metonymies (*read Needham*) did. (Notwithstanding, introducing *Needham* as an author in prior context results in no difficulty for unfamiliar metonymies.)

Another counterexample to the direct access model is found in Gibbs (1990), who showed that understanding figurative referring expressions took longer to understand than literal referring expressions retrieving the same antecedent. In his study, participants read short narratives ending with either a figurative (metaphoric or metonymic) or a literal referring expression (see following example 2). Participants were fastest at reinstating the antecedent of the literal description. They were also faster at reinstating the antecedent of the metaphoric expression than the antecedent of the metonymic expression. These findings are consistent with the predictions of the traditional view, which posits the priority of literal meanings. They are also accountable by the graded salience hypothesis, which posits the superiority of salient meanings (which here coincide with literal meanings). While the intended meaning of the literal referring expressions is salient (conventional), the intended figurative meanings of both the metaphoric and the metonymic referring expressions is somewhat novel. The difference in reading times, then, might have been induced by salience difference (although this has not been controlled):

(2)   a. *Metaphoric referring expression*
        Stu went to see the Saturday night fights. There was a boxer that Stu hated. This
        guy always lost. Just as the match was supposed to start, Stu went to get some
        snacks. He stood in the line for ten minutes. When he returned, the bout had
        been canceled. "What happened?" Stu asked a friend. The friend replied,
            "The creampuff didn't even show up." [*Metaphoric reinstatement*]
            "The fighter didn't even show up." [*Literal reinstatement*]
            "The referee didn't even show up." [*Baseline control*]
            Boxer (probe word)

      b. *Metonymic referring expression*
        Mr. Bloom was manager of a high school baseball team. He was concerned
        about the poor condition of the field. He also was worried about one athlete. His
        third baseman wasn't a very good fielder. This concerned the manager a good
        deal. The team needed all the help it could get. At one point, Mr. Bloom said to
        his assistant coach,
            "The glove at third base has to be replaced." [*Metonymic reinstatement*]
            "The player at third base has to be replaced." [*Literal reinstatement*]
            "The grass at third base has to be replaced." [*Baseline control*]
            Athlete (probe word)

Onishi and Murphy (1993) attempted to explain Gibbs's (1990) findings in terms of information structure. Using different materials, they first replicated Gibbs's findings concerning metaphoric versus literal referring expressions. However, they also manipulated information ordering by placing the highly informative message in predicate, noninitial position (as in "*He's such a creampuff that he didn't even show up*," *said Tracey; "He's such a loser that he didn't even show up," said Tracey*) rather than in topic, initial position as did Gibbs (as in *The creampuff didn't even show up*). When the information was presented noninitially, equal reading times were obtained for literal and metaphoric targets. Onishi and Murphy (1993: 770) concluded that the longer reading times found for metaphoric than for literal referring expressions in Gibbs's study "may be a property not of metaphor alone, but of any reference in which the referring expression's meaning is not highly related to the properties of the referent." Recall, however, that placing targets in sentence noninitial position has been shown to mask lexical processes and neutralize differences between salient and less salient language (Giora, Peleg, & Fein, 2001; Peleg et al., 2001, in press; chapter 3 in this volume).

On the face of it, the work of Blasko and Connine (1993) could also be problematic for the direct access view, showing that tne salient, literal meaning of metaphors was always activated initially. In the case of less familiar metaphors, it also became available before the metaphoric meaning. (This was not true for less familiar but apt metaphors, however; see also Gentner & Wolff, 1997). In all, however, their findings cannot forcefully argue against the direct access view, since their contexts are very dull and cannot induce context effects (for a more thorough critique of Blasko & Connine, see chapter 5 in this volume; Gibbs, 2001; Glucksberg, 2001). This, however, has been remedied by Brisard et al. (2001), who showed that novel metaphors embedded in a rich and supportive context are interpreted literally first.

These findings tie up with findings by Blank (1988), Gregory and Mergler (1990), and Pexman, Ferretti, and Katz (2000). These studies examined processing strategies of conventional versus novel metaphors, and their findings suggest that, as predicted by the graded salience hypothesis, comprehension of unfamiliar metaphors involves more complex inferential processes. In contrast, conventional metaphors are understood as fast as literals.

More compelling are findings by Williams (1992), who showed that both the literal and the metaphoric meanings of conventional, metaphor-based polysemies were accessed initially regardless of context; these meanings remained active even after a long delay (for an extensive review, see chapter 5 in this volume). These findings, showing that the salient (literal) meaning of the metaphoric word was active for a while, allude to the possibility that the literal meaning of the sentence as a whole was activated and retained. Such findings cannot be accounted for by the direct access view (Gibbs, 2001).

McGlone, Glucksberg, and Cacciari (1994) also examined figurative language which varied in what I would term "degree" of salience. They provided evidence for the parallel process of figurative language and showed that, in understanding idioms such as *spill the beans*, but particularly in understanding less conventional (variant) idioms such as *didn't spill a single bean*, the literal meanings of the words themselves and the idiomatic meanings are simultaneously apprehended. McGlone et al. suggest that the hypothesis that two kinds of meanings are simultaneously apprehended also accounts for the findings in Peterson, Burgess, Dell, and Eberhard (1989).

Peterson et al. found that in literally biasing contexts (*kick the ball*), lexical decisions to concrete words were faster than to abstract words. In contrast, in idiomatically biasing contexts (*kick the bucket*), there was no difference between concrete and abstract targets. Moreover, lexical decisions to both concrete and abstract targets were faster than the decisions to abstract targets in the literally biasing contexts. McGlone et al. suggest that in the idiomatic context, both abstract and concrete noun targets are primed, because an idiomatic phrase such as *kick the bucket* has both a concrete ('bucket') and an abstract ('die') meaning.

Keysar and Bly's (1995, 1999) findings are consistent with the hypothesis that it is the more salient (whether literal or figurative) meaning that is activated first. They showed that transparency of idioms is a consequence of familiarity. In their research, participants became acquainted with the original and the contrived meanings (which were sometimes the opposite of the original meanings) of unfamiliar idioms. Results showed that it was the recently learned (and hence the more salient) meaning that was perceived as more transparent, regardless of whether participants learned the original meaning or its opposite.[1]

Another counterexample to the direct access view is Gernsbacher, Keysar, Robertson, and Werner (2001). They show that understanding metaphors such as *My uncle's surgeon is a butcher* involves activating the literal meaning of the vehicle. Such a metaphor facilitated the reading times of the literal meaning of the vehicle *Butchers use knives* to a greater extent than did the literal prime *My father's brother is a butcher*.[2]

Recent research into ironic language also suggests that, contrary to the direct access view, irony comprehension involves more complex processes than comprehending the same utterances intended literally. A reanalysis of Gibbs's (1986b) findings (see Giora, 1995), as well as findings by Dews and Winner (1997, 1999), Giora and Fein (1999a), Giora, Fein, and Schwartz (1998), Pexman et al. (2000), and Schwoebel, Dews, Winner, and Srinivas (2000), reveal that less and nonsalient ironic interpretations take longer to process than salient, literal ones. Dews and Winner (1995, 1997, 1999) and Giora et al. (1998) show that irony comprehension involves processing the salient, literal meaning as well (for a similar view, see also Bredin, 1997). Moreover, findings in Giora et al. (1998) and in Giora and Fein (1999a) attest that the salient literal meaning of irony is induced initially by both familiar and unfamiliar ironies. However in the case of familiar ironies, this meaning is activated alongside the similarly salient ironic meaning, while less familiar ironies give rise to the compatible (ironic) interpretation only after a delay (Giora & Fein, 1999a; chapter 4 in this volume).

Further evidence comes from Colston and Gibbs (2002) and Gibbs (1998a). Colston and Gibbs presented participants with utterances such as *This one's really sharp* embedded at the end of stories that biased their meaning either toward their metaphoric (3a) or toward their ironic meaning (3b):

(3) a. You are a teacher at an elementary school. You are discussing a new student with
       your assistant teacher. The student did extremely well on her entrance examina-
       tions. You say to your assistant,
       "This one's really sharp."

   b. You are a teacher at an elementary school. You are gathering teaching supplies
      with your assistant teacher. Some of the scissors you have are in really bad shape.
      You find one pair that won't cut anything. You say to your assistant,
      "This one's really sharp."

Participants took longer to read the ironic than the metaphoric utterances. According to Colston and Gibbs, such findings suggest that metaphor and irony involve different processes (see also Winner, 1988). However, an alternative explanation seems no less plausible. Because many of the metaphoric utterances involve conventional metaphors while the ironic interpretations do not, Colston and Gibbs's findings might demonstrate that salient meanings are faster to process than are less salient ones. These findings cannot be accounted for by either the direct access view, according to which, in a supportive context, salient and less salient meanings should be equally accessible (cf. Ortony et al., 1978), or the traditional view, which posits the priority of literal meanings. They are accountable by the graded salience hypothesis, which posits the superiority of salient over less salient meanings, regardless of literality or context.

In all, the evidence adduced here is only partly consistent with the traditional view, and only partly consistent with the direct access view. However, it is almost entirely consistent with the graded salience hypothesis. It demonstrates that salient meanings are not inhibited by context but are always activated upon encounter. The only finding that is not predicted by the graded salience hypothesis concerns the relative ease of processing of somewhat novel but apt metaphors compared to novel but less apt metaphors (but see the discussion in chapter 5 in this volume and in Giora, 2002b).

3. On the Superiority of the Salient Meaning: The Case of Literal Language

Gerrig (1989) provides an opportunity to examine the applicability of the graded salience hypothesis to literal language comprehension. His data concern (what is termed here) "degrees" of salience of literal language. He looked into the processes invoked by conventional versus less conventional language used innovatively. He proposed that processing conventional (salient) meanings involves sense-selection operating via a direct look up in the mental lexicon, while processing novel (nonsalient) meanings involves both sense selection and sense creation which operate in parallel, the latter depending on contextual processes. Gerrig's findings are consistent with the graded salience hypothesis (which similarly assumes two distinct mechanisms that operate simultaneously). They may be taken to show that even a heavily weighted context biased in favor of nonsalient meanings does not block salient meanings (see also Binder & Rayner, 1998, 1999; Giora, Peleg, & Fein, 2001; Peleg et al. 2001, in press; Rayner et al., 1994).

Gerrig (1989) contrasted the traditional sequential process model (labeled error-recovery) with a parallel process model of sense creation. According to the parallel process model, sense creation (4b) should not be sensitive to the time it takes to process the conventional meaning (4a) of the expression in question. Innovative interpretations of any conventional expression should involve the same processing strategies. In contrast, the sequential process model, he suggests, predicts that novel interpretations should be sensitive to the processing time of their conventional uses. If a certain conventionally intended utterance is faster to understand than another conventionally intended utterance, derivation of their respective novel meaning should exhibit the same difference.

As illustration, consider the following discourses cited in Gerrig (1989), repeated here for convenience, which give rise to both conventional and innovative interpretations of the same utterances, differing in degree of conventionality:

4)   a. *Conventional story*

The people of Marni, France, have an unusual celebration every year. Over four hundred years ago, Louis X visited their town. He started the tradition of having annual sports events. The town's teenagers race on foot all the way around the town. The older sportsmen race horses around the same course. The foot/horse race is the more popular event.

b. *Innovative story*

Over four hundred years ago, Louis X visited the town of Marni, France. He started the tradition of racing snails in the town square. The town's people still gather every year for races of two lengths. By tradition, the short course is made just as long as King Louis's foot. The longer race is made the length of Louis's favorite horse. The foot/horse race is the more popular event.

According to the sequential processing model, contends Gerrig, if *foot race* is understood faster than *horse race* in their conventional use (4a), it should be also understood more swiftly in their innovative use (4b). In contrast, according to the parallel process model, the reading times of both compounds used innovatively should be roughly the same, irrespective of which took longer to read in its conventional use.

The graded salience and retention/suppression hypotheses (see chapter 2 in this volume) have different predictions, however. Although a strong context is allowed to be predictive of nonsalient, contextually compatible meanings (cf. Giora, Peleg, & Fein, 2001; Peleg et al., 2001; chapters 2–3 in this volume), it further predicts that difficulty in suppressing disruptive salient meanings increases relative to increase in salience (see chapter 2). Therefore, it predicts longer processing times for high than for low salience expressions used innovatively in Gerrig's experiments.[3]

Results indeed show that sentences containing salient and innovative interpretations of low conventionality expressions exhibited no reading time difference when used conventionally or innovatively. In contrast, sentences biased toward the nonsalient, innovative interpretations of high conventionality expressions took longer to read than when biased toward their salient interpretation (for similar findings, see Coulson & Kutas, 1998; cf. chapter 6 in this volume). Such findings can be accounted for by the suppression hypothesis (cf. chapters 2 and 5, showing that highly salient meanings are more difficult to suppress than less salient ones).

Gerrig interpreted these results as disconfirming the sequential model and supporting "an elaborated" parallel process model:

> [According to] an elaborated concurrent processing model, when readers understand preempting innovations, they are dividing their resources between the processes of examining a conventional reading and creating an innovative meaning. The greater the demands of the conventional readings, the fewer resources remain for constructing the innovative meaning. If a conventional meaning is highly available, resources are divided between two processes—sense selection and sense creation—for a lengthy period of time. (1989: 199)

In spite of some different assumptions, both processing models assume that the salient (conventional) meaning should be activated on encounter, regardless of context. Findings in Gerrig (1989), then, support the view that salience plays a major role in language comprehension: salient meanings cannot be obstructed by contextual information.

Additional support for the graded salience hypothesis comes from Gibbs (1982). His findings show that the compositional, less conventional (question) meaning ('Are you unable to be friendly?') of utterances such as *Can't you be friendly?* took longer to comprehend than their conventional (request) meaning ('Please be friendly to other people'), regardless of contextual bias. As predicted by the graded salience hypothesis, readers' decisions as to whether a word string was or was not an English sentence was much faster when it instantiated the salient, conventional interpretation than when it instantiated the compositional, less conventional, less salient interpretation, regardless of whether it followed a context biasing the utterance toward the conventional (5b) or toward the less conventional (5a) interpretation:

(5)   a. *Literal context*
        Martin was talking with his psychiatrist.
        He was having many problems with his relations.
        He always seemed hostile to other people.
        Martin commented to the psychiatrist,
        "Everybody I meet I seem to alienate."

The shrink said,
"Can't you be more friendly?"
   "Are you unable to be friendly?" [*Literal*]
   "Please be friendly to other people." [*Conventional*]
   "The weather was quite hot today." [*Unrelated*]
   "Have you never car the?" [*False*]

b. *Indirect context*
Mrs. Connor was watching her kids play in the backyard.
One of the neighbor's children had come over to play.
But Mrs. Connor's son refused to share his toys.
This made Mrs. Connor upset.
She angrily walked outside and said in a stern voice to her son,
"Can't you be more friendly?"
   "Are you unable to be friendly?" [*Literal*]
   "Please be friendly to other people." [*Conventional*]
   "The weather was quite hot today." [*Unrelated*]
   "Have you never car the?" [*False*]

In sum, the plethora of findings regarding comprehension of literal and nonliteral language is best explained by the graded salience hypothesis. The vast array of apparently conflicting findings is consistent with the view that salient meanings are always accessed automatically, regardless of either literality or contextual information. This view renders the metaphoric/literal distinction inapplicable to initial processes. As shown earlier, figurative and literal utterances involve different processes when they diverge in salience, with nonsalient meanings, whether literal or figurative, taking longer to process (e.g., less salient or novel metaphors vs. their literal interpretation, literal uses of salient idioms vs. their idiomatic use, innovative use of highly salient literal language vs. its conventional use, nonsalient ironies vs. their literal interpretation). Indeed, although both familiar and unfamiliar utterances activate their salient meaning initially, nonsalient language mostly involves an additional process of redressing the incompatible meaning. Figurative and literal utterances involve similar processes when they converge in salience (e.g., less familiar idioms and their literal interpretation, less familiar literal language vs. its innovative use, familiar ironies and their literal interpretation, familiar metaphors and their literal use). They activate their salient, literal and nonliteral, meanings in parallel, regardless of context. Thus, the graded salience hypothesis enables the reconciliation of views that have until now been in disagreement.

9

Coda

Unaddressed Questions—
Food for Future Thought

1. Is Salience a Property of Linguistic Input Only?

Given enough exposure and individual experience, any information can become foremost on our mind to the extent that it resists contextual information (see Zajonc, 2000). Many examples spring to mind—whether perceptual, social, or emotional. Consider, for instance, the visual example in figure 9.1. Given our previous experience with Arik Sharon, currently the Israeli prime minister, there is no way we can ignore or inhibit this salient response even though the portrait is carved of bloody minced meat. Along the same lines, it is unthinkable that Holocaust survivors' interpretation of the swastika will ever be desensitized, regardless of how often they encounter a positive or a neutral interpretation of it (as an ancient symbol). On a different note, will Joan Collins ever be un-Alexised? To *Dynasty*'s viewers, the memory of the character she played so prominently will probably always spring to mind when she is encountered

Feelings we have been brought up to entertain may also pop up automatically upon facing the relevant stimulus, regardless of contextual information (see also Öhman & Wiens, 2003; Levenson, 2003; Zajonc, 1980, 2000). For instance, even a radical feminist like myself has not rid herself entirely of "women hate." I notice that on certain occasions I still feel automatically prejudiced against women—an emotion I hasten to adjust to contextual information, my feminist awareness, and understanding.

Given that salience is the product of learning and exposure (cf. chapter 2 in this volume), more than one kind of information (e.g., linguistic) is amenable to consolidation and to automatic retrieval (cf. Dudai, 1989; Zajonc, 2000 and references therein).

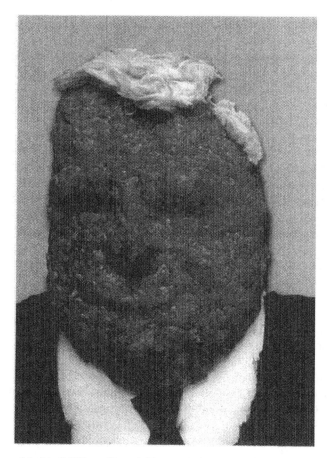

Figure 9.1 "Arik." From Hanoch Piven (1999). Copyright by Hanoch Piven.
Reproduced with permission.

2. Are Literality and Figurativeness Linguistic or Conceptual?

The question whether literality is linguistic or conceptual has not yet attracted enough attention (but see Coulson and Van Petten, 1999, in press; Gibbs, 1994: chap. 2; Lakoff, 1986; and particularly Sperber & Wilson, 1986/1995: 231–237, in which the resemblance obtaining between a propositional form of an utterance and the thought it represents forms the basis of literality). In contrast, it is almost consensual now (following Fauconnier, 1994, 1997; Fauconnier, & Turner, 1998; Gibbs, 1994; Lakoff, 1987; Lakoff & Johnson, 1980) that figurativeness, particularly metaphor, is not necessarily linguistic. Indeed, it is not, as can be also deduced from research into nonverbal metaphor (Carroll, 1994, 1996; Forceville, 1996; Kennedy & Kennedy, 1993).

Research into nonverbal irony still lags behind (but see Ducas, 1998, for an initiation; see also Heyd, 1986; Hutcheon, 1991; Lars, 1996 and references therein). The following examples, however, are quite suggestive. Consider Matthew Bourne's all-male production of the classic *Swan Lake*; Duchamp's *Fountain*[1] or *Mona Lisa* (entitled *L.H.O.O.Q.*,[2]); Magritte's *Elective Affinities* or *This Is Not a Pipe*; or even a common gesture, such as when trying to "disarm" a domineering father, the daughter gives him the military salute.

In Ducas (1998), some ironic stills (as Duchamp's) and cinematic examples are discussed. Such is the scene in *The Godfather* (Coppola, 1972) in which the new Mafia head, Michael Corleone, decorously participates in baptizing his newly born nephew in a hugely majestic Gothic church that is filled with religious aura and music. While Corleone is piously reassuring the priest that he believes in God and in the Holy Ghost, and rejects Satan, in the other parts of the city, his men are brutally and persistently slaughtering his rivals. The intercuts portraying the executions, which stand in a stark contrast to the foreground scene, result in an ironic interpretation of that "pious" scene proceeding in the foreground (as attested by viewers' judgments).

3. Are Different Representations of the Same Meaning/Concept Similarly Salient?

The different representations of the same meaning/concept need not be similarly salient. Their salience depends on the experiential familiarity an individual has with the stimulus in question (written, vocal, or other; see Gernsbacher, 1984).

4. Is Salient Information a Factor in Language Acquisition?

Kecskés (2000a, b; 2002a, b; Kecskés & Papp, 2000) proposes that some of the difficulties in second-language acquisition can be accounted for by the graded salience hypothesis. Learners have more difficulties acquiring the proper meaning of words and expressions than the syntax of the target language. This is particularly true of situation-bound utterances (SBUs). SBUs are formulaic, highly conventionalized, prefabricated pragmatic units that occur in standardized communicative situations (Kecskés, 1999, 2000a, b). Generally, SBUs have a pragmatic function specific to a given situation, such as *talk to you later* used to mean 'good bye'. Many of them can have both salient literal and nonliteral meanings. However, the most salient meaning is usually the nonliteral one: "Using the principle of salience, L1 [first-language] speakers process functional meanings of SBUs directly without falling back on the literal meaning. Adult L2 [second-language] speakers, however, can hardly ignore the literal meaning of SBUs" (Kecskés, 2000: 621), since it is more salient to them than the more conventional meaning.[3]

5. Is Salient Information True?

Though this question must sound strange, it is not entirely out of place. Consider, McGlone and Tofighbakhsh (2000), who provide evidence suggesting that "beauty is truth." They show that when clad in rhyme, unfamiliar aphorisms sound more reasonable and convincing than equivalent unrhymed utterances. In the same way, salient information can "feel" more truthful than less or nonsalient information. Apparently, salient information includes several factors that might make it "feel right": it springs to mind first, it is familiar, it is likable (see chapter 7 in this volume), and it resists change (that is, it is hard to eradicate or attenuate). No wonder it makes one feel "at home" even when it comes to prejudices. Provoking or de-automatizing salient meanings, concepts, and ideas is, therefore, one of the most important roles of art and science (cf. Reinhart, 2000; chapter 7 in this volume). I can only end here with the hope that this book may be helpful in this direction and evoke counterthinking.

6. On Our Mind

In the final analysis, what does our salience-sensitive behavior tell us about the mind? Encapsulated processes that are blind to contextual information can indeed be viewed as "stupid" (as perceived by Fodor, 1983). However, they can also be viewed as reflecting aspects of the autonomy of the mind—its independence of and resistance to contextual processes. The evidence attesting to the superiority and autonomy of salient meanings suggests that compliance with contextual information is not automatic but a matter of deliberation. Contextual information cannot dominate our thinking entirely.[4] Instead, alternative concepts will be made available despite apparent evidence to the contrary and allow the individual to keep an open mind in face of biasing or manipulative information (Giora, Peleg, & Fein, 2001).

NOTES

CHAPTER 1

1. On how one views ingroup as opposed to outgroup members, see Ariel and Giora (1992a,b, 1998) and references therein. On perspective taking, see Keysar, Barr, and Horton (1998).

2. On the possibility that pragmatic knowledge may be modular in a limited sense, see Kasher (1991, 1998); Kasher, Batori, Soroker, Graves, and Zaidel (1999); Zaidel, Kasher, Soroker, and Batori (2002); Zaidel, Kasher, Giora, Batori, Soroker, and Graves (2000).

CHAPTER 2

1. The assumption that information about gender is coded in the mental lexicon is not consensual (for a different view, see, e.g., Bates, Hernandez, & Pizzamilglio, 1996).

2. On rigidity and lack of adaptability as a source of the comic, see Bergson (1956: 67).

3. Consolidation is the progressive stabilization of newly acquired internal representations and of processes that ensure its retrieval. Gradual consolidation is a general property of biological learning (cf. Dudai, 1989, 1996).

4. For the accessibility distinction between stored and inferred information, see Ariel (1990: 100), Kintsch (1998), and Sperber and Wilson (1986/1995).

5. Needless to say, a *piece of paper* also echoes another (un)eventful agreement between Chamberlain and Hitler:

> While Chamberlain returned to England with a piece of paper in his hand, Hitler was laughing. (www.pagesz.net/~stevek/europe/lecture11.html), accessed July 2001.

I remember how a desperate Chamberlain got a piece of paper from Hitler, and declared, "Peace in our Time." . . . That was the last gasp before the world exploded into another war. (www.nysec.org/essays/MayOutlook.html), accessed July 2001.

6. It is possible that the past tense of *do* (i.e., *did*), or the conventional greeting 'hello' (among other seemingly arbitrary conventions) are in some (mysterious?) way motivated. However, their conventionality seems independent of what may have motivated them. In fact, it is quite possible that the more arbitrary the convention, the more salient it is (on account of its frequency of use that made dispensing with its motivation possible). I owe this remark to Andrew Wedel (personal communication, 20 October 1998). On the "dual mechanism" view proposing that regular forms are handled by rule-based systems while irregular forms rely more heavily on memory, see Pinker (1999) and Ullman et al. (1997), among others.

7. It is possible that frozen idioms (*kick the bucket*) which are restricted to a specific word order in that they do not retain their idiomatic meaning in case of, for example, passivization (*the bucket was kicked*) are more salient than flexible idioms that are less amenable to loss of idiomaticity under similar conditions (*make up one's mind* versus *her mind was made up*). They were found by some to be read faster than flexible idioms (Connine, Blasko, Brandt, & Kaplan Layer, 1992; Gibbs & Gonzales, 1985; but see Gibbs, Nayak, & Cutting, 1989).

8. There was significant priming only in the literal condition ('solid), which was unaffected by delay. Priming in the metaphoric condition ('strict') "was numerically present at all three delays (decreasing over delay) but the effect was only significant when data were collapsed over delay" (Williams, 1992: 201).

9. A homonym is a word having multiple distinct, allegedly unrelated meanings (*bank* denoting 'financial institution' and 'riverside'). In fact, homonymy may be viewed as two words that have the same pronunciation or spelling (Lehrer, 1990: 211); a polysemy is a word that has multiple related meanings (*hand* denoting 'the human limb', 'helper', 'deliver', etc.) See also Brugman (1997).

10. In my previous writings (Giora, 1997b) I said that context can contribute to the salience of meanings. I should have said instead that context may contribute to the availability or accessibility of a concept.

11. However, it is plausible to assume that since the appropriate (literal) meaning of these targets was available immediately, the incompatible (ironic) meaning could not disrupt comprehension. Hence no suppression was triggered. I thank Orna Peleg for this comment.

12. While grounding may make a meaning transparent, convention is most operative when meanings are not transparent and need the glue of convention and entrenchment to keep intact (see also Wedel & Sherman (Ussishkin), 1999).

13. For a meaning to become grammaticized, the evolution of its interpretation or function must be stabilized, so that it is generalized or bleached. High frequency is a prerequisite for grammaticization (on processes of grammaticization of grammatical items, see Ariel, 1999b; Bybee, 1985; Bybee, Perkins, & Pagliuca, 1994). A process of grammaticization may turn inferred meanings into lexicalized meanings, as are the meanings of opaque idioms (*kick the bucket*) which no longer hinge on the transparency of their lexical parts (for a discussion, see Clausner & Croft, 1997).

14. Note that the term of *salience* is also used by Hudson (1998) and Verschueren (1995, 1998) to denote different notions (such as "communicative transparency" and "degrees of awareness").

15. "'Enduring' and 'lasting' mean at least a few seconds, but in most cases much longer, and in some cases up to a lifetime" (Dudai, 1989: 6).

CHAPTER 3

1. So far, there is no evidence showing that context biased toward the more salient meaning of a word allows for the less salient meaning to be activated as well, as would be predicted by any exhaustive access model.

2. This specific experiment was run in Hebrew in which the demonstrative follows the noun.

3. But see Pritchett (1988, 1991) for a different view.

4. According to Pritchett (1988, 1991), this does not hold for languages other than English (e.g., Japanese, in which the verb occupies sentence final position).

5. The late closure principle—the tendency to append oncoming information to the structure currently being built—is also explained in terms of comprehenders' sensitivity to distributional information. The assumption is that speakers and writers tend to produce utterances in order of accessibility. Consequently, elements more accessible to them (on account of their frequency or brevity) precede those of lower accessibility (which require more processing). Comprehenders, who are sensitive to distributional information, interpret ambiguities in a way that is consistent with frequency of occurrence (MacDonald, 1999).

6. The garden-path models have also been challenged by findings that eliminate the processing difficulties for garden-path clauses in the presence of referentially supportive context (Altmann, 1988; Altmann & Steedman, 1988; Altmann, Garnham, & Dennis, 1992). For instance, in the absence of an appropriate context, the preferred reading of *He told the woman he was having trouble with to leave* led to a garden-path error, and hence to long reading times. However, with a preceding context such as *The therapist saw two women* reading time was faster. Note that these studies used self-paced reading techniques, which are suspect (for a review, see Rayner & Sereno, 1994; for an overview, see Mitchell, 1994; for a critique, see Clifton & Ferreira, 1989).

CHAPTER 4

1. The field of irony research has received an immense boost in the last decade. For a review of the field (which is beyond the scope of this chapter), see Attardo, 1998, 2000; Giora, 1998b.

2. On a direct access view that posits that the literal interpretation of a nonliteral utterance as a whole need not be retrieved, see Gibbs, 2002; Utsumi, 2000.

3. On the processes/products distinction and the different phases involved in utterance interpretation, see Gibbs (1994: 115–119).

4. However, while overpolite requests that were perceived as ironic were rated as less rude than their (nonironic) underpolite counterparts, they were not rated as less insulting (Kumon-Nakamura, Glucksberg, & Brown, 1995). According to some accounts, irony may be a politeness strategy without muting the criticism. In fact, Colston (1997) and Toplak and Katz (2000) argue that irony is used to enhance rather than to dilute condemnation. On how to reconcile these inconsistent findings, see Kotthoff (1996) and Pexman and Olineck (2002).

5. Here we are talking about the literal and ironing meanings of the whole phrase. These ironies and their literal interpretations have been found to be equally salient in Hebrew (cf. Giora & Fein, 1999a); however, they may not be equally salient in English.

6. Because the graded salience hypothesis allows for parallel context effects (cf. chapters 2–3 in this volume), strong contextual information may predict the appropriate meaning very early on, even before encountering the key element on which the irony

hinges. With respect to familiar ironies, speedier processes for the ironic than the literal meaning are anticipated, since this meaning is probably listed as a fixed unit in the mental lexicon, while this is not always the case with regard to the literal counterpart (but see, e.g., *Read my lips; Very funny*).

7. That speakers are not always after a full propositional meaning is made manifest in the following naturally occurring conversation (taken from Tsuyoshi & Thompson 1996: 77; numbers in square brackets indicate overlap) in which speakers respond by agreeing even before hearing the full propositional content:

D: .. she [4 always was,   .. you know 4].
G: [4 yeah.   .. exactly 4].
D: ... pretty much uh,   ... able to do anything that I wanted to do.

8. Irony need not have only a salient literal meaning. Its nonironic meaning can also be figurative, as when the conventional metaphor *Children are precious gems* can be used ironically. In such cases, it is also the metaphoric meaning that should be processed initially on account of it salience (cf. Pexman, Ferretti, & Katz, 2000).

9. This evaluation has not been confirmed by native speakers' intuitions, but see a discussion of it in Giora (1995).

10. Another measure of ease of processing applied by Gibbs in the same experiment involved participants' paraphrase judgments of the target sentences tested. Results showed that it took participants longer to make paraphrase judgments for the nonsarcastic than for the sarcastic remarks. Although Gibbs considered this supportive of the relative ease of processing for ironic language, it is possible that these findings attest to the double (explicit and implicit) meaning of sarcasm. If an utterance involves a double meaning, it seems rather easy to make a given, implicit meaning explicit, or recognize it. Nonambiguous utterances, on the other hand, do not have a ready-made, already perceived extra paraphrase at their disposal. In addition, it is probable that every paraphrase is a much worse version of the original.

11. In Gibbs, O'Brien, & Doolittle (1995), verbal irony (termed "intended irony") took longer to read than an equivalent situational irony (termed "unintended irony"), which is intended literally:

(i) *Intended irony*
     John and Bill were taking a statistics class together. Before the final exam, they decided to cooperate during the test so they worked out a system so they could secretly share answers. After the exam, John and Bill were really pleased with themselves. They thought they were pretty clever for beating the system. Later that night, a friend happened to ask them if they ever tried to cheat. John and Bill looked at each other and laughed, then John said,
     "I would never be involved in any cheating".

(ii) *Unintended irony*
     John and Bill were taking a statistics class together. They studied hard together, but John was clearly better prepared than Bill. During the exam, Bill panicked and started to copy answers from John. John did not see Bill do this and so did not know he was actually helping Bill. John took the school's honor code very seriously. Later that night, a friend happened to ask them if they ever tried to cheat. John and Bill looked at each other, then John said,
     "I would never be involved in any cheating".

Although in an offline task subjects perceived the unintended irony and considered it even more ironic than the intended irony, it is possible that their reading times reflect only their comprehension of the original salient, literally intended interpretation. Such findings, then, would be consistent with the graded salience and literal first hypotheses.

12. This claim, of course, is too simplistic and is put in this way for purposes of presentation. It is quite plausible to use a conventional metaphor ironically. Under such circumstances, it would be the metaphoric meaning that would be salient, as when *Children are precious gems* is used ironically (cf. Pexman et al., 2000).

13. Previous research has shown that children under this age misunderstand irony (Ackerman, 1981, 1983; Winner, 1988, Winner, Levy, Kaplan, & Rosenblatt, 1988). However, children as old as nine have been shown to understand irony (Milosky & Ford, 1997; Rosenblatt et al. 1987, cited in Winner 1988: 155, and see Gibbs, 1994 for a review).

14. Legend follows Du Bois, Schuetze-Coburn, Cumming, & Paolino (1993).

15. Guerrilla Girls are an anonymous group of women who protest women's marginalization in society and in the arts. They use the names of women artists of the past and appear in gorilla masks. For over a decade they have created numerous posters which, principally by means of irony, address taboo topics, challenge men's values, and protest women's discrimination.

16. This latter finding is true of the retention phase as well and is somewhat surprising there. It is inconsistent with the view that contextually incompatible meanings, which have no role in constructing the utterance interpretation, should be discarded. It is, indeed, unclear what role the ironic meaning of a familiar irony could have in the literally biasing context (e.g., the ironic meaning 'known' in the literally biasing context of *Tell me about it*). It is possible, however, that the ironic meaning of a familiar/conventional irony is so salient that it is hard to suppress entirely, despite its irrelevance.

CHAPTER 5

1. "In 1985 Israeli defense minister Rabin of the National Unity Government formed in 1984 announced Iron Fist II. This program stepped up the presence and power of the military in the West Bank and Gaza Strip. It was designed to crush, once and for all, Palestinian resistance. Within one month a dozen political leaders were deported without formal trials, sixty-two activists were placed under administrative detention, and the military killed five people. Documented reports of human rights violations, including collective punishment, arrests, and killings, rose dramatically from 1984 onward" (Samih & Zacharia, 1997: 233). After the outbreak of the Intifada on 8 December 1987, "the defense minister of Israel, Yitzhak Rabin . . . pledged that 'the disturbances in the territories will not occur again. . . . Even if we are forced to use massive force, under no circumstances will we allow last week's events to repeat themselves'" (Samih & Zacharia, 1997: 214, quoting J. Kifner, "Israel Vows to Stress Riot Training," *New York Times*, 30 December 1987, A6).

2. In what follows, reference to "metaphors" and "idioms" or "metaphoric" and "idiomatic" statements should be taken as a shortcut to utterances embedded in either metaphorically or idiomatically biasing contexts. The same holds for their "literal" interpretation, which is, likewise, a consequence of these same utterances being embedded in literally biasing contexts. The items this chapter focuses on are the ones that have both a literal and a nonliteral interpretation.

3. See also chapter 3 for similar ongoing debates over lexical and syntactic ambiguity resolution, chapter 4 for such debates regarding irony comprehension, and chapter

8 for an overview. Readers familiar with these debates can go directly to section 3 in this chapter.

4. On the possibility that context might be predictive enough to avail the contextually compatible but (less or) nonsalient meaning before the contextually incompatible salient meaning is accessed, without blocking it though, see Peleg, Giora, and Fein (2001, in press) and Rayner, Binder, and Duffy (1999). Indeed, in Peleg et al. (2001, in press) and Giora, Peleg, and Fein (2001), we provide evidence showing that even such a strong context cannot block salient meanings, not even when its effects are speedier and precede lexical accessing.

5. As mentioned earlier, both the explicature—the meaning of utterances made up of the literal meanings of their individual words enriched by pragmatic inferencing—and the literal meaning of the individual words will indistinguishably be referred to as "literal meaning" (see chapter 2 in this volume). This ambiguity between word and sentence meaning has not yet been teased apart in the literature and is hard to resolve experimentally (see Ariel, 2002a). For instance, when investigating the processes involved in comprehension of nonliteral language, a probe (test word) such as 'pail', which is literally related to the idiom *He kicked the bucket*, can be primed by the literal meaning of the word *bucket* rather than by the literal interpretation of the utterance as a whole. In contrast, the idiomatically related probe 'die' must rely on the message-level interpretation for its priming. This difference in the priming conditions may render the comparison between responses to literally and nonliterally related test words vacuous (Gibbs, 2001). The problem is hard to solve, since it is hard to envisage a way to tap the literal message while bypassing the literal meaning of the words that make it up. In an attempt to overcome this difficulty, Gibbs (1986c) tested classifications of paraphrases of literal and nonliteral targets. But this methodology may not be flawless, either. While idioms may have a ready-made literal interpretation at their disposal, which is different from their literal compositional meaning, literal utterances do not. Thus, while *kick the bucket* has a coded interpretation ('die') that can be computed directly from the mental lexicon, its literal interpretation does not have a ready-made literal paraphrase ('tip the pail') that can be similarly retrieved. In addition, or maybe as a result, literal paraphrases tend to be made up of less salient or frequent words. Consider the commonality of the interpretation/paraphrase of the nonliteral meaning ('He didn't tell anyone') of the idiom *He kept it under his hat*, as opposed to the oddity and low salience of its literal interpretation/paraphrase and words ('It's beneath his cap'). This could be one reason literal paraphrases took longer to read than nonliteral ones (Gibbs, 1986c). Thus, even though the literal meaning of an utterance usually hinges on the literality of its individual words while its nonliteral meaning depends on the message-level interpretation, the experiments reported here have not warranted this much needed distinction (cf. chapter 2 in this volume).

6. Williams (1992) did not directly discuss metaphors but, rather, polysemous words—words having multiple meanings that are interrelated (as opposed to ambiguous words whose multiple meanings do not seem related, such as the various meanings of *bank*). However, most of his polysemous items are metaphorically based: for example, *dirty* ('soiled'; *'obscene'*) and *smooth* ('even'; *'slick'*). (For a metaphor-based explanation of polysemy, see, e.g., Brugman & Lakoff, 1988; Gibbs, 1994; Lee, 1990; Matlock, 1998, 1989; Sweetser, 1990).

7. As noted earlier, there was significant priming only in the literal condition ('solid'), which was unaffected by extra processing time. Priming in the metaphoric condition ('strict') "was numerically present at all three delays (decreasing over delay) but the effect was only significant when data were collapsed over delay" (Williams, 1992: 201).

8. For similar findings regarding literal language, see Balaban (2002); Giora, Balaban, and Fein (2002); Giora, Balaban, Fein, and Alkabets (in press). For a different view, see MacDonald and Just (1989). For the limited inhibitory effect of negation on inferencing, see Lea and Mulligan (2002).

9. For a discussion of the processing difficulties at the end of sentences see, for instance, Balogh, Zurif, Prather, Swinney, and Finkel, 1998).

10. LOW FAMILIAR/HIGH APT METAPHOR   METAPHORIC TEST WORD
(Test words highly associated with the meaning of both the topic
and metaphoric constituents are italicized.)

A dusty and crowded attic is a paradise	memories
The *fall* of an empire is the sunset	decline
A sea *captain* is a quarterback	leader
Her boyfriend's *look of hate* was a laser	piercing
Anger was a blizzard	blinding
The *thunderclouds* were wild horses	rampage
Purgatory is a lobby	waiting
The rocky mountains were a spine	foundation
Perjury is a boomerang	backfires
Indecision was a whirlpool	confusion
Smog is a shroud	engulfing
Greed is a buzzard	consuming

11. LOW FAMILIAR/MODERATE APT METAPHOR   METAPHORICTEST WORD
(Test words highly associated with the meaning of both the topic
and metaphoric constituents are italicized.)

A long distance swimmer is a warrior	stamina
A good professor is an oasis	fulfilling
The stars were snowflakes	unique
Ritual is a prison	restricting
A *well trained* fighter is a knight	skillful
Her thoughts were a boiling kettle	turmoil
Dictionaries are microscopes	detail
Darkness is a gloved hand	unknown
The bible is cement	unchanging
The stars were signposts	navigate
The *automobile* is a horse	transportation
Garden *weeds* are a case of the measles	spreading

12. Similar problems concerning suitability of test words were also found in Giora and Fein (1999c) for the set of unfamiliar (but not for the set of less familiar) metaphors.

13. Although Gildea and Glucksberg (1983) and Glucksberg et al. (1982) showed that apt metaphors are understood instantly and require no contextual information, whereas less apt metaphors rely on contextual information for their interpretation, they did not look into the salience/familiarity variable. But consider the possibility that aptness might not be a factor when familiar metaphors are concerned, as might be deduced from Pynte et al. (1996; see also section 2.1.4 in this chapter).

14. It should be noted that Glucksberg et al. (2001) did not find priming for any property in a word–word priming test, which indeed often fails to show differences.

15. Legend follows Du Bois, Schuetze-Coburn, Cumming, and Paolino (1993).

16. True, the availability of the salient literal meaning of novel metaphors has hardly been disputed, inconsistently though. There is no reason why, upon the direct ac-

cess view, in a rich and supportive context like this one, novel metaphors should not be accessed directly. Obviously, the intended meaning cannot escape the speaker herself who "knows her mind." Her choice to attend to the literal meaning must be motivated by something other than getting across her point.

17. Judgments of familiarity have been collected from three native speakers.

18. Ariel (2002b) shows that whenever people regress to the unintended (incompatible) meanings, it is the salient meaning they pick up. For instance, in the following examples (i–ii), originally in Hebrew, the respective speakers (the manager; Maya) can still insist that they are right in their respective arguments, because they come up with the salient (rather than the enriched pragmatic) reading of the numbers:

(i)   "A young couple went into the Allegro record store and offered to sell two CDs. The store manager offered the couple 40 sheqels. The guy, who looked like a Kibbutznik, said that in the store across the street he can get **50 sheqels**. The manager of the store said that not on his life will he get **such a sum**. They took a bet. . . . The guy . . . sold the CDs and got **55 sheqels** for them. He took a receipt and went back to Allegro. Sorry, said the manager, you lost. I said you won't get **50 sheqels**, and indeed, you did not get **such a sum**. I got more, explained the astonished Kibbutznik, but the sales woman laughed him in the face." (A story in the magazine *Hair*, 3 September 1990)

(ii)   Mom: You're big kids now, 11 and 9.
       Maya: I am big. I'm 11 and a half. But Iddo is not. He's only 9.
       Iddo: Maya, if anything, then I'm more 9 and a half than you are 11 and a half.
       Maya: **You're not 9 and a half**.
       Mom: Maya, he's right!
       [Calculations follow, and it turns out that Maya is just over 11 years 5 months old and Iddo is 9 years 9 months old.]
       Maya: Well, I said he's not 9 and a half, because he's more! (26 February 2000).

19. Seana Coulson (personal communication) has a different view of examples such as (13). She suggests that once a metaphor has been used to set up connections between domains, it makes it easier to establish mappings between other elements in the source domain with counterpart candidates in the target. Thus, instead of resonating with the literal meaning, such examples may indicate resonating with the metaphoric meaning.

20. Gentner and Wolff (1997) and Wolff and Gentner (2000) found that conventional metaphors were more likely to behave like class inclusion statements when the similarity between the topic and vehicle was low than when it was high. However, when the similarity between the topic and vehicle was high—that is, when metaphors were apt—alignment processes dominated, regardless of salience. In a similar vein, Chiappe and Kennedy (2001) found that it is aptness (number of common features) rather than familiarity (salience) that is the more important factor in determining speakers' preference of metaphor over simile.

21. We also examined the correlations between sarcasm and metaphor comprehension and lesion extent in "anterior" and "posterior" peri-sylvian regions separately for left-brain-damaged and right-brain-damaged individuals. Significant negative correlations between test scores and lesion extent were found for Sarcasm Comprehension in the left middle and inferior frontal gyri and for Metaphor Comprehension in the left middle temporal gyrus and the junctional area of the superior temporal and supramarginal

gyri on the left. Lesion extent in right-hemisphere regions did not correlate with either test performance. The distinct correlation patterns further support the claim that sarcasm comprehension and metaphor comprehension are functionally dissociated if they diverge in salience.

22. Only the literal and figurative meanings were examined, and only they were subject to any analysis reviewed here. Other meanings might have been involved as well, but they were not looked into.

23. This conclusion need not be always true. Consider, for instance, the following modified idiom—*At least I will have something to write home about*—which I used with the intention that my addressee would process it both literally and figuratively ('what I will write home about will be interesting'). Although I cued my addressee as to my literal intention (using a less salient, modified version of the idiom), I also counted on her to access the salient, idiomatic meaning alongside the literal meaning. Since both meanings made sense in the given context, they were most probably retained. (For similar examples, see chapter 2 in this volume.)

CHAPTER 6

1. The jokes dealt with here include either polysemous or ambiguous interpretations. Polysemies involve related meanings (see example 2); ambiguities involve unrelated meanings (see example 1). According to Attardo et al. (1994), such jokes are the most common ones and highly typical among verbal jokes.

2. Obviously, the preceding example may serve to question the notion of "opposition." Although there is some incongruity between the two scripts involved, no opposition relation obtains between them.

3. On the categorial organization of informative texts, see Giora (1985b, 1988).

4. It is questionable, though, whether example (1) is accountable within the categorial view of jokes. For a comprehensive review of the theories of humor and joke interpretation, see Attardo (1994, 1996a, 1998) and Giora (1991).

5. Even if the processing model assumed here should be somewhat revised by incorporating an initial suppression stage that affects salience imbalance, the overall picture remains the same. After all, it is also possible that the contextually appropriate meaning of a joke is hard to retrieve not because it is less salient (less frequent), but because it has been discarded earlier as inappropriate and is consequently less available when called upon. Indeed, a supportive context, while enhancing the salient meaning, also attenuates alternative candidates of similar salience that have been activated on account of their relative salience. Suppression of such contextually incompatible meanings makes them a lot less available when they are required to render a text meaningful (Gernsbacher, 1990; Gernsbacher & Robertson, 1995). As illustration, consider the following joke: "Two men walk into a bar and a third man ducks." It is possible that processing *bar* in the context of the initial clause involves activating a set of similarly salient meanings ('pub', 'legal profession', 'candy'). For certain addressees, this set can also include 'rod'. However, the context of 'walking into a bar', while supporting only the contextually compatible meaning ('pub'), simultaneously suppresses the alternative contextually incompatible meanings. On this account, too, the contextually compatible meaning ('rod') is hardly accessible at the punch line and is consequently hard to retrieve at that point.

6. Indeed, most jokes involve salient, contextually compatible meanings initially that will have to be reinterpreted at the disjunctor point. Some involve less salient meanings initially, however. It is hypothesized that, as a result, their reinterpretation will be less surprising.

7. Indeed, not all jokes involve suppression of incompatible meanings. Some appear to retain them and expose their relatedness to the compatible meanings. For instance, the following joke seems to maintain both the salient (nonliteral) and nonsalient (literal) meanings of the punch line to be funny:

An old Jew was asked how it makes him feel to go to the Wailing Wall every day for 25 years and pray. The old man sadly replied: "Like I'm talking to a wall."

Research has not yet teased apart the differences between the various types of joke texts and the comprehension processes involved.

8. It should be noted that we did not control for the salience of the meanings of the key words, which were selected on the basis of intuitions.

9. Morton A. Gernsbacher has expressed the same view (personal communication).

10. It could be argued, though, that the humorous and nonhumorous examples are not akin in frame shifting and that jokes involve more complex frame shifting than nonjokes (Seana Coulson, personal communication).

11. Compared to the notion of salience, frame shifting is loosely defined. At times it is difficult to see what frame shift is involved in a joke. For instance, blaming the birth of a child on the husband (example 2) may very well be part of a childbirth frame (although not a stereotypical/salient component of it). Similarly, the assumption that noodles are long is part of the frame of cooking noodles (cf. example 10). Rather than frame shift, some jokes involve a reorganization of a given frame. Even so, neither frame shifting nor frame reorganization can account for the overall findings in Coulson and Kutas. Particularly they cannot account for the relative ease of processing nonjokes, involving a frame shift, compared to jokes; nor can they account for the difficulty of joke comprehension among participants who understood the jokes compared to those who did not.

CHAPTER 7

1. On the aesthetic as deviating from a given aesthetic norm or involving old and new forms, see Brinker, 1988; Mukařovský, 1978; Shklovsky, 1917/1965; for a review, see Renan, 1984). On the aesthetic being structured by general cognitive constraints, which makes it easier rather than more difficult to understand, see Shen (1995, 1997).

2. It is questionable whether there are indeed "pure" innovations at all. Consider Zuckermann (1999), who shows that, in many languages, coining new words tends to consist in echoing familiar meanings and sounds. Such lexical enrichment, accomplished via the mechanism termed "phono-semantic matching," allows for a familiar foreign word to be reproduced in the native language, using native preexisting elements that are similar to the foreign word in both meaning and sound. For instance, the Hebrew *dibuv* has been selected to match the salient English *dub*. Similarly, the Hebrew *kef* takes after *cape*, *ashaf* matches *chef*, etc. (See also Pisani, 1967).

The examples provided here might be pure innovations, but they are rare. *Grok* means 'get it', or 'grasp'; taken from *A Stranger in a Strange Land*, a novel by Robert Heinlein (1963), and so might *spandy-wear* (as in "Lanka girls in spandy-wear dancing around"; taken from *Weetzie Bat*, by Francesca Lia Block, 1989: 8).

An innovation may be considered "pure" to the extent that when it is encountered for the first time, the salient, original stem (if it has one) is not made transparent instantly. However, if it is, it will not be "optimal" as long as the novel coin does not involve a change of the original meaning (e.g., *cat sledge*; cf. Gerrig, 1989, where the new compound does not involve a change of the original meanings of its components).

3. For a different assessment see Moon (1998) see also Hudson (1998)

CHAPTER 8

1. But see Gibbs, 1998b, for a critique suggesting that most of the idioms used by Keysar and Bly are based on metonymy, which is often less transparent about its meaning and is viewed as arbitrary.

2. The possibility that the enhancement of the literal meaning of the vehicle by the metaphoric prime may be attributed to the salience of *use knives* which, in the metaphoric prime, could be facilitated by both *surgeon* and *butcher* while, in the literal prime, could be facilitated only by a single constituent (*butcher*), has been disconfirmed by experiment 2.

3. Gerrig's innovative materials are ambiguous rather than polysemous and seem to require suppression. Where polysemies are involved (as in Giora, Kronrod et al., 2001), no such suppression is anticipated. For similar views, see Frazier and Rayner (1990), Frisson and Pickering (2001).

CHAPTER 9

1. In 1917, Duchamp sent a "work" called *Fountain* to the New York "Independent Show," signed with the name "R. Mutt". It was nothing but a common urinal.

2. In 1919, Duchamp presented his version of the *Mona Lisa*: the symbol of femininity was given a moustache (crayon on a reproduction of the original). Its title, *L.H.O.O.Q*, when read in French, has a debasing meaning.

3. This must also be true of translation errors.

4. If it did, it would undermine the code involved in language. While contextual meanings account for language change, salient meanings account for language stability. Change, indeed, occurs constantly, but its pace is slow, since we cannot accommodate a flux of innovation (Mira Ariel, personal communication; on optimal innovation, see chapter 7 in this volume).

REFERENCES

Abdullaev, Y. G., & Posner, M. I. (1997). Time course of activating brain areas in generating verbal associations. *Psychological Science, 8*, 56–59.

Abrams, K., & Bever, T. G. (1969). Syntactic structures modifies attention during speech perception and recognition. *Quarterly Journal of Experimental Psychology, 21*, 280–290.

Abrahams, J., Zucker, D., & Zucker, J. (1980). *Flying high*. USA: Paramount.

Ackerman, B. P. (1981). Young children's understanding of a speaker's intentional use of a false utterance. *Developmental Psychology, 17*, 472–480.

Ackerman, B. P. (1983). Form and function in children's understanding of ironic utterances. *Journal of Experimental Child Psychology, 35*, 487–508.

Altmann, G. T. M. (1988). Ambiguity, parsing strategies, and computational models. *Language and Cognitive Processes, 3*, 73–97.

Altmann, G. T. M., & Steedman, M. (1988). Interacting with context during human sentence processing. *Cognition, 30*, 191–238.

Altmann, G. T. M., Garnham, A., & Dennis, Y. (1992). Avoiding the garden path: Eye movements in context. *Journal of Memory and Language, 31*, 685–712.

Anaki, D., Faust, M., & Kravetz, S. (1998). Cerebral hemispheric asymmetries in processing lexical metaphors. *Neuropsychologia, 36*, 691–700.

Ariel, M. (1988). Referring and accessibility. *Journal of Linguistics, 24*, 65–87.

Ariel, M. (1990). *Accessing NP antecedents*. London: Routledge.

Ariel, M. (1991). The function of accessibility in a theory of grammar. *Journal of Pragmatics, 16*, 443–463.

Ariel, M. (1998). Discourse markers and form-function correlations. In A. H. Jucker & Y. Ziv (Eds.), *Discourse markers* (pp. 217–253). Amsterdam: John Benjamins.

Ariel, M. (1999a, June). Against a unique literal meanings. Paper presented at Pragma99: International Conference on Pragmatics and Negotiations, Tel Aviv University.

Ariel, M. (1999b). Mapping so-called "pragmatic" phenomena according to a "linguistic-extralinguistic" distinction: The case of propositions marked "accessible." In M. Darnell, E. Moravcsik, F. Newmeyer, M. Noonan, & K. Wheatley (Eds.), *Functionalism and formalism in linguistics.* Vol. 2: *Case studies* (pp. 11–38). Amsterdam: John Benjamins.

Ariel, M. (2000). The development of person agreement markers: From pronouns to higher accessibility markers. In M. Barlow & S. Kemmer (Eds.), *Usage based models of language* (pp. 197–260). Stanford: CSLI

Ariel, M. (2002a). The demise of a unique literal meaning. *Journal of Pragmatics, 34,* 361–402. Special issue on "Literal, minimal, salient, and privileged meanings," ed. M. Ariel.

Ariel, M. (2002b). Privileged interactional interpretations. *Journal of Pragmatics, 34,* 1003–1044.

Ariel, M. (In press). *Pragmatics and language.* Cambridge: Cambridge University Press

Ariel, M., & Giora, R. (1992a). Gender versus group-relation analysis of impositive speech acts. In K. Hall, M. Bucholtz, & B. Moonwomon (Eds.), *Locating power: Proceedings of the Second Berkeley Women and Language Conference, April 4 and 5, 1992* (Vol. 1, pp. 11–22). Berkeley: Berkeley Linguistic Society

Ariel, M., & Giora, R. (1992b). The role of women in linguistic and narrative change: A study of the Hebrew pre-state literature. *Journal of Narrative and Life History, 2,* 309–332.

Ariel, M., & Giora, R. (1998). A Self versus Other point of view in language: Redefining femininity and masculinity. *International Journal of the Sociology of Language, 129,* 59–86.

Ariel, M., & Giora, R. (2000). Pragmatics. In A. Kazdin (Ed.), *Encyclopedia of psychology* (Vol. 6, pp. 272–275). New York and Washington, DC: Oxford University Press and American Psychological Association.

Armstrong, S., Gleitman, L., & Gleitman, H. (1983). What some concepts might not be. *Cognition, 13,* 263–308.

Attardo, S. (1994). *Linguistic theories of humor.* Berlin: Mouton de Gruyter.

Attardo, S. (1996a). Humor. In J. Verschueren, J-O. Östman, J. Blommaert, & C. Bulcaen (Eds.), *Handbook of pragmatics* (pp. 1–18). Amsterdam: John Benjamins.

Attardo, S. (1996b). Humor theory beyond jokes: The treatment of humorous texts at large. In J. Hulstijn & A. Nijholt (Eds.), *Automatic interpretation and generation of verbal humor.* IWCH '96. Twente Workshop on Language and Technology 12 (pp. 87–101). Enschede: University of Twente.

Attardo, S. (1998). Theoretical pragmatics. Unpublished manuscript.

Attardo, S. (2000). Irony as relevant inappropriateness. *Journal of Pragmatics, 32,* 793–826.

Attardo, S. (2001). *Humorous texts: A semantics and pragmatics analysis.* Berlin: Mouton de Gruyter.

Attardo, S., Attardo, D. H., Baltes, P., & Petray, M. J. (1994). The linear organization of jokes: Analysis of two thousand texts. *Humor, 7,* 27–54.

Bakhtin, M. M. (1981). *The dialogic imagination.* C. Emerson & M. Holquist (Eds.). Austin: University of Texas Press.

Balaban, N. (2002). Negation: Lexical access and integration. Unpublished M.A. thesis, Tel Aviv University.

Ball, C. N., & Ariel, M. (1978). Or something, etc. *Penn Review of Linguistics, 3,* 35–45.

Balogh, J., Zurif, E., Prather, P., Swinney, D., & Finkel, L. (1998). End-of-sentence effects in real-time language processing: A new perspective on Blumstein et al.'s findings. *Brain and Language, 61*, 169–182.

Balota, D. A. (1994). Visual word recognition: The journey from features to meaning. In M. A. Gernsbacher (Ed.), *Handbook of psycholinguistics* (pp. 303–358). San Diego: Academic Press.

Balota, D. A., & Duchek, J. M. (1991). Semantic priming effects, lexical repetition effects and contextual disambiguation effects in healthy aged individuals and individuals with senile dementia of the Alzheimer type. *Brain and Language, 40*, 181–201.

Barsalou, L. W., & Prinz, J. J. (1997). Mundane creativity in perceptual symbol systems. In T. B. Ward, S. M. Smith, & J. Vaid (Eds.), *Conceptual structures and processes: Emergence, discovery, and change* (pp. 267–307).Washington, DC: American Psychological Association Press.

Bassili, J. N. (1989). Trait encoding in behavior identification and dispositional inference. *Personality and Social Psychology Bulletin, 15*, 285–296.

Bassili, J. N. & Smith, M. C. (1986). On the spontaneity of trait attribution: Converging evidence for the role of cognitive strategy. *Journal of Personality and Social Psychology, 50*, 239–245.

Bassili, John N., Smith, M. C., & MacLeod, C. M. (1989). Auditory and visual word stem completion: Separating data-driven and conceptually-driven processes. *Quarterly Journal of Experimental Psychology, 41A*, 439–453.

Bates, E. (1999). On the nature and nurture of language. In E. Bizzi, P. Calissano, & V. Volterra (Eds.), *Frontiere della biologia Il cervello di Homo sapiens* [Frontiers of biology: The brain of homo sapiens] (pp. 241–265). Rome: Istituto della Enciclopedia Italiana fondata da Giovanni Trecanni S.p.A.

Bates, E., Hernandez, A., & Pizzamilglio, L. (1996). Gender priming in Italian. *Perception & Psychophysics, 58*, 992–1004.

Bates, E., & MacWhinney, B. (1989). Functionalism and the competition model. In B. MacWhinney & E. Bates (Eds.), *The crosslinguistic study of language processing* (pp. 3–73). Cambridge: Cambridge University Press.

Beauvillain, C., & Grainger, J. (1987). Accessing interlexical homographs: Some limitations of a language-selective access. *Journal of Memory and Language, 26*, 658–672.

Beeman, M., Friedman, R., Grafman, J., Perez, E., Diamond, S., & Lindsey, M. (1994). Summation priming and coarse semantic coding in the right hemisphere. *Journal of Cognitive Neuroscience, 6*, 26–45.

Berg, J. (1993). Literal meaning and context. *Iyyun, 42*, 397–411. (In Hebrew).

Bergson, H. (1956). Laughter. In W. Sypher (Ed.), *Comedy* (pp. 61–190). New York: Anchor Books.

Bergvall, V. L., Bing, J. M., & Freed, F. A (1996). *Rethinking language and gender: Theory and practice.* London: Longman.

Berlyne, D. E. (1971). *Aesthetics and psychobiology.* New York: Appleton-Century-Crofts.

Bever, T. G. (1970). The cognitive basis for linguistic structure. In J. R. Hays (Ed.), *Cognitive and the development of language.* New York: Wiley.

Bihrle, A. M., Brownell, H. H., Powelson, J., & Gardner, H. (1986). Comprehension of humorous and non-humorous materials by left and right brain-damaged patients. *Brain and Cognition, 5*, 399–411.

Binder, K. S., & Morris, R. K. (1995). Eye movement and lexical ambiguity resolution: Effects of prior encounter and discourse topic. *Journal of Experimental Psychology: Learning, Memory, and Cognition, 21*, 1186–1196.

Binder, K. S., & Rayner, K. (1998). Contextual strength does not modulate the subordinate bias effect: Evidence from eye fixations and self-paced reading. *Psychonomic Bulletin and Review, 5,* 217–276.

Binder, K. S., & Rayner, K. (1999). Does contextual strength modulate the subordinate bias effect? A reply to Kellas and Vu. *Psychonomic Bulletin and Review, 6,* 518–522.

Blank, G. D. (1988). Metaphors in the lexicon. *Metaphor and Symbolic Activity, 3,* 21–36.

Blasko, G. D., & Connine, C. (1993). Effects of familiarity and aptness on metaphor processing. *Journal of Experimental Psychology: Learning, Memory, and Cognition, 19,* 295–308.

Blaxton, T. A. (1989). Investigating dissociations among memory measures: Support for a transfer-appropriate processing framework. *Journal of Experimental Psychology: Learning, Memory and Cognition, 15,* 657–668.

Block, F. L. (1989). *Weetzie bat.* New York: Harper Trophy.

Boland, J. E., Tanenhaus, M. K., & Garnsey, S. M. (1990). Evidence from the immediate use of verb control information in sentence processing. *Journal of Memory and Language, 29,* 413–432.

Booth, W. (1974). *A rhetoric of irony.* Chicago: University of Chicago Press.

Bornstein, R. F., & D'Agostino, P. R. (1992). Stimulus recognition and the mere exposure effect. *Journal of Personality and Social Psychology, 63,* 545–552.

Bottini, G., Corcoran, R., Sterzi, R., Paulesu, E., Schenone, P., Scarpa, P., Frackowiak, R. S. J., & Frith, C. D. (1994). The role of the right hemisphere in the interpretation of figurative aspects of language: A positron emission tomography activation study. *Brain, 117,* 1241–1253.

Bowdle, B. F., & Gentner, D. (1995, November). The career of metaphor. Poster presented at the Thirty-sixth Annual Meeting of the Psychonomic Society, Los Angeles, California.

Bowdle, F. B., & Gentner, D. (1999). Metaphor comprehension: From comparison to categorization. In M. Hahn & S. C. Stoness (Eds.), *Proceedings of the Twenty-first Annual Conference of the Cognitive Science Society* (pp. 90–95). Mahwah, NJ: Lawrence Erlbaum Associates.

Bowdle, B. F., & Gentner, D. (2001). The career of metaphor: Patterns of change in figurative language and figurative thought. Unpublished ms.

Bradley, D. C., & Forster, K. I. (1987). A reader's view of listening. *Cognition, 25,* 103–134.

Bredin, H. (1997). The semantic structure of verbal irony. *Journal of Literary Semantics, 26,* 1–19.

Brinker, M. (1988). *Aesthetics as the theory of criticism.* Tel Aviv: Broadcast University and the Ministry of Defense, Israel.

Brisard, F., Frisson, S., & Sandra, D. (2001). Processing unfamiliar metaphors in a self-paced reading task. *Metaphor and Symbol, 16,* 87–108.

Brown, P., & Levinson, S. (1987). *Politeness.* Cambridge: Cambridge University Press.

Brownell, H. H. (1988). Appreciation of metaphoric and connotative word meaning by brain damaged patients. In C. Chiarello (Ed.), *Right hemisphere contributions to lexical semantics* (pp. 19–31). New York: Springer.

Brownell, H. H., Michel, D., Powelson, J., & Gardner, H. (1983). Surprise but not coherence: Sensitivity to verbal humor in right hemisphere patients. *Brain and Language, 18,* 20–27.

Brownell, H. H., Potter, H. H., Michelow, D., & Gardner, H. (1984). Sensitivity to lexical denotation and connotation in brain-damaged patients: A double dissociation. *Brain and Language, 22,* 253–265.

Brownell, H. H., Potter, H. H., Bihrle, A. M., & Gardner, H. (1986). Inference deficits in right brain damaged patients. *Brain and Language, 27,* 310–321

Brugman, C. (1997). Polysemy. In J. Verschueren, J-O. Östman, J. Blommaert, & C. Bulcaen (Eds.), *Handbook of pragmatics* (pp. 1–26). Amsterdam: John Benjamins.

Brugman, C. & Lakoff, G. (1988). Cognitive topology and lexical networks. In S. Small, G. Cottrell, & M. Tannenhaus (Eds.), *Lexical ambiguity resolution* (pp. 477–508). Palo Alto, CA: Morgan Kaufman.

Burgess, C., & Lund, K. (1997). Modeling parsing constraints with high-dimensional context space. *Language and Cognitive Processes, 12,* 177–210.

Burgess, C., & Simpson, G. B. (1988a). Cerebral hemispheric mechanisms in the retrieval of ambiguous word meanings. *Brain and Language, 33,* 86–103.

Burgess, C., & Simpson, G. B. (1988b). Neuropsychology of lexical ambiguity resolution: The contribution of divided visual field studies. In S. L. Small, G. W. Cottrell, & M. K. Tanenhaus (Eds.), *Lexical ambiguity resolution: Perspectives from psycholinguistics, neuropsychology, and artificial intelligence* (pp. 411–430). San Mateo, CA: Morgan Kaufmann.

Burgess, C., Tanenhaus, M. K., & Seidenberg, M. S. (1989). Context and lexical access: Implication of nonword interference for lexical ambiguity resolution. *Journal of Experimental Psychology: Learning, Memory and Cognition, 15,* 620–632.

Bybee, J. L. (1985). *Morphology.* Amsterdam: John Benjamins.

Bybee, J. L., Perkins, R., & Pagliuca, W. (1994). *The evolution of grammar.* Chicago: University of Chicago Press.

Cairns, H. S. (1984). Current issues in language comprehension. In R. Naremore (Ed.), *Recent advances in language science* (pp. 221–237). San Diego: College Hill Press.

Cameron, D. (1995). *Verbal hygiene.* London: Routledge.

Carpenter, P. A., & Daneman, M. (1981). Lexical retrieval and error recovery in reading: A model based on eye fixations. *Journal of Verbal Learning and Verbal Behavior, 8,* 737–744.

Carreiras, M. (1992). Estrategias de análisis sintáctico en el procesamiento de frases: Cierre temprano versus cierre tradío. *Cognitiva, 4,* 3–27.

Carreiras, M., Garnham, A., Oakhill, J., & Cain, K. (1996). The use of stereotypical gender information in constructing a mental model: Evidence from English and Spanish. *Quarterly Journal of Experimental Psychology, 49A,* 639–663.

Carroll G., & Rooth, M. (1998, June). *Valence induction with a head-lexicalized PCFG.* Paper presented at the Third Conference on Empirical Methods in Natural Language Processing, Granada, Spain.

Carroll, J., Davis, P., & Richman, B. (1976). *Word frequency book.* New York: Houghton Mifflin.

Carroll, N. (1994). Visual metaphor. In J. Hintikka (Ed.), *Aspects of metaphor* (pp. 189–218). Dordrecht: Kluwer.

Carroll, N. (1996). A note on film metaphor. *Journal of Pragmatics, 26,* 809–822. Special issue "On the Cognitive and Cinematic Visual Discourse," ed. R. Giora.

Carston, R. (1988). Implicature, explicature, and truth-theoretic semantics. In R. Kempson (Ed.), *Mental representations: The interface between language and reality* (pp.155–181). Cambridge: Cambridge University Press.

Carston, R. (1993). Conjunction, explanation, and relevance. *Lingua, 90,* 27–48.

Castel-Bloom, O. (1992). *Dolly city.* Tel Aviv: Zmora Bitan. (In Hebrew).

Challis B. H., & Brodbeck, D. R. (1992). Levels of processing affects priming in word fragment completion. *Journal of Experimental Psychology: Learning, Memory and Cognition, 18,* 595–607.

Chiappe, D. L., & Kennedy, J. M. (1999). Aptness predicts preference for metaphors or similes, as well as recall bias. *Psychonomic Bulletin & Review, 6,* 668–676.

Chiappe, D. L., & Kennedy, J. M. (2001). Literal bases for metaphor and simile. *Metaphor and Symbol, 16,* 249–276. Special issue "On Models of Figurative Language," ed. R. Giora.

Chiappe, D. L., Kennedy, J. M., & Chiappe, P. (1999). Aptness is more important than comprehensibility in predicting recognition bias and preference for metaphors and similes. Unpublished ms.

Chiarello, C. (1991). Interpretation of word meanings by the cerebral hemispheres: One is not enough. In P. J. Schwanenflugel (Ed.), *The psychology of word meanings* (pp. 251–278). Hillsdale, NJ: Lawrence Erlbaum Associates.

Chiarello, C. (1998). On codes of meaning and the meaning of codes: Semantic access of retrieval within and between hemispheres. In M. Beeman & C. Chiarello (Eds.), *Right hemisphere language comprehension: Perspectives from cognitive neuroscience* (pp. 141–160). Mahwah, NJ: Lawrence Erlbaum Associates.

Chwilla, D. J., Hagoort, P., & Brown, C. M. (1998). The mechanism underlying backward priming in a lexical decision task: Spreading activation versus semantic matching. *Quarterly Journal of Experimental Psychology: Human Experimental Psychology, 51A,* 531–560.

Clark, H. H. (1979). Responding to indirect speech acts. *Cognitive Psychology, 11,* 430–477.

Clark, H. H. (1996). *Using language.* Cambridge: Cambridge University Press.

Clark, H. H. & Carlson, T. B. (1982). Hearers and speech acts. *Language, 58,* 332–373.

Clark, H. H., & Gerrig, R. (1983). Understanding old words with new meanings. *Journal of Verbal Learning and Verbal Behavior, 22,* 591–608.

Clark, H. H., & Gerrig, R. (1984). On the pretense theory of irony. *Journal of Experimental Psychology: General, 113,* 121–126.

Clausner, T. C., & Croft, W. (1997). Productivity and schematicity in metaphors. *Cognitive Science, 21,* 247–282.

Clifton, C. Jr., & Ferreira, F. (1989). Ambiguity in context. *Language and Cognitive Processes, 12,* 77–103.

Coates, J. (1986). *Women, men and language.* London: Longman.

Coates, J. (1996). *Women talk.* Oxford: Blackwell.

Colston, H. L. (1997). Salting a wound or sugaring a pill: The pragmatic functions of ironic criticism. *Discourse Processes, 23,* 25–45.

Colston, H. L., Giora, R., & Katz, A. (2000, July). *Joke comprehension: Salience and context effects.* Paper presented at the Seventh International Pragmatics Conference, Budapest.

Colston, H. L., & O'Brien, J. (2000). Contrast and pragmatics in figurative language: Anything understatement can do, irony can do better. *Journal of Pragmatics, 32,* 1557–1583.

Connine, M. C., Blasko, D., Brandt, R., & Kaplan Layer, J. (1992). Idiomatic processing: Syntactic frozenness and subjective familiarity. *Psychological Research, 54,* 225–232.

Connine, C. M., Blasko, D., & Wang, J. (1994). Vertical similarity in spoken word recognition: Multiple lexical activation, individual differences, and the role of sentence context. *Perception & Psychophysics, 56,* 624–636.

Conrad, C. (1974). Context effects in sentence comprehension: A study of the subjective lexicon. *Memory & Cognition, 2*, 130–138.

Coppola, F. F. (1972). *The godfather*. Paramount Pictures.

Coulson, S. (2001). *Semantic leaps*. Cambridge: Cambridge University Press.

Coulson, S. & Kutas, M. (1998). Frame-shifting and sentential integration. University of California, San Diego: Cognitive Science Technical Report 98.03.

Coulson, S. & Kutas, M. (2001). Getting it: Human event-related response to jokes in good and poor comprehenders. *Neuroscience Letters, 316*, 71–74.

Coulson, S., & Van Petten, C. (1999). Conceptual integration and metaphor: An ERP study. *Cognitive Neuroscience Society Annual Meeting Program 1999: A Supplement of the Journal of Cognitive Neuroscience*, 50.

Coulson, S. & Van Petten, C. (in press). Conceptual integration and metaphor comprehension: An ERP Study. *Memory & Cognition*.

Crawford, M. (1995). *Talking difference: On gender and language*. London: Sage.

Creusere, M. A. (1999). Theories of adults' understanding and use of irony and sarcasm: Applications to and evidence from research with children. *Developmental Review, 19*, 213–261.

Creusere, M. A. (2000). A developmental test of theoretical perspectives on the understanding of verbal irony: Children's recognition of allusion and pragmatic insincerity. *Metaphor and Symbol, 15*, 29–45.

Cronk, B. C., Lima, S. D., & Schweigert, W. A. (1993). Idioms in sentences: Effects of frequency, literalness, and familiarity. *Journal of Psycholinguistic Research, 22*, 59–82.

Cronk, B. C., & Schweigert, W. A. (1992). The comprehension of idioms: Effects of familiarity, literalness, and usage. *Applied Psycholinguistics, 13*, 131–146.

Curcó, C. (1995). Some observations on the pragmatics of humorous interpretations: A relevance theoretic approach. *UCL Working Papers in Linguistics, 7*, 27–47.

Curcó, C. (1996a). The implicit expression of attitudes, mutual manifestness, and verbal humor. *UCL Working Papers in Linguistics, 8*, 89–99.

Curcó, C. (1996b). Relevance theory and humorous interpretations. In N. Hulstijn & A. Nijholt (Eds.), *Automatic interpretation and generation of verbal humor* (pp. 53–68). Twente: University of Twente.

Curcó, C. (1997). *The pragmatics of humorous interpretations: A relevance-theoretic approach*. Unpublished ms.

Curcó, C. (1998). Indirect echoes and verbal humor. In V. Rouchota & A. H. Jucker (Eds.), *Current issues in relevance theory* (pp. 305–325). Amsterdam: John Benjamins.

Curcó, C. (2000). Irony: negation, echo and metarepresentation. *Lingua, 110*, 257–280.

Cutler, A. (1974). On saying what you mean without meaning what you say. In M. W. Lagaly, R. A. Fox, & A. Bruck (Eds.), *Papers from the Tenth Regional Meeting* (pp. 117–127). Chicago: Chicago Linguistic Society.

Daly, M. (1978). *Gyn/ecology: The metaethics of radical feminism*. Boston: Beacon Press.

Dascal, M. (1987). Defining literal meaning. *Cognitive Science, 11*, 259–281.

Dascal, M. (1989). On the role of context and literal meaning in understanding. *Cognitive Science, 13*, 253–257.

De Palma, P., & Weiner E. J. (1990, July). "When a riddle is not a riddle?" Paper presented at the International Pragmatics Conference, Barcelona.

Dews, S., Kaplan, J. & Winner, E. (1995). Why not say it directly? The social functions of irony. *Discourse Processes, 19*, 347–368.

Dews, S. & Winner, E. (1995). Muting the meaning: A social function of irony. *Metaphor and Symbolic Activity, 10*, 3–19.

Dews, S., & Winner, E. (1997). Attributing meaning to deliberately false utterances: The case of irony. In C. Mandell & A. McCabe (Eds.), *The problem of meaning: Behavioral and cognitive perspectives* (pp. 377–414). Amsterdam: Elsevier.

Dews, S., & Winner, E. (1999). Obligatory processing of the literal and nonliteral meanings of ironic utterances. *Journal of Pragmatics, 31*, 1579–1599.

Dopkins, S., Morris, R. K., & Rayner, K. (1992). Lexical ambiguity and eye fixation in reading: A test of competing models of lexical ambiguity. *Journal of Memory and Language, 31*, 461–477.

Drew, P. (1987). Po-faced receipts of teases. *Linguistics, 25*, 219–253.

Du Bois, W. J. (1998, January). *Dialogic syntax*. Paper presented at the Cognitive Theories of Intertextuality Meeting, Tel Aviv University.

Du Bois, W. J. (2000a, May). *Reusable syntax: Socially distributed cognition in dialogic interaction*. Paper presented at CSDL 2000: Fifth Conference on Conceptual Structure, Discourse, and Language, University of California, Santa Barbara.

Du Bois, W. J. (2000b). *Santa Barbara corpus of spoken American English*. CD-ROM. Philadelphia: Linguistic Data Consortium.[www.ldc.upnn.edu/publications.sbc/]

Du Bois, W. J., Schuetze-Coburn, S., Cumming, S., & Paolino, D. (1993). Outline of discourse transcription. In J. A. Edwards & M. D. Lampert (Eds.), *Talking data: Transcription and coding in discourse research* (pp. 45–87). Hillsdale, NJ: Lawrence Erlbaum Associates.

Ducas, G. (1998).Irony aptness: The case of visual and cinematic discourse. M.A. thesis, Tel Aviv University.

Dudai, Y. (1989). *The neurobiology of memory*. Oxford: Oxford University Press.

Dudai, Y. (1996). Consolidation: Fragility on the road to the engram. *Neuron, 17*, 367–370.

Duffy, S. A., Morris, R. K., & Rayner, K. (1988). Lexical ambiguity and fixations times in reading. *Journal of Memory and Language, 27*, 429–446.

Elnatan, I. (2002). Degree of innovation and pleasure rating. Unpublished M.A. thesis, Tel Aviv University (in Hebrew).

Erman, B., & Warren, B. (2001). The idiom principle and the open choice principle. *Text, 20*, 29–62.

Fauconnier, G. (1994). *Mental spaces*. Cambridge: Cambridge University Press.

Fauconnier, G. (1997). *Mappings in language and thought*. Cambridge: Cambridge University Press.

Fauconnier, G., & Turner, M. (1996). Blending as a central processes of grammar. In A.Goldberg (Ed.), *Conceptual structure, discourse, and language* (pp. 113–130). Stanford: Center for the Study of Language and Information.

Fauconnier, G., & Turner, M. (1998). Conceptual integration networks. *Cognitive Science, 22*, 133–187.

Faust, M. (1998). Obtaining evidence of language comprehension from sentence priming. In M. Beeman & C. Chiarello (Eds.), *Right hemisphere language comprehension: Perspectives from cognitive neuroscience* (pp. 161–185). Hillsdale NJ: Lawrence Erlbaum Associates.

Faust, M., & Chiarello, C. (1998). Sentence context and lexical resolution by the two hemispheres. *Neuropsychologia, 36*, 827–836.

Faust, M., & Gernsbacher, M. A. (1995). Cerebral mechanisms for suppression of inappropriate information during sentence comprehension. *Brain and Language, 53*, 234–259.

Faust, M., & Kahane, A. (2002). Summation of activation in the cerebral hemisphere: Evidence from semantically convergent and semantically divergent primes. *Neuropsychologia, 40*, 892–901.

Ferreira, F., & Clifton, C. Jr. (1986). The independence of syntactic processing. *Journal of Memory and Language, 30*, 725–745.

Fodor, J. (1983). *The modularity of mind*. Cambridge, MA: MIT Press.

Fodor, J. D. (1990). Thematic roles and modularity: Comments on the chapters by Frazier and Tanenhaus et al. In G. T. M. Altmann (Ed.), *Cognitive models of speech processing: Psycholinguistic and computational perspectives* (pp. 434–456). Cambridge, MA: MIT Press.

Forceville, C. F. (1996). *Pictorial metaphor in advertising*. London: Routledge & Kegan Paul.

Forster, K. I. (1981). Priming and the effects of sentence and lexical contexts on naming time: Evidence for autonomous lexical processing. *Quarterly Journal of Experimental Psychology, 33A*, 465–495.

Forster, K. I. (1989). Basic issues in lexical processing. In W. Marslen-Wilson (Ed.), *Lexical representation and process* (pp. 75–107). Cambridge, MA: MIT Press.

Forster, K. I., & Bednall, E. S. (1976). Terminating and exhaustive search in lexical access. *Memory & Cognition, 4*, 53–61.

Frazier, L. (1978). *On comprehending sentences: Syntactic parsing strategies*. Ph.D. dissertation, University of Connecticut, Storrs, CT. Distributed by Indiana University Linguistics Club.

Frazier, L. (1987a). Sentence processing: A tutorial review. In M. Coltheart (Ed.), *Attention and performance XII: The psychology of reading* (pp. 559–586). Hillsdale, NJ: Lawrence Erlbaum Associates.

Frazier, L. (1987b). Syntactic processing: Evidence from Dutch. *Natural Language and Linguistic Theory, 5*, 519–560.

Frazier, L. (1990). Exploring the architecture of the language-processing system. In G. T. M. Altmann (Ed.), *Cognitive models of speech processing: Psycholinguistic and computational perspectives* (pp. 409–433). Cambridge, MA: MIT Press.

Frazier, L., & Clifton, C. (1996). *Construal*. Cambridge, MA: MIT Press.

Frazier, L., Pacht, J. M., & Rayner, K. (1999). Taking on semantic commitments, II: Collective versus distributive readings. *Cognition, 70*, 87–104.

Frazier, L., & Rayner, K. (1987). Resolution of syntactic category ambiguities: Eye movements in parsing lexical ambiguous sentences. *Journal of Memory and Language, 26*, 505–526.

Frazier, L., & Rayner, K. (1990). Taking on semantic commitments: Processing multiple meanings vs. multiple senses. *Journal of Memory and Language, 29*, 181–200.

French, M. (1977). *The women's room*. New York: Summit Books.

Freud, S. (1905/1960). *Jokes and their relation to the unconscious*. New York: Norton.

Frisson, S., & Pickering M. (2001). Obtaining a figurative interpretation of a word: Support for underspecification. *Metaphor and Symbol, 16*, 149–172. Special issue "On Models of Figurative Language," ed. R. Giora.

Galbraith, G. G., & Taschman, C. S. (1969). Homophone units: A normative methodological investigation of the strength of component elements. *Journal of Verbal Learning and Verbal Behavior, 8*, 737–744.

Gardner, H. & Brownell, H. H. (1986). *The right hemispheric communication battery*. Boston: Psychology Service.

Garrod, S., & Terras, M. (2000). The contribution of lexical and situational knowledge to resolving discourse roles: Bonding and resolution. *Journal of Memory and Language, 42*, 526–544.

Gentner, D., & Bowdle, F. B. (2001). Convention, form, and figurative language processing. *Metaphor and Symbol,* 223–247. Special issue "On Models of Figurative Language," ed. R. Giora.

Gentner, D., & Wolff, P. (1997). Alignment in the processing of metaphor. *Journal of Memory and Language, 37*, 331–355.

Gentner, D., & Wolff, P. (2000). Metaphor and knowledge change. In E. Dietrich & A. Markman (Eds.), *Cognitive dynamics: Conceptual change in humans and machines* (pp. 295–342). Mahwah, NJ: Erlbaum.

Gernsbacher, M. A. (1984). Resolving twenty years of inconsistent interactions between lexical familiarity and orthography, concreteness, and polysemy. *Journal of Experimental Psychology: General, 113*, 256–281.

Gernsbacher, M. A. (1989). Mechanisms that improve referential access. *Cognition, 32(2)*, 99–156.

Gernsbacher, M. A. (1990). *Language comprehension as structure building.* Hillsdale NJ: Lawrence Erlbaum Associates.

Gernsbacher, M. A. (1993). Less skilled readers have less efficient suppression mechanisms. *Psychological Science, 4*, 294–298.

Gernsbacher, M. A., & Faust, M. E. (1990). The role of suppression in sentence comprehension. In G. B. Simpson (Ed.), *Understanding word and sentence* (pp. 97–128). Amsterdam: North Holland.

Gernsbacher, M. A., & Faust, M. E. (1991). The mechanism of suppression: A component of general comprehension skill. *Journal of Experimental Psychology: Learning Memory and Cognition, 17*, 245–262.

Gernsbacher, M. A., Keysar, B., Robertson, R. W., & Werner, N. K. (2001). The role of suppression and enhancement in understanding metaphors. *Journal of Memory and Language, 45*, 433–450.

Gernsbacher, M. A., & Robertson, R. W. (1995). Reading skill and suppression revisited. *Psychological Science, 6*, 165–169.

Gernsbacher, M. A., & Robertson, R. W. (1999). *Parallel form affects sentence comprehension.* Unpublished ms.

Gerrig, R. J. (1989). The time course of sense creation. *Memory & Cognition, 17*, 194–207.

Gerrig, R. J., & Healy, A. F. (1983). Dual process in metaphor understanding: Comprehension and appreciation. *Journal of Experimental Psychology: Learning, Memory and Cognition, 9(4)*, 667–675.

Gibbs, R.W. Jr. (1980). Spilling the beans on understanding and memory for idioms in conversation. *Memory & Cognition, 8*, 449–456.

Gibbs, R. W. Jr. (1982). A critical examination of the contribution of literal meaning to understanding nonliteral discourse. *Text, 2*, 9–27.

Gibbs, R. W. Jr. (1983). Do people always process the literal meanings of indirect requests? *Journal of Experimental Psychology: Learning, Memory, and Cognition, 9*, 524–533.

Gibbs, R. W. Jr. (1984). Literal meaning and psychological theory. *Cognitive Science, 8*, 575–304.

Gibbs, R. W. Jr. (1986a). Comprehension and memory for nonliteral utterances: The problem of sarcastic indirect requests. *Acta Psychologica, 62*, 41–57.

Gibbs, R. W. Jr. (1986b). On the psycholinguistics of sarcasm. *Journal of Experimental Psychology: General, 115*, 3–15.

Gibbs, R. W. Jr. (1986c). Skating on thin ice: Literal meaning and understanding idioms in conversation. *Discourse Processes, 9*, 17–30.

Gibbs, R. W. Jr. (1986d). What makes some indirect speech acts conventional? *Journal of Memory and Language, 25*, 181–196.

Gibbs, R. W. Jr. (1990). Comprehending figurative referential descriptions. *Journal of Experimental Psychology: Learning, Memory and Cognition, 16*, 56–66.

Gibbs, R. W. Jr. (1991). Metaphor as constraint on individual creativity. *Creativity Research Journal, 4*, 86–88.

Gibbs, R. W. Jr. (1993). Processes and products in making sense of tropes. In A. Ortony (Ed.), *Metaphor and thought* (2nd ed., pp. 252–276). Cambridge: Cambridge University Press.

Gibbs, R. W. Jr. (1994). *The poetics of mind.* Cambridge: Cambridge University Press.

Gibbs, R. W. Jr. (1998a). Counter point commentary. In A. Katz, C. Cacciari, R. Gibbs, & M. Turner (Eds.), *Figurative language and thought* (pp. 158–192). New York: Oxford University Press.

Gibbs, R. W. Jr. (1998b). The fight over metaphor in thought and language. In A. Katz, C. Cacciari, R. Gibbs, & M. Turner (Eds.), *Figurative language and thought* (pp. 88–118). New York: Oxford University Press.

Gibbs, R. W. Jr. (2001). Evaluating contemporary models of figurative language understanding. *Metaphor and Symbol, 16*, 317–333.

Gibbs, R. W. Jr. (2002). A new look at literal meaning in understanding what is said and implicated. *Journal of Pragmatics, 34*, 457–486. Special issue on "Literal, minimal, salient, and privileged meanings," ed. M. Ariel.

Gibbs, R. W. Jr., Buchalter, D. L., Moise, J. F., & Farrar W. T. (1993). Literal meaning and figurative language. *Discourse Processes, 16*, 387–403.

Gibbs, R. W. Jr., & Gerrig, R. J. (1989). How context makes metaphor comprehension seem "special." *Metaphor and Symbolic Activity, 4*, 145–158.

Gibbs, R. W. Jr., & Gonzales, G. (1985). Syntactic frozenness in processing and remembering idioms. *Cognition, 20*, 243–259.

Gibbs, R. W. Jr., & Moise, J. F. (1997). Pragmatics in understanding what is said. *Cognition, 62*, 51–74.

Gibbs, R. W. Jr., Nayak, N. P., & Cutting, C. (1989). How to kick the bucket and not decompose: Analyzability and idiom processing. *Journal of Memory and Language, 28*, 576–593.

Gibbs, R.W. Jr., O'Brien, J., & Doolittle S. (1995). Inferring meanings that are not intended: Speakers' intentions and irony comprehension. *Discourse Processes, 20*, 187–203.

Gildea, P., & Glucksberg, S. (1983). On understanding metaphor: The role of context. *Journal of Verbal Learning and Verbal Behavior, 22*, 577–590.

Giles, H. (Ed.) (1984). The dynamics of speech accommodation. *International Journal of the Sociology of Language, 46.*

Giora, R. (1985a). A text-based analysis of nonnarrative texts. *Theoretical Linguistics, 12*, 115–135.

Giora, R. (1985b). Towards a theory of coherence. *Poetics Today, 6*, 699–716.

Giora, R. (1988). On the informativeness requirement. *Journal of Pragmatics, 12*, 547–565.

Giora, R. (1991). On the cognitive aspects of the joke. *Journal of Pragmatics, 16*, 465–486. Special issue on "Cognitive Perspectives of Language Use," ed. R. Giora and A. Kasher.

Giora, R. (1995). On irony and negation. *Discourse Processes, 19*, 239–264.

Giora, R. (1997a). Discourse coherence and theory of relevance: Stumbling blocks in search of a unified theory. *Journal of Pragmatics, 27*, 17–34.

Giora, R. (1997b). Understanding figurative and literal language: The graded salience hypothesis. *Cognitive Linguistics, 7*, 183–206.

Giora, R. (1998a). Discourse coherence is an independent notion: A reply to Deirdre Wilson. *Journal of Pragmatics, 29*, 75–86.

Giora, R. (1998b). Irony. In J. Verschueren, J-O. Östman, J. Blommaert, & C. Bulcaen (Eds.), *Handbook of pragmatics* (pp. 1–21). Amsterdam: John Benjamins.

Giora, R. (1998c). When is relevance? On the role of salience in utterance interpretation. *Revista Alicantina de Estudios Ingleses, 11*, 85–94.

Giora, R. (1999a). Indirect negation view of irony: Dolly City—a compassionate city. In Z. Ben Porat (Ed.), *An overcoat of Benjamin: Papers on literature for Benjamin Harshav, on his seventieth birthday* (pp. 187–192). Porter Institute, Tel Aviv University—Hakibbutz Hameuchad. (In Hebrew).

Giora, R. (1999b). On the priority of salient meanings: Studies of literal and figurative language. *Journal of Pragmatics, 31*, 919–929.

Giora, R. (2001). Irony and its discontent. In D. Schram & G. Steen (Eds.), *Psychology of language: In honour of Elrud Ibsch* (pp. 165–184). Amsterdam: John Benjamins.

Giora, R. (2002a). Literal vs. figurative language: Different or equal? *Journal of Pragmatics, 34*, 487–506. Special issue on "Literal, minimal, salient, and privileged meanings," ed. M. Ariel.

Giora, R. (2002b). Masking one's themes: Irony and the politics of indirectness. In M. M. Louwerse & W. van Peer (Eds.), *Thematics in psychology and literary studies* (pp. 283–300). Amsterdam: John Benjamins.

Giora, R. (2002c). Optimal innovation and pleasure. In O. Stock, C. Strapparava & A. Nijholt (Eds.), *Proceedings of The April Fools' Day Workshop on Computational Humour, April 2002, ITC-itst, Trento* (pp. 11–28). Trento: ITC-itst.

Giora, R. (2002d). Theorizing gender: Feminist awareness and language change. In B. Baron & H. Kotthoff (Eds.), *Gender in interaction* (pp. 329–347). Amsterdam: John Benjamins.

Giora, R., & Balaban, N. (2001). Lexical access in text production: On the role of salience in metaphor resonance. In T. Sanders, J. Schilperoord, & W. Spooren's (Eds.), *Text representation* (pp.111–124). Amsterdam: John Benjamins.

Giora, R., Balaban, N., & Fein, O. (2002, June). *Explicit negation as positivity in disguise*. Paper presented at the Twelfth Annual Meeting of The Society for Text and Discourse. Chicago.

Giora, R., Balaban, N., Fein, O., & Alkabets, I. (in press). Negation as positivity in disguise. In H. L. Colston, & A. Katz (Eds.), *Figurative language comprehension: Social and cultural influences*. Hillsdale, NJ: Erlbaum.

Giora, R., & Fein, O. (1999a). Irony: Context and salience. *Metaphor and Symbol, 14*, 241–257.

Giora, R., & Fein, O. (1999b). Irony comprehension: The graded salience hypothesis. *Humor, 12*, 425–436.

Giora, R., & Fein, O. (1999c). On understanding familiar and less-familiar figurative language. *Journal of Pragmatics, 31*, 1601–1618. Special issue on "Figurative and Literal Language," ed. R. Giora.

Giora, R., Fein, O., Kronrod, A., Elnatan, I., & Zur, A. (2002, April). *Optimal innovation and affect*. April Fools' Day Workshop. Trento, Italy.

Giora, R., Fein O., & Schwartz, T. (1997). *On the time course of understanding metaphor*. Unpublished ms.

Giora, R., Fein O., & Schwartz, T. (1998). Irony: Graded salience and indirect negation. *Metaphor and Symbol, 13*, 83–101.

Giora R., & Gur, I. (in press). Irony in conversation: Salience and context effects. In B. Nerlich, Z. Todd, V. Herman, & D. Clarke (Eds.), *Polysemy*. Berlin: Mouton de Gruyter.

Giora, R., Kronrod, A., Elnatan, I., & Fein, O. (2001, July). *The role of salience in aesthetic creativity*. Paper presented at the Eleventh Annual Meeting of the Society for Text and Discourse, University of California, Santa Barbara.

Giora, R., Peleg, O., & Fein, O. (2001, May). *Resisting contextual information: You can't put a salient meaning down*. Paper presented at the International Workshop on Towards an Experimental Pragmatics, University of Lyon.

Giora, R., Zaidel, E., Soroker, N., Batori, G., & Kasher, A. (2000). Differential effects of right and left hemispheric damage on understanding sarcasm and metaphor. *Metaphor and Symbol, 15*, 63–83.

Glenberg, A. M. (1997). What memory is for. *Behavioral and Brain Sciences, 20*, 1–55.

Glenberg, A. M., & Robertson, D. A. (2000). Symbol grounding and meaning: A comparison of high-dimensional and embodied theory of meaning. *Journal of Memory and Language, 43*, 379–401.

Glucksberg, S. (1989). Metaphors in conversation: How are they understood? Why are they used? *Metaphor and Symbolic Activity, 4*, 125–143.

Glucksberg, S. (1991). Beyond literal meanings: The psychology of allusion. *Psychological Science, 2*, 146–152.

Glucksberg, S. (1995). Commentary on nonliteral language: Processing and use. *Metaphor and Symbolic Activity, 10*, 47–57.

Glucksberg, S. (1998). Understanding metaphors. *Current Directions in Psychological Science, 7*, 39–43.

Glucksberg, S. (2001). *Understanding figurative language: From metaphors to idioms*. New York: Oxford University Press.

Glucksberg, S., Gildea, P., & Bookin, H. B. (1982). On understanding nonliteral speech: Can people ignore metaphors? *Journal of Verbal Learning and Verbal Behavior, 21*, 85–98.

Glucksberg, S., & Keysar, B. (1990). Understanding metaphorical comparisons: Beyond similarity. *Psychological Review, 97*, 3–18.

Glucksberg, S., Kreuz, R., & Rho, S. H. (1986). Context can constrain lexical access: Implications for models of language comprehension. *Journal of Experimental Psychology: Learning, Memory, and Cognition, 12*, 323–335.

Glucksberg, S., McGlone, M. S., & Manfredi, D. (1997). Property attribution in metaphor comprehension. *Journal of Memory and Language, 36*, 50–67.

Glucksberg, S., Newsome, M. R., & Goldvarg, Y. (2001). Inhibition of the literal: Filtering metaphor-irrelevant information during metaphor comprehension. *Metaphor and Symbol, 16*, 277–294.

Goldenberg, J., Mazursky, D., & Solomon, S. (1999a). Creative sparks. *Science, 258*, 1495–1496.

Goldenberg, J., Mazursky, D., & Solomon, S. (1999b). The fundamental templates of quality ads. *Marketing Science, 18*, 333–351.

Gorfein, D. S. (Ed.) (1989). *Resolving semantic ambiguity*. New York: Springer Verlag.

Gow, D. W., & Gordon, P. C. (1995). Lexical and prelexical influences on word segmentation: Evidence from priming. *Journal of Experimental Psychology: Human Perception and Performance, 21*, 344–359.

Gregory, M. E., & Mergler, N. L. (1990). Metaphor comprehension: In search of literal truth, possible sense, and metaphoricity. *Metaphor and Symbolic Activity, 5*, 151–173.

Grice, H. P. (1975). Logic and conversation. In P. Cole & J. Morgan (Eds.), *Speech acts: Syntax and semantics* (Vol. 3, pp. 41–58). New York: Academic Press.

Grice, H. P. (1978). Some further notes on logic and conversation. In P. Cole & J. Morgan (Eds.), *Pragmatics: Syntax and semantics* (Vol. 9, pp. 113–127). New York: Academic Press.

Grosjean, F. (1980). Spoken word recognition processes and the gating paradigm. *Perception & Psychophysics, 28,* 267–283.

Hagoort, P. (1989). Processing lexical ambiguities: A comment on Milberg, Blumstein, and Dworetzky (1987). *Brain and Language, 36,* 335–348.

Haiman, J. (1998). *Talk is cheap: Sarcasm, alienation, and the evolution of language.* New York: Oxford University Press.

Hamblin, J. & Gibbs, R. W. Jr. (2001, May). *Processing the meanings of what speakers say and implicate.* Paper presented at the International Workshop on Towards an Experimental Pragmatics, University of Lyon.

Hareven, S. (1982). *Bdidut.* [Loneliness]. Tel-Aviv: Am-Oved. (In Hebrew).

Harnad, S. (1990). The symbol grounding problem. *Physica, 42,* 335–346.

Harnad, S. (1993). Grounding symbols in the analog world with neural nets. *Think, 2,* 12–78.

Harrison, A. A. (1977). Mere exposure. In L. Berkowitz (Ed.), *Advances in experimental social psychology* (Vol. 10, pp. 610–646). New York: Academic Press.

Hasson, U. (2000). Comprehension of negation in negated metaphors. M.A. thesis, Princeton University, New Jersey.

Haviland, S. E., & Clark, H. H. (1974). What's new? Acquiring new information as a process in comprehension. *Journal of Verbal Learning and Verbal Behavior, 13,* 512–521.

Heinlein, R. A. (1963). *Stranger in a strange land.* New York: Putnam.

Hernandez, A. E., Fennema-Notestine, C., Udell, C., & Bates, E. (2001). Lexical and sentential priming in competition: Implications for two-stage theories of lexical access. *Applied Psycholinguistics, 22,* 191–215.

Heyd, M. (1986). *Aubrey Beardsley: Symbol, mask and self-irony.* New York: Peter Lang.

Hillert, D., & Swinney, D. (2001). The processing of fixed expressions during sentence comprehension. In A. Cienki, B. Luka, & M. Smith (Eds.), *Conceptual and discourse factors in linguistic structure* (pp. 107–122). Stanford, CA: CSLI.

Hindle, D., & Rooth, M. (1993). Structural ambiguity and lexical relations. *Computational Linguistics, 19,* 103–120.

Hintzman, D. L., & Curran, T. (1994). Retrieval dynamics of recognition and frequency judgements: Evidence for separate processes of familiarity and recall. *Journal of Memory and Language, 33,* 1–18.

Hirshman, E., Snodgrass, J. G., Mindes, J., & Feenan, K. (1990). Conceptual priming in word fragment completion. *Journal of Experimental Psychology: Learning, Memory and Cognition, 16,* 634–647.

Hogaboam, T. W., & Perfetti, C. A. (1975). Lexical ambiguity and sentence comprehension. *Journal of Verbal Learning and Verbal Behavior, 14,* 265–274.

Holtgraves, T. (1998). Interpersonal foundations of conversation indirectness. In S. Fussell & R. Kreuz (Eds.), *Social and cognitive approaches to interpersonal communication* (pp. 71–90). Mahwah, NJ: Lawrence Erlbaum Associates.

Honeck, R. P., Welge, J., & Temple, J. G. (1998). The symmetry control in tests of the standard pragmatic model: The case of proverb comprehension. *Metaphor and Symbol, 13,* 257–273.

Hopper, P. J., & Traugott, E. C. 1993. *Grammaticalization*. Cambridge: Cambridge University Press.

Horn, L. R., & Bayer, S. (1984). Short-circuited implicature: A negative contribution. *Linguistics and Philosophy, 7*, 397–414.

Horton, W. S., & Keysar, B. (1996). When do speakers take into account common ground? *Cognition, 59*, 91–117.

Howes, D., & Soloman, R. L. (1951). Visual duration thresholds as a function of word probability. *Journal of Experimental Psychology, 41*, 401–410.

Hubbell, J. A., & O'Boyle, M. W. (1995). The effects of metaphorical and literal comprehension processes on lexical decision latency of sentence components. *Journal of Psycholinguistic Research, 24*, 269–287.

Hudson, J. (1998). *Perspectives on fixedness: Applied and theoretical.* Lund, Sweden: Lund University Press.

Hutcheon, L. (1991). *Splitting images: Contemporary Canadian ironies.* Toronto: Oxford University Press.

Inhoff, A. W., Lima, S. D., & Carroll, P. J. (1984). Contextual effects on metaphor comprehension in reading. *Memory & Cognition, 12*, 558–567.

Ivanko, S., & Pexman, P. M. (2001, July). Understanding irony: On-line processing of figurative and literal meaning. Poster presented at the Eleventh Annual Meeting of the Society for Text and Discourse, University of California, Santa Barbara.

Jakobson, R. (1960). Closing statement: Linguistics and poetics. In T. Sebeok (Ed.), *Style in language* (pp. 350–377). Cambridge, MA: MIT Press.

Janus, R. A., & Bever, T. G. (1985). Processing of metaphoric language: An investigation of the three stage model of metaphor comprehension. *Journal of Psycholinguistic Research, 14*, 473–487.

Johnson, M. (1987). *The body in the mind: The bodily basis of meaning, imagination, and reason.* Chicago: University of Chicago Press.

Johnson, M. G., & Malgady, R. G. (1979). Some cognitive aspects of figurative language: Association and metaphor. *Journal of Psycholinguistic Research, 8*, 249–265.

Jones, J. L. (1991). Early integration of context during lexical access of homonym meanings. *Current Psychology: Research and Reviews, 10*, 163–181.

Jorgensen, J., Miller, G., & Sperber, D. (1984). Test of the mention theory of irony. *Journal of Experimental Psychology: General, 113*, 112–120.

Juliano, C., & Tanenhaus, M. K. (1993). Contingent frequency effects in syntactic ambiguity resolution. In *Proceedings of the fifteenth annual conference of the Cognitive Science Society* (pp. 593–598). Mahwah, NJ: Lawrence Erlbaum Associates.

Juliano, C., & Tanenhaus, M. K. (1994). A constraint based lexicalist account of the subject-object attachment preference. *Journal of Psycholinguistic Research, 23*, 459–471.

Jurafsky, D. (1996). A probabilistic model of lexical and syntactic access and disambiguation. *Cognitive Science, 20*, 137–194.

Just, M. A., & Carpenter, P. A. (1980). A theory of reading: From eye fixation to comprehension. *Psychological Review, 4*, 329–354.

Just, M. A., & Carpenter, P. A. (1992). A capacity theory of comprehension: Individual differences in working memory. *Psychological Review, 99*, 122–149.

Just, M. A., Carpenter, P. A., & Wooley, J. D. (1982). Paradigms and processes in reading comprehension. *Journal of Experimental Psychology: General, 111*, 228–238.

Kaplan, J. & Zaidel, E. (2001). Error monitoring in the hemispheres: The effect of feedback on lateralized lexical decision. *Cognition, 82*, 157–178

Kasher, A. (1991). On the pragmatic modules: A lecture. *Journal of Pragmatics, 16,* 381–397.

Kasher, A. (1998). Pragmatics and the modularity of mind. In A. Kasher (Ed.), *Pragmatics: Critical concepts* (Vol. 6, pp. 230–252). London: Routledge.

Kasher, A., Batori, G., Soroker, N., Graves, D., & Zaidel, E. (1999). Effects of right- and left-hemisphere damage on understanding conversational implicatures. *Brain and Language, 68,* 566–590.

Katz, A. N. (1986). On choosing the vehicles for metaphors: Referential concreteness, semantic distances, and individual differences. *Journal of Memory and Language, 28,* 486–499.

Katz, A. N. (1998). Figurative language and figurative thought. In A. N. Katz, C. Cacciari, R. W. Gibbs Jr., & M. Turner (Eds.), *Figurative language and thought* (pp. 3–43). New York: Oxford University Press.

Katz A. N., & T. Ferretti (2000, November). Reading proverbs in context: The role of explicit markers. Poster presented at the Forty-first Annual Meeting of the Psychonomic Society, New Orleans, Louisiana.

Katz, A. N., & T. Ferretti (2001). Moment-by-moment reading of proverbs in literal and nonliteral contexts. *Metaphor and Symbol, 16,* 193–221.

Katz, A. N., Ferretti, T., & Taylor, T. (1999, November). "Moment-by-moment comprehension of proverbs." Paper presented at the Fortieth Annual Meeting of the Psychonomic Society, Los Angeles.

Katz, A. N. & Pexman, P. (1997). Interpreting figurative statements: Speaker occupation can change metaphor into irony. *Metaphor and Symbolic Activity, 12,* 19–41.

Katz, J. J. (1977). *Propositional structure and illocutionary force.* New York: Thomas Y. Crowell.

Kawamoto, A. H. (1988). Distributed representations of ambiguous words and their resolution in a connectionist network. In S. I. Small, G. W. Cottrell, & M. K. Tanenhaus (Eds.), *Lexical ambiguity resolution: Perspectives from psycholinguistics, neuropsychology, and artificial intelligence* (pp. 195–228). San Mateo, CA: Morgan Kaufmann.

Kawamoto, A. H. (1993). Nonlinear dynamics in the resolution of lexical ambiguity: A parallel distributed processing account. *Journal of Memory and Language, 32,* 474–516.

Kecskés, I. (1999). The use of situation-bound utterances from an interlanguage perspective. In J. Verscheuren (Ed.), *Pragmatics in 1998: Selected papers from the 6th International Pragmatics Conference* (Vol. 2, pp. 299–310). Antwerp: International Pragmatics Association.

Kecskés, I. (2000). A cognitive-pragmatic approach to situation-bound utterances. *Journal of Pragmatics, 32,* 605–625.

Kecskés, I. (2002a). The "graded salience hypothesis" in second language acquisition. In S. Niemeier & M. Puetz (Eds.), *Applied cognitive linguistics* (pp. 249–271). Berlin: Mouton de Gruyter.

Kecskés, I. (2002b). *Situation-bound utterances in L1 and L2.* Berlin: Mouton de Gruyter.

Kecskés, I., & Papp, T. (2000). *Foreign language and mother tongue.* Mahwah, NJ: Lawrence Erlbaum Associates.

Keenan, J. (1978). *Inferring causal connections in prose comprehension.* Paper presented at the American Psychological Association Convention.

Kemper, S. (1981). Comprehension and interpretation of proverbs. *Journal of Psycholinguistic Research, 10,* 179–183.

Kennedy, V. R., & Kennedy, J. M. (1993). Metaphor and visual rhetoric. *Metaphor and Symbolic Activity, 8,* 149–255.

Keysar, B. (1989). On the functional equivalence of literal and metaphorical interpretations in discourse. *Journal of Memory and Language, 28*, 375–385.

Keysar, B. (1994a). Discourse context effects: Metaphorical and literal interpretations. *Discourse Processes, 18*, 247–269.

Keysar, B. (1994b). The illusory transparency of intention: Linguistic perspective taking in text. *Cognitive Psychology, 26*, 165–208.

Keysar, B. (1998). Language users as problem solvers: Just what ambiguity problem do they solve? In S. Fussell & R. Kreuz (Eds.), *Social and cognitive approaches to interpersonal communication* (pp. 175–200). Mahwah, NJ: Lawrence Erlbaum Associates.

Keysar, B. (2000). The illusory transparency of intention: Does June understand what Mark means because he means it? *Discourse Processes, 29*, 161–172.

Keysar, B., Barr, D. J., Balin J. A., & Brauner, J. S. (2000). Taking perspective in conversation: The role of mutual knowledge in comprehension. *Psychological Sciences, 11*, 32–38.

Keysar, B., Barr, D. J., Balin J. A., & Paek, T. S. (1998). Definite reference and mutual knowledge: Process models of common ground in comprehension. *Journal of Memory and Language, 39*, 1–20.

Keysar, B., Barr, D. J., & Horton, W. S. (1998). The egocentric basis of language use: Insights from a processing approach. *Current Directions in Psychological Sciences, 7*, 46–50.

Keysar, B., & Bly, B. (1995). Intuitions of the transparency of idioms: Can one keep a secret by spilling the beans? *Journal of Memory and Language, 34*, 89–109.

Keysar, B., & Bly, B. (1999). Swimming against the current: Do idioms reflect conceptual structure? *Journal of Pragmatics, 31*, 1559–1578.

Keysar, B., & Glucksberg, S. (1992). Metaphor and communication. *Poetics Today, 13*, 633–658.

Keysar, B., Shen, Y., Glucksberg, S., & Horton, S. W. (2000). Conventional language: How metaphorical is it? *Journal of Memory and Language, 43*, 576–593.

Kiger, J. I. & Glass, A. L. (1983). The facilitation of lexical decisions by a prime occurring after the target. *Memory & Cognition, 11*, 356–365.

Kintsch, W. (1998). *Comprehension: A paradigm for cognition.* Cambridge: Cambridge University Press.

Kintsch, W., & Mross, E. F. (1985). Context effects in word identification. *Journal of Memory and Language, 24*, 336–349.

Koivisto, M. (1997). Time course of semantic activation in the cerebral hemispheres. *Neuropsychologia, 35*, 497–504.

Koriat, A. (1981). Semantic facilitation in lexical decision as a function of prime-target association. *Memory & Cognition, 9*, 587–598.

Kotthoff, H. (1996). Impoliteness and conversational joking: On relational politics. *Folia Linguistica, 30*, 299–325.

Kotthoff, H. (1998). Irony, quotation, and other forms of staged intertextuality: Double or contrastive perspectivation in conversation. *Interaction and Linguistic Structures, 5*, 1–27.

Kotthoff, H. (in press). Responding to irony in different contexts: cognition and conversation. *Journal of Pragmatics.*

Krasin, M. (1992a). A prize to Anita Hill. *Noga, 23*, 8. (In Hebrew).

Krasin, M. (1992b). In spite of everything, we don't give up. *Noga, 23*, 9. (In Hebrew).

Kreuz R., & Glucksberg, S. (1989). How to be sarcastic: The reminder theory of verbal irony. *Journal of Experimental Psychology: General, 118*, 347–386.

Kronrod, A. (2001). On the role of salience in optimal innovation: Aesthetics as a function of the old/new ratio. M.A. thesis, Tel Aviv University.

Kronrod, A., Giora, R., & Fein, O. (2000, September). *Creative writing: The optimal creative innovation in fixed expressions.* Paper presented at the EARLI special interest group writing conference, Università degli Studi di Verona

Kucera, H. & Francis, W. (1967). *Computational analysis of present-day American English.* Providence, RI: Brown University Press.

Kumon-Nakamura, S., Glucksberg, S., & Brown, M. (1995). How about another piece of the pie: The allusional pretense theory of discourse irony. *Journal of Experimental Psychology: General, 124,* 3–21.

Kunst-Wilson, W. R., & Zajonc, R. B. (1980). Affective discrimination of stimuli that cannot be recognized. *Science, 207,* 1019–1024.

Lakoff, G. (1986). The meanings of literal. *Metaphor and Symbolic Activity, 1,* 291–296.

Lakoff, G. (1987). *Women, fire, and dangerous things: What categories reveal about the mind.* Chicago: University of Chicago Press.

Lakoff, G., & Johnson, M. (1980). *Metaphors we live by.* Chicago: University of Chicago Press.

Lakoff, G., & Turner, M. (1989). *More than cool reason: A field guide to poetic metaphor.* Chicago: University of Chicago Press.

Landauer, T. K. (1999). Latent semantic analysis: A theory of the psychology of language and mind. *Discourse Processes, 27,* 303–310.

Landauer, T. K., & Dumais, S.T. (1997). A solution to Plato's problem: The latent semantic analysis theory of acquisition, induction and representation of knowledge. *Psychological Review, 104,* 211–240.

Landauer, T. K., Foltz, P. W., & Laham, D. (1998). An introduction to latent semantic analysis. *Discourse Processes, 25,* 259–284.

Lars, E. (1996). Some notes on irony in the visual arts and music: The examples of Magritte and Shostakovich. *Word and Image, 12(2),* 197–208.

Larson, G. (1984). *The far side gallery.* Kansas City: Andrews, McMeel & Parker.

Lea, B. R. & Mulligan, E. J. (2002). The effect of negation on deductive inferences. *Journal of Experimental Psychology: Learning, Memory, and Cognition, 28,* 303–317.

Lee, J. C. (1990). Some hypothesis concerning the evolution of polysemous words. *Journal of Psycholinguistic Research, 19,* 211–219.

Lehrer, A. E. (1990). Polysemy, conventionality, and the structure of the lexicon. *Cognitive Linguistics, 1–2,* 207–246.

Levenson, R. W. (2003). Autonomic specificity and emotion. In R. J. Davidson, K. R. Scherer, & H. H. Goldsmith (Eds.), *The handbook of affective sciences* (pp. 212–224). New York: Oxford University Press.

Levinson, C. S. (1983). *Pragmatics.* Cambridge: Cambridge University Press.

Levinson, C. S. (1987a). Minimization and conversational inference. In: J. Verschueren & M. Bertuccelli-Papi (Eds.), *The pragmatic perspective* (pp. 61–130). Philadelphia: John Benjamins.

Levinson, C. S. (1987b). Pragmatics and the grammar of anaphora. *Journal of Linguistics, 23,* 379–434.

Levinson, C. S. (2000). *Presumptive meanings: The theory of generalized conversational implicature.* Cambridge, MA: MIT Press.

Lewis, D. K. (1969). *Convention: A philosophical study.* Cambridge, MA: Harvard University Press.

Li, P., & M. C. Yip (1996). Lexical ambiguity and context effects in spoken word recognition: Evidence from Chinese. In G. W. Cottrell (Ed.), *Proceedings of the eigh-*

teenth annual conference of the Cognitive Science Society (pp. 228–232). Mahwah, NJ: Lawrence Erlbaum Associates.

Liu, H., Bates, E., Powell, T., & Wulfeck, B. (1997). Single-word shadowing and the study of lexical access. *Applied Psycholinguistics, 18*, 157–180.

Long, D. L. & Graesser, A. (1988). Wit and humor in discourse processing. *Discourse Processes, 11*, 35–60.

Long, D. L., Oppy, B. J., & Seely, M. R. (1994). Individual differences in the time course of differential processing. *Journal of Experimental Psychology: Learning, Memory, and Cognition, 20*, 1456–1470.

Long, D. L., Seely, M. R., & Oppy, B. J. (1999). The strategic nature of less skilled readers' suppression problems. *Discourse Processes, 27*, 281–302.

Lucas, M. M. (1987). Context effects on the processing of ambiguous words in sentence context. *Language and Speech, 30*, 25–46.

Lund, K., Burgess, C., & Atchley, R. A. (1995). Semantic and associative priming in high dimensional semantic space. In J. D. Moore & J. F. Lehman (Eds.), *Proceedings of the seventeenth annual meeting of the Cognitive Science Society* (pp. 660–665). Pittsburgh, PA: Erlbaum.

MacDonald, M. C. (1994). Probabilistic constraints and syntactic ambiguity resolution. *Language and Cognitive Processes, 9*, 157–201.

MacDonald, M. C. (1999). Distributional information in language comprehension, production, and acquisition: Three puzzles and a moral. In B. MacWhinney (Ed.), *The emergence of language* (pp. 177–196). Mahwah, NJ: Lawrence Erlbaum Associates.

MacDonald, M. C., & Just, M. A. (1989). Changes in activation levels with negation. *Journal of Experimental Psychology: Learning, Memory, and Cognition, 15*, 633–642.

MacDonald, M. C., Just, M. A., & Carpenter, P. A. (1992). Working memory constraints on the processing of syntactic ambiguity. *Cognitive Psychology, 24*, 56–98.

MacDonald, M. C., Pearlmutter, N. J., & Seidenberg, M. S. (1994). Lexical nature of syntactic ambiguity resolution. *Psychological Review, 101*, 676–703.

MacWhinney, B. (1987). The competition model. In B. MacWhinney (Ed.), *Mechanisms of language acquisition* (pp. 249–308). Hillsdale, NJ: Lawrence Erlbaum Associates.

Malgady, R., & Johnson, M. (1976). Modifiers in metaphors: effects of constituent phrase similarity on the interpretation of figurative sentences. *Journal of Psycholinguistic Research, 5*, 43–52.

Mandler, G., Graf, P. & Kraft, D. (1986). Activation and elaboration effects in recognition and word priming. *Quarterly Journal of Experimental Psychology, 38A*, 645–662.

Mandler, G., Hamson, C. O., Dorfman, J. (1990). Tests of dual process theory: Word priming and recognition. *Quarterly Journal of Experimental Psychology, 42A*, 713–739.

Marschark, M., Katz, A. N., & Paivio, A. (1983). Dimensions of metaphor. *Journal of Psycholinguistic Research, 12*, 17–39.

Marslen-Wilson, W. D., & Tyler, L. K. (1980). The temporal structure of spoken language understanding. *Cognition, 8*, 1–71.

Martin, C., Vu, H., Kellas, G., & Metcalf, K. (1999). Strength of discourse context as a determinant of the subordinate bias effect. *Quarterly Journal of Experimental Psychology, 52A*, 813–839.

Matlock, T. (1988). The metaphorical extensions of "see." In J. Emonds, P. J. Mistry, V. Samiian, & L. Thornburg (Eds.), *Proceedings of the Western Conference on Linguistics* (Vol. 1, pp. 185–195). Department of Linguistics, California State University, Fresno, CA.

Matlock, T. (1989). Metaphor and the grammaticalization of evidentials. In K. Hall, M. Meacham, & R. Shapiro (Eds.), *Proceedings of the Fifteenth Annual Meeting of the Berkeley Linguistics Society: General Session and Parasession on Theoretical Issues in Language Reconstruction* (pp. 215–25). Berkeley: Berkeley Linguistics Society.

Matzkel, Y. (1999, January–May). *Nolad met (Born dead)*. Ramat Gan: Museum of Israeli Art.

McGlone, M. S., Glucksberg, S., & Cacciari, C. (1994). Semantic productivity and idiom comprehension. *Discourse Processes, 17*, 167–190.

McGlone, M. S., & Tofighbakhsh, J. (2000). Birds of a feather flock conjointly(?): Rhyme *as* reason in aphorisms. *Psychological Science, 11*, 424–428.

McNaughton, I. (1972). *And now for something completely different*. Columbia TriStar Home Video.

McRae, K., Ferretti, T. R., & Amyote, L. (1997). Thematic roles as verb-specific concepts. *Language and Cognitive Processes, 12*, 137–176.

McRae, K., Spivey-Knowlton, M. J., & Tanenhaus, M. K. (1998). Modeling the influence of thematic fit (and other constraints) in on line sentence comprehension. *Journal of Memory and Language, 38*, 283–312.

Meehan, M. (1991). Men oh pause. In D. Taylor & A. Coverdale Sumrall (Eds.), *Women in the 14th moon: Writings on menopause* (p. 247). Freedom, CA: Crossing Press.

Merlo, P. (1994). A corpus based analysis of verb continuation frequencies for syntactic processing. *Journal of Psycholinguistic Research, 23*, 435–457.

Meyer, D. E., & Schvaneveldt, R. W. (1971). Facilitation in recognizing word pairs of words: Evidence of a dependence between retrieval operations. *Journal of Experimental Psychology, 90*, 227–234.

Miall, D. S., & Kuiken, D. (1994). Foregrounding, defamiliarization, and affect response to literary stories. *Poetics, 22*, 389–407.

Milosky, L. M., & Ford, J. A (1997). The role of prosody in children's inferences of ironic intent. *Discourse Processes, 23*, 47–61.

Mishori, E. (1999). The wall of motherhood. Trans. R. T. Back. In S. Kaufman, G. Hasan-Rokem, & T. S. Hess (Eds.), *The defiant muse: Hebrew feminist poems from antiquity to the present* (p. 237). New York: Feminist Press.

Mitchell, D. C. (1994). Sentence parsing. In M. A. Gernsbacher (Ed.), *Handbook of psycholinguistics* (pp. 375–409). San Diego: Academic Press.

Miyake, A., Just, M. A., & Carpenter, A. P. (1994). Working memory constraints on the resolution of lexical ambiguity: Maintaining multiple interpretations in neutral contexts. *Journal of Memory and Language, 33*, 175–202.

Moon R. (1998). *Fixed expressions and idioms in English: A corpus-based approach*. Oxford: Clarendon Press.

Morgan, J. (1978). Two types of convention in indirect speech acts. In P. Cole (Ed.), *Pragmatics*, Syntax and Semantics 9 (pp. 261–280). New York: Academic Press.

Morris, R. K., & Binder, K. S. (2002). What do skilled readers do with the unselected meaning of an ambiguous word? In D. S. Gorfein (Ed.), *On the consequences of meaning selection: Perspectives on ambiguity resolution* (pp. 139–153). Washington, DC: American Psychological Association.

Mukařovský, J (1932/1964). Standard language and poetic language. In P. L. Garvin (Ed.), *A Prague School reader on esthetics, literary structure, and style* (pp. 17–30). Washington, DC: Georgetown University Press.

Mukařovský, J. (1978). *Structure, sign and function*. New Haven, CT: Yale University Press.

Needham, W. P. (1992). Limits on literal processing during idiom interpretation. *Journal of Psycholinguistic Research, 21*, 1–16.

Neill, W. T., Hilliard, D. V., & Cooper, E. (1988). The detection of lexical ambiguity: Evidence for context-sensitive parallel access. *Journal of Memory and Language, 27*, 279–287.

Nerlich, B., & Clarke D. D. (2001). Ambiguities we live by: Towards a pragmatics of polysemy. *Journal of Pragmatics, 33*, 1–20.

Ni, W., Crain, S., & Shankweiler, D. (1996). Sidestepping the garden paths: Assessing the contributions of syntax, semantics and plausibility in resolving ambiguities. *Language and Cognitive Processes, 11*, 283–334.

Nicolle, S., & Clark B. (1999). Experimental pragmatics and what is said: A response to Gibbs and Moise. *Cognition, 69*, 337–354.

Nunberg, G., Sag, I., & Wasow, T. (1994). Idioms. *Language, 70*, 491–538.

Oakhill, J. Garnham, A., & Reynolds, D. (1999, August). *Evidence of immediate activation of gender information from a social role name.* Paper presented at the Ninth Annual Meeting of the Society for Text and Discourse, Vancouver.

Oden, G., & Spria, J. (1983). Influence of context on the activation and selection of ambiguous word senses. *Quarterly Journal of Experimental Psychology, 35A*, 51–64.

Öhman, A. & Wiens, S. (2003). On the automaticity of autonomic responses in emotion: An evolutionary perspective. In R. J. Davidson, K. R. Scherer, & H. H. Goldsmith (Eds.), *The handbook of affective sciences* (pp. 256–275). New York: Oxford University Press.

Onifer, W., & Swinney, D. A. (1981). Accessing lexical ambiguities during sentence comprehension: Effects of frequency of meaning and contextual bias. *Memory & Cognition, 9*, 225–236.

Onishi, K. H., & Murphy, G. L. (1993). Metaphoric reference: When metaphors are not understood as easily as literal expressions. *Memory & Cognition, 21*, 763–772.

Ortony, A., Schallert, D. L., Reynolds, R. E., & Antos, S. J. (1978). Interpreting metaphors and idioms: Some effects of context on comprehension. *Journal of Verbal Learning and Verbal Behavior, 17*, 465–477.

Ortony, A., Vondruska, R. J., Foss, M. A., & Jones, L. E. (1985). Salience, similes, and asymmetry of similarity. *Journal of Memory and Language, 24*, 569–594.

Overson, C., & Mandler, M. (1987). Indirect word priming in connected and phonological contexts. *Bulletin of the Psychonomic Society, 25*, 229–232.

Pacht, J. M., & Rayner, K. (1993). The processing of homophonic homographs during reading: Evidence from eye movement studies. *Journal of Psycholinguistic Research, 22*, 251–271.

Pearlmutter, N. J., & MacDonald, M. C. (1992). Plausibility and syntactic ambiguity resolution. In *Proceedings of the Fourteenth Annual Conference of the Cognitive Science Society* (pp. 699–704). Hillsdale, NJ: Lawrence Erlbaum Associates.

Pearlmutter, N. J., & MacDonald, M. C. (1995). Individual differences and probabilistic constraints in syntactic ambiguity resolution. *Journal of Memory and Language, 34*, 521–542.

Peleg, O. (1992). The relationship between linguistic divergence and social identity among Israelis of oriental origin. M.A. thesis, Tel Aviv University.

Peleg, O. (2002). Linguistic and nonlinguistic mechanisms in language comprehension. Ph.D. dissertation, Tel Aviv University.

Peleg, O., Giora, R., & Fein, O. (2001). Salience and context effects: Two are better than one. *Metaphor and Symbol, 16*, 173–192.

Peleg, O., Giora, R., & Fein, O. (in press). Contextual strength: The whens and hows of context effects. In I. Noveck& D. Sperber (Eds.), *Experimental Pragmatics*. Basingstoke: Palgrave.

Peterson, R. R., Burgess, C., Dell, G. S., & Eberhard, K. (1989). *Dissociation of syntactic and semantic analyses during idiom processing.* Paper presented at the Second Annual CUNY Conference on Human Sentence Processing, New York City.

Pexman P. M., Ferretti, T., & Katz, A. (2000). Discourse factors that influence irony detection during on-line reading. *Discourse Processes, 29*, 201–222.

Pexman, P. M, & Olineck, K. M. (2002). Does sarcasm always sting? Investigating the impact of ironic insults and ironic compliments. *Discourse Processes, 33*, 199–217.

Pickering, M., & Frisson, S. (2001a). "Familiarity, not literalness, affects language comprehension." Unpublished ms.

Pickering, M., & Frisson, S. (2001b). Processing of verbs: Evidence from eye movements. *Journal of Experimental Psychology: Learning, Memory, and Cognition, 27*, 556–573

Pickering, M., Traxler, M. J., & Crocker, M. W. (2000). Ambiguity resolution in sentence processing: Evidence against frequency-based accounts. *Journal of Memory and Language, 43*, 447–475.

Picoult, J., & Johnson, M. K. (1992). Controlling for homophone polarity and prime target relatedness in the cross-modal lexical decision task. *Bulletin of the Psychonomic Society, 30*, 15–18.

Pinker, S. (1999). *Words and rules: The ingredients of language.* New York: Basic Books.

Pisani, V. (1967). *L'Etimologia: Storia—questioni—metodo.* Brescia: Paideia.

Piven, H. (1999). *Piven, Avodot 1990–1999 [Piven, Works 1990–1999].* Tel Aviv: Am Oved.

Popiel, S. J., & McRae, K. (1988). The figurative and literal senses of idioms, or all idioms are not used equally. *Journal of Psycholinguistic Research, 17*, 475–487.

Prather, P. A., & Swinney, D. A.. (1988). Lexical processing and ambiguity resolution: An autonomous process in an interactive box. In S. I. Small, G. W. Cottrell, & M. K. Tanenhaus (Eds.), *Lexical ambiguity resolution: Perspectives from psycholinguistics, neuropsychology, and artificial intelligence* (pp. 289–310). San Mateo, CA: Morgan Kaufmann.

Prinz, J. J., & Barsalou, L. W. (2002). Acquisition and productivity in perceptual symbol systems: An account of mundane creativity. In T. Dartnall (Ed.), *Creativity, cognition and knowledge* (pp. 105–107). Westport, CT: Praeger.

Pritchett, B. L. (1988). Garden path phenomena and the grammatical basis of language processing. *Language, 64*, 539–576.

Pritchett, B. L. (1991). Head position and parsing ambiguity. *Journal of Psycholinguistic Research, 20*, 251–270.

Pynte J., Besson, M., Robichon, F-H., & Poli J. (1996). The time-course of metaphor comprehension: An event-related potential study. *Brain and Language, 55*, 293–316.

Rajaram, S., & Roediger, H. L. (1993). Direct comparison of four implicit memory tests. *Journal of Experimental Psychology: Learning, Memory and Cognition, 19*, 765–776.

Raskin, V. (1985). *Semantic mechanisms of humor*. Dordrecht: Reidel.

Rattok, L. (1997). *Angel of fire: The poetry of Yona Wallach*. Tel Aviv: Hakibbutz Hameuchad. (In Hebrew).

Rayner, K., Binder, K. S., & Duffy, S. (1999). Contextual strength and subordinate bias effect. *Quarterly Journal of Experimental Psychology, 52A*, 841–852.

Rayner, K., Carlson, M., & Frazier, L. (1983). The interaction of syntax and semantics during sentence processing: Eye movements in the analysis of semantically biased sentences. *Journal of Verbal Learning and Verbal Behavior, 22*, 358–374.

Rayner, K., & Frazier, L. (1989). Selection mechanisms in reading lexically ambiguous words. *Journal of Experimental Psychology: Learning, Memory, and Cognition, 15*, 779–790.

Rayner, K., Garrod, S., & Perfetti, C. A. (1992). Discourse influences during parsing are delayed. *Cognition, 45*, 109–139.

Rayner, K., & Morris, R. K. (1991). Comprehension processes in reading ambiguous sentences: Reflections from eye movements. In G. B. Simpson (Ed.), *Understanding word and sentence* (pp. 175–198). Amsterdam: North Holland.

Rayner, K., Pacht J. M., & Duffy, S. A. (1994). Effects of prior encounter and global discourse bias on the processing of lexically ambiguous words: Evidence from eye fixations. *Journal of Memory and Language, 33*, 527–544.

Rayner, K., & Sereno C. S. (1994). Eye movement in reading. In M. A. Gernsbacher (Ed.), *Handbook of psycholinguistics* (pp. 57–81). San Diego: Academic Press.

Rayner, K., Sereno, C. S., Morris, R. K., Schmauder, A. R., & Clifton, C. Jr. (1989). Eye movement and on-line language comprehension processes. *Language and Cognitive Processes, 4*, 21–49.

Récanati, F. (1989). The pragmatics of what is said. *Mind and Behavior, 4*, 295–329.

Récanati, F. (1993). *Direct reference: From language to thought*. Oxford: Blackwell.

Récanati, F. (1995). The alleged priority of literal meaning. *Cognitive Science, 19*, 207–232.

Reinhart, T. (1976). On understanding poetic metaphor. *Poetics, 5*, 383–402.

Reinhart, T. (1980). Conditions for text coherence. *Poetics Today, 1*, 161–180.

Reinhart, T. (2000). *Self-inspection in the art of the 20th century*. Tel Aviv: Hakibbutz Hameuchad. (In Hebrew).

Renan, Y. (1984). Disautomatization and comic deviations from models of organizing experience. *Style, 18*, 160–176.

Richards, A., & French, C. C. (1991). Effects of encoding and anxiety on implicit and explicit memory performance. *Personality and Individual Differences, 12*, 131–139.

Roediger, H. L., & Blaxton, T. A. (1987). Effects of varying modality, surface features, and retention interval on priming in word-fragment completion. *Memory & Cognition, 15*, 379–388.

Roediger, H. L., & Challis, B. H. (1992). Effects of exact repetition and conceptual repetition on free recall and primed word-fragment completion. *Journal of Experimental Psychology: Learning, Memory and Cognition, 18*, 3–14.

Roos, D. (1998). *The opposite of sex*. Rysher Entertainment, Inc.

Rosch, E. H. (1973). On the internal structure of perceptual and semantic categories. In T. E. Moore (Ed.), *Cognitive development and the acquisition of language* (pp. 111–144). New York: Academic Press.

Rosch, E., & Mervis, C. B. (1975). Family resemblance: Studies in the internal structure of categories. *Cognitive Psychology, 8*, 382–439.

Rubenstein, H., Garfield, L., & Millikan, J. A. (1970). Homographic entries in the internal lexicon. *Journal of Verbal Learning and Verbal Behavior, 9,* 487–494.

Samih K. F., & Zacharia, C. E. (1997). *Palestine and the Palestinians.* Boulder, CO: Westview Press.

Sanford, A., & Garrod, S. (1981). *Understanding written language.* Chichester, U.K.: Wiley.

Sapir, E. (1921). *Language.* New York: Harcourt.

Schopenhauer, A. (1997 [1969]). The world as will and representation. In D. Cooper (Ed.), *Aesthetics: The classical readings* (pp. 150–163). Oxford, U. K.: Blackwell.

Schraw, G., Trather, W., Reynolds, R. E., & Lapan, R. T. (1988). Preferences for idioms: restrictions due to lexicalization and familiarity. *Journal of Psycholinguistic Research, 17,* 413–424.

Schvaneveldt, R. W., Meyer, D. E., & Becker, C. A. (1976). Lexical ambiguity, semantic context, and visual word recognition. *Journal of Experimental Psychology: Human Perception and Performance, 2,* 243–256.

Schwanenflugel, P. J. (1991). *The psychology of word meanings.* Hillsdale, NJ: Lawrence Erlbaum Associates.

Schwanenflugel, P. J., & Shoben, E. J. (1985). The influence of sentence constraint on the scope of facilitation for upcoming words. *Journal of Memory and Language, 24,* 253–270.

Schweigert, W. A. (1986). The comprehension of familiar and less familiar idioms. *Journal of Psycholinguistic Research, 15,* 33–45.

Schweigert, W. A. (1991). The muddy waters of idiom comprehension. *Journal of Psycholinguistic Research, 17,* 305–314.

Schwoebel, J., Dews, S., Winner, E., & Srinivas, K. (2000). Obligatory processing of the literal meaning of ironic utterances: Further evidence. *Metaphor and Symbol, 15,* 47–61.

Searle, J. R. (1978). Literal meaning. *Erkenntnis, 13,* 207–24.

Searle, J. R. (1979). *Expression and meaning.* Cambridge: Cambridge University Press.

Seidenberg, M. S., Tanenhaus, M. K., Leiman, J. M., & Bienkowski, M. (1982). Automatic access of the meaning of ambiguous words in context: Some limitations of knowledge based processing. *Cognitive Psychology, 14,* 489–537.

Seidenberg, M. S., Waters, G. S., Barnes, M. A., & Tanenhaus, M. K. (1984). When does irregular spelling or pronunciation influence word recognition? *Journal of Verbal Learning and Verbal Behavior, 23,* 383–404.

Sela, I., & Mazali, R. (1993). *Testimonies.* A Film by Eduyot Association. Les Films D'Ici in Association with Channel 4, Commissioning Editor—Alan Fountain.

Sereno C. S., Pacht, J. M., & Rayner, K. (1992). The effect of meaning frequency on processing lexically ambiguous words: Evidence from eye fixations. *Psychological Science, 3,* 269–300.

Sereno, C. S. (1995). Resolution of lexical ambiguity: Evidence from an eye movement priming paradigm. *Journal of Experimental Psychology: Learning, Memory and Cognition, 21,* 582–595

Shen, Y. (1989). Symmetric and asymmetric comparisons. *Poetics, 18,* 517–536.

Shen, Y. (1991). Schemata, categories, and metaphor comprehension. *Poetics Today, 12,* 111–124.

Shen, Y. (1992). Metaphors and categories. *Poetics Today, 13,* 771–794.

Shen, Y. (1995). Cognitive constraints on directionality in the semantic structure of poetic vs. non-poetic metaphors. *Poetics, 23,* 255–274.

Shen, Y., & Balaban, N. (1999). Metaphorical (in)coherence in discourse. *Discourse Processes*, *28*, 139–154.

Shinjo, M., & Myers, J. L. (1987). The role of context in metaphor comprehension. *Journal of Memory and Language*, *26*, 226–241.

Shklovsky, V. (1917/1965). Art as technique. In L. T. Lemon & M. J. Reis (Eds. and Trans.), *Russian formalist criticism: Four essays* (pp. 3–57). Lincoln: University of Nebraska Press.

Simpson, G. B. (1981). Meaning dominance and semantic context in the processing of lexical ambiguity. *Journal of Verbal Learning and Verbal Behavior*, *20*, 120–136.

Simpson, G. B. (1984). Lexical ambiguity and its role in models of word recognition. *Psychological Bulletin*, *96*, 316–340.

Simpson, G. B. (1994). Context and the processing of ambiguous words. In M. A. Gernsbacher (Ed.), *Handbook of psycholinguistics* (pp. 359–374). San Diego: Academic Press.

Simpson, G. B., & C. Burgess (1985). Activation and selection processes in the recognition of ambiguous words. *Journal of Experimental Psychology: Human Perception and Performance*, *11*, 28–39.

Simpson, G. B., & Foster, M. R. (1986). Lexical ambiguity and children's word recognition. *Developmental Psychology*, *22*, 147–154.

Simpson, G. B., & Krueger, M. A. (1991), Selective access of homograph in sentence context. *Journal of Memory and Language*, *30*, 627–643.

Small, S. I., Cottrell, G. W., & Tanenhaus, M. K. (1988). *Lexical ambiguity resolution: Perspectives from psycholinguistics, neuropsychology, and artificial intelligence*. San Mateo, CA: Morgan Kaufmann.

Smith, M. C. (1991). On the recruitment of semantic information for word fragment completion: evidence from bilingual priming. *Journal of Experimental Psychology: Learning, Memory and Cognition*, *17*, 234–244.

Smith, N. & Wilson, D. (1992). Introduction. *Lingua*, *87*, 1–10.

Solomon, K. O., & Barsalou, L. W. (1997). Productivity and propositional construal as the meshing of embodied representations. *Behavioral and Brain Sciences*, *20*, 38–39.

Spence, S., Zaidel, E., & Kasher, A. (1990). The right hemisphere communication battery: Results from commissurotomy patients and normal subjects reveal only partial right hemisphere contribution. *Journal of Comparative and Experimental Neuropsychology*, *12*, 42.

Sperber, D. (1984). Verbal irony: Pretense or echoic mention. *Journal of Experimental Psychology: General*, *113*, 130–136.

Sperber, D. & Wilson, D. (1981). Irony and the use-mention distinction. In P. Cole (Ed.), *Radical pragmatics* (pp. 295–318). New York: Academic Press.

Sperber, D., & Wilson, D. (1986/1995). *Relevance: Communication and cognition*. Oxford: Blackwell.

Spivey-Knowlton, M. J., & Sedivy, J. C. (1995). Resolving attachment ambiguity with multiple constraints. *Cognition*, *55*, 227–267.

Stanovich, K. E., & West, R. F. (1983). On priming by a sentence context. *Journal of Experimental Psychology: General*, *112*, 1–36.

Stein, G. (1922/1975). Miss Furr and Miss Skeene. In S. Cahill (Ed.), *Women and fiction* (pp. 42–48). New York: New American Library.

Stern, C., Prather, P., Swinney, D., & Zurif, E. B. (1991). The time course of automatic lexical access and aging. *Brain and Language*, *40*, 359–372.

Stroop, J. R. (1935). Studies of interference in serial verbal reactions. *Journal of Experimental Psychology*, *18*, 643–662.

Sundermeier, A. B., Marsolek, J. C., van den Broek, P., & Virtue, S. (2002, June). "Familiarity of causal inference scenarios during comprehension: Evidence for dissociable neural mechanisms." Paper presented at the Twelfth Annual Meeting of The Society for Text and Discourse, Chicago.

Sweetser, E. (1990). *From etymology to pragmatics: The mind-body metaphor in semantic structure and semantic change.* Cambridge: Cambridge University Press.

Swift, J. (1729/1971). A modest proposal for preventing the children of the poor from being a burthen to their parents or country, and for making them beneficial to the public. In T. Scott (Ed.), *The prose works of Jonathan Swift* (pp. 205–216). New York: American Mathematical Society Press.

Swinney, D. A. (1979). Lexical access during sentence comprehension: (Re)consideration of context effects. *Journal of Verbal Learning and Verbal Behavior, 18,* 645–659.

Swinney, D. A., & Prather, P. A. (1989). On the comprehension of lexical ambiguity by young children: Investigations into development of mental modularity. In D. S. Gorfein (Ed.), *Resolving semantic ambiguity* (pp. 225–238). New York: Springer Verlag.

Swinney, D., Zurif, E., & Nicol, J. (1989). The effects of focal brain damage on sentence processing: An examination of the neurological organization of a mental module. *Journal of Cognitive Neuroscience, 1,* 25–37

Tabossi, P. (1988). Accessing lexical ambiguity in different types of sentential contexts. *Journal of Memory and Language, 27,* 324–340.

Tabossi, P., Colombo, L., & Job, R. (1987). Accessing lexical ambiguity: Effects of context and dominance. *Psychological Research, 49,* 161–167.

Tabossi, P., Spivey-Knowlton, M. J., McRae, K., & Tanenhaus, M. K. (1994). Semantic effects on syntactic ambiguity resolution: Evidence for a constraint-based resolution process. In C. Ultima & M. Moscovitch (Eds.), *Attention and performance XV* (pp. 589–616). Cambridge, MA: MIT Press.

Tabossi, P., & Zardon, F. (1993). The activation of idiomatic meaning in spoken language comprehension. In C. Cacciari & P. Tabossi (Eds.), *Idioms: Processing, structure and interpretation* (pp. 145–162). Hillsdale, NJ: Lawrence Erlbaum Associates.

Talmy, L. (2000). *Toward a cognitive semantics.* Vol. 2: *Typology and process in concept structuring.* Cambridge, MA: MIT Press.

Tanenhaus, M. K., Carlson, G. N., & Seidenberg, M. S. (1985). Do listeners compute linguistic representations? In D. Dowty, L. Kartunnen, & A. Zwicky (Eds.), *Natural language parsing: Psychological, theoretical and computational perspectives* (pp. 359–408). Cambridge: Cambridge University Press.

Tanenhaus, M. K., Garnsey, S. M., & Boland, J. (1990). Combinatory lexical information and language comprehension. In G. T. M. Altamnn (Ed.), *Cognitive models of speech processing: Psycholinguistic and computational perspectives* (pp. 383–408). Cambridge, MA: MIT Press.

Tanenhaus, M. K., Leiman, J. M., & Seidenberg, M. S. (1979). Evidence for multiple stages in the processing of ambiguous words in syntactic contexts. *Journal of Verbal Learning and Verbal Behavior, 18,* 161–167.

Tanenhaus, M. K., Spivey-Knowlton, M. J., Eberhard, K. M., & Sedivy, J. C. (1995). Integration of visual and linguistic information in spoken language comprehension. *Science, 268,* 1632–1634.

Tanenhaus, M. K., & Trueswell, J. C. (1995). Sentence comprehension. In J. Miller & P. Eimas (Eds.), *Handbook of perception and cognition*. Vol. 11: *Speech, language and communication* (pp. 217–262). San Diego: Academic Press.

Till, R. E., Mross, E. F., & Kintsch, W. (1988). Time course of priming for associate and inference words in a discourse context. *Journal of Verbal Learning and Verbal Behavior, 16*, 283–298.

Titone, D. (1998). Hemispheric differences in context sensitivity during lexical ambiguity resolution. *Brain and Language, 65*, 361–394.

Toplak, M., & Katz, A. N. (2000). On the uses of sarcastic irony. *Journal of Pragmatics, 32*, 1467–1488.

Tourangeau, R., & Rips, L. (1991). Interpreting and evaluating metaphors. *Journal of Memory and Language, 30*, 454–472.

Tourangeau, R., & Sternberg, R. J. (1981). Aptness in metaphor. *Cognitive Psychology, 13*, 27–55.

Tourangeau, R., & Sternberg, R. J. (1982). Understanding and appreciating metaphor. *Cognition, 11*, 203–244.

Traugott, E. C., & Dasher, R. B. (2002). *Regularity in semantic change*. Cambridge Studies in Linguistics 97. Cambridge: Cambridge University Press.

Traugott, E. C., & König, E. (1991). The semantics-pragmatics of grammaticalization revisited. In E. C. Traugott & B. Heine (Eds.), *Approaches to grammaticalization* (Vol. 1, pp. 189–219). Amsterdam: John Benjamins.

Trueswell, J. C. (1996). The role of frequency in syntactic ambiguity resolution. *Journal of Memory and Language, 35*, 566–585.

Trueswell, J. C., Tanenhaus, M. K., & Garnsey, S. M. (1994). Semantic influences on parsing: Use of thematic role information in syntactic ambiguity resolution. *Journal of Memory and Language, 33*, 285–318.

Trueswell, J. C., Tanenhaus, M. K., & Kello, C. (1993). Verb specific constraints in sentence processing: Separating effects of lexical preference from garden paths. *Journal of Experimental Psychology: Learning, Memory, and Cognition, 19*, 528–553.

Tsuyoshi, O., & Thompson, S. A. (1996). Interaction and syntax in the structure of conversational discourse: Collaboration, overlap, and syntactic dissociation. In E. H. Hovy & D. R. Scott (Eds.), *Computational and conversational discourse: Burning issues—An interdisciplinary account* (pp. 67–96). Berlin: Springer.

Tulving, E., & Gold, C. (1963). Stimulus information and contextual information as determinants of tachistoscopic recognition of words. *Journal of Experimental Psychology, 66*, 319–327.

Turner, N. E., & Katz, A. (1997). Evidence for the availability of conventional and of literal meaning during the comprehension of proverbs. *Pragmatics and Cognition, 5*, 203–237.

Tyler, L. K., & Wessels, J. (1983). Quantifying contextual contributions to word recognition processes. *Perception & Psychophysics, 34*, 409–420.

Tyler, L. K., & Wessels, J. (1985). Is gating an on-line task? Evidence from naming latency data. *Perception & Psychophysics, 38*, 217–222.

Ullman, M., Corkin, S., Coppola, M., Hickok, G., Growdon J. H., Koroshetz, W. J., & Pinker, S. (1997). A neural dissociation within language: Evidence that the mental dictionary is part of declarative memory, and the grammatical rules are processed by the procedural system. *Journal of Cognition and Neuroscience, 9*, 266–276.

Utsumi, A. (2000). Verbal irony as implicit display of ironic environment: Distinguishing ironic utterances from nonirony. *Journal of Pragmatics, 32*, 1777–1807.

Vaid, J., Heredia, R., Hull, R., Martinez, F., & Gerkens, D. (2001, November). On getting a joke: Multiple meaning activation in humor comprehension. Poster presented at the Forty-second Annual meeting of the Psychonomic Society. Orlando, Florida.

Vaid, J., Hull, R., Gerkens, D., & Heredia, R. R. (2000, November). *The time course of script activation in verbal humor processing.* Poster presented at the Forty-first Annual meeting of the Psychonomic Society. New Orleans, Louisiana.

Vaid, J., Hull, R., Heredia, R., Gerkens, D., & Martinez, F. (in press). Getting a joke: The time course of meaning activation in verbal humor. *Journal of Pragmatics.*

Van Lancker D. R. & Kempler, D. (1987). Comprehension of familiar phrases by left-but not by right-hemisphere damaged patients. *Brain and Language, 32,* 265–277.

Van Lancker D. R. & Kempler, D. (1993). Acquisition and loss of familiar language: Idiom and proverb comprehension. In F. R. Eckman (Ed.), *Confluence: Linguistics, l2 acquisition and speech pathology* (pp. 249–257). Amsterdam: John Benjamins.

Van de Voort, M. E. C., & Vonk, W. (1995). You don't die immediately when you kick an empty bucket: A processing view on semantic and syntactic characteristics of idioms. In M. Everaert, E-J. van der Linden, A. Schenk, & R. Schreuder (Eds.), *Idioms: Structural and psychological perspectives* (pp. 283–299). Hillsdale, NJ: Lawrence Erlbaum Associates.

Van Petten, C. (1995). Words and sentences: Event-related brain potential measures. *Pyschophysiology, 32,* 511–525.

Van Petten, C., Coulson, S., Rubin, S., Plante, E., & Parks, M. (1999). The course of word identification and semantic integration in spoken language. *Journal of Experimental Psychology: Learning, Memory, and Cognition, 25,* 1–24.

Van Petten, C., & Kutas, M. (1991). Electrophysiological evidence for the flexibility of lexical processing. In G. B. Simpson (Ed.), *Understanding word and sentence* (pp. 129–174). Amsterdam: Elsevier.

Verschueren, J. (1995). The pragmatic return to meaning: Notes on the dynamics of communication, degrees of salience, and communicative transparency. *Journal of Anthropology, 5,* 127–153.

Verschueren, J. (1998). *Understanding pragmatics.* London: Arnold.

Vu, H., Kellas, G., Metcalf, K., & Herman, R. (2000). The influence of global discourse on lexical ambiguity resolution. *Memory & Cognition, 28,* 236–252.

Vu, H., Kellas, G., & Paul, S. T. (1998). Sources of sentence constraint in lexical ambiguity resolution. *Memory & Cognition, 26,* 979–1001.

Wallach, Y. (1997). *Wild light.* Trans. Linda Zisquit. Riverdale-on-Hudson, NY: Sheep Meadow Press.

Wedel, A., & Sherman-Ussishkin, A. (1999, July). *Entropy and language structure: Toward an explanation of regularity in Creole grammar.* Paper presented at the Sixth International Cognitive Linguistics Conference, Stockholm, Sweden.

Weiner, J. E. (1996). Why is a riddle not like a metaphor? In J. Hulstijn & A. Nijholt (Eds.), *Automatic interpretation and generation of verbal humor* (pp. 111–119). IWCH '96. Twente Workshop on Language and Technology 12. Enschede: University of Twente.

Weldon, M. S. (1991). Mechanisms underlying priming on perceptual tests. *Journal of Experimental Psychology: Learning, Memory and Cognition, 17,* 526–541.

Weldon, M. S., Roediger H. L., & Challis, B. H. (1989). The properties of retrieval cues constrain in picture superiority effect. *Memory & Cognition, 17,* 95–105.

West, R. F., & Stanovich, K. E. (1988). How much of sentence priming is word priming? *Bulletin of the Psychonomic Society, 26,* 1–4.

Whaley, C. P. (1978). Word nonword classification time. *Journal of Verbal Learning and Verbal Behavior, 17,* 143–154.

Whitney, P., Waring, D. A., & Zingmark, B. (1992). Task effects on the spontaneous activation of trait concepts. *Social Cognition, 10,* 377–396.

Wiley, J., & Rayner, K. (2000). Effects of titles on the processing of text and lexically ambiguous words: Evidence from eye movements. *Memory & Cognition, 28,* 1011–1021.

Williams, J. N. (1992). Processing polysemous words in context: Evidence from interrelated meanings. *Journal of Psycholinguistic Research, 21,* 193–218.

Wilson, D. (1998). Discourse, coherence and relevance: A reply to Rachel Giora. *Journal of Pragmatics, 29,* 57–74.

Wilson, D., & Sperber, D. (1992). On verbal irony. *Lingua, 87,* 53–76.

Wilson, D., & Sperber, D. (1993). Linguistic form and relevance. *Lingua, 90,* 1–25.

Winner, E. (1988). *The point of words: Children's understanding of metaphor and irony.* Cambridge, MA: Harvard University Press.

Winner, E., Levy, J., Kaplan, J., & Rosenblatt, E. (1988). Children's understanding of nonliteral language. *Journal of Aesthetic Education, 22,* 51–63.

Wolff, P., & Gentner, D. (2000). Evidence for role-neutral initial processing of metaphors. *Journal of Experimental Psychology: Learning, Memory, and Cognition, 26,* 529–541.

Wu, L. (1995). Perceptual representation in conceptual combination. Ph.D. dissertation, University of Chicago.

Yus, F. (1998). A decade of relevance theory. *Journal of Pragmatics, 30,* 305–345.

Yus, F. (2001). On reaching the intended ironic interpretation. *International Journal of Communication, 10,* 27–78.

Zaidel, D. W., & Kasher, A. (1989). Hemispheric memory for surrealistic versus realistic paintings. *Cortex, 25,* 617–641.

Zaidel, D. W., Zaidel, E., Oxbury, S. M., & Oxbury, J. M. (1995). The interpretation of sentence ambiguity in patients with unilateral focal brain surgery. *Brain and Language, 51,* 458–468.

Zaidel, E. (1979). Performance on the ITPA following cerebral commissurotomy and hemispherectomy. *Neuropsychologia, 17,* 259–280.

Zaidel, E. (1987). Hemispheric monitoring. In D. Ottoson (Ed.), *Duality and unity of the brain,* 247–281. Hampshire: Macmillan.

Zaidel, E., Kasher, A., Giora, R., Batori, G., Soroker, N., & Graves, D.(2000). *Hemispheric control of basic speech acts: Evidence from unilateral brain damage.* Unpublished ms.

Zaidel, E., Kasher, A., Soroker, N., & Batori, G. (2002). Effects of right and left hemisphere damage on performance of the "Right Hemisphere Communication Battery." *Brain and Language, 80,* 510–535.

Zajonc, R. B. (1968). Attitudinal effects of mere exposure. *Journal of Personality and Social Psychology, 9,* 1–27.

Zajonc, R. B. (1980). Feeling and thinking: Preference need no inferences. *American Psychologist, 35,* 151–175.

Zajonc, R. B. (2000). Closing the debate over the independence of affect. In J. P. Forgas (Ed.), *Feeling and thinking: The role of affect in social cognition* (pp.31–58). Cambridge: Cambridge University Press.

Zuckerman, G. (1999, December). *"Phono-semantic matching" as a means of lexical enrichment: Comparative analysis of Ivrit, Turkish, Chinese, and Japanese.* Paper presented at the Linguistics Colloquium, Tel Aviv University.

Zwitserlood, P. (1989). The locus of the effects of sentential-semantic context in spoken-word processing. *Cognition, 32,* 25–64.

AUTHOR INDEX

GENERAL INDEX